The Voice Beneath the Skin

The Voice Beneath the Skin

Besmira Stermilli

Written by Besmira Stermilli

ISBN (Paperback): 979-8-9933948-2-4
ISBN (Hardback): 979-8-9933948-1-7
ISBN (eBook): 979-8-9933948-0-0

Layout by Arash Jahani
Cover Design by Arash Jahani

Dedication

To my daughters, Maya, Zoe, and Bliss—my galaxies, my brightest constellations.

You are the rhythm of my tides, the starlight threaded through my veins, the songs the universe keeps teaching me to hear.

You orbit in ways both ancient and new, pulling me toward wonder, stretching me into futures I never dreamed were mine to live.

You are whole universes disguised as children, and it is your light that turned my darkness into sky.

To Oerti—my anchor and my horizon, the axis around which my galaxies turn.

The one who stayed when staying was hardest, who carried fire beside me without wavering, who steadied me when the ground gave way.

But also the one who laughed with me when nothing else made sense, who surprised me with tenderness in the middle of ordinary days, who turned even silence into companionship.

You are the man who keeps choosing me not only in grief, but in joy, not only in fire, but in celebration.

You are my fiercest mirror, my softest refuge, my proof that love is not only survival but delight, devotion, and renewal.

To my mother—who held it all when everything was breaking, who taught me what endurance looks like even when it came at great cost.

To my father—guiding from above, your unseen hand steady at my back, your quiet blessing carried in my bones.

To my sisters, nieces and nephew and kin—threads in the great weaving, too many for one page, deserving their own book, their own sky.

To the ancestors whose prayers I walk upon, and to the ones not yet born, who will one day carry this story further than I can imagine.

This book is for you.

This book is because of you.

This book is you.

Prologue

The Voice Beneath the Skin

There has always been a voice moving through us—not the kind that shouts from stages or hides in libraries, but the kind that startles us mid-laughter, the kind that ripples across the skin when a child's giggle bursts too loud and we realize, if only for a breath, that joy itself is holy. It is the same voice that rises in tears when we think we are alone, that hums low in the chest when we press our palm to the earth, that flickers like starlight just beneath the surface of things.

I have heard it in the simplest places—in the clatter of dishes, in the stubborn ache of grief that refused to loosen, in the questions whispered into pillows in the middle of the night. I have heard it in my daughters' play, their voices weaving whole worlds out of nothing but air and imagination, reminding me that creation was never complicated, only alive. I have heard it in the quiet of love, in the way two bodies who have walked through fire still find one another, skin to skin, breath to breath, choosing to open where it would be easier to close. I have heard it in the pulse of union, when love itself becomes a vow spoken without words, a fire that does not consume but keeps us alive. And I have heard it in the spaces where language breaks open, where the body trembles with too much feeling to contain, and something larger spills through.

It is not mine. It is not yours. It is ours, ancient and childlike at once, fierce as fire and tender as breath. It runs barefoot through the fields of our days, scattering light like dandelion seeds, waiting to be caught in our cupped hands. If you listen, truly listen, you may feel it tugging at you now—playful, wild, alive—the voice beneath the skin, calling you to play your part in the great game of being.

Table of Contents

A Note Before We Begin

This book may feel a little different. Not because it's trying hard to be, but because I stopped trying so hard to make it something it wasn't. I stopped forcing what I knew into neat little boxes and just let it come the way it wanted.

These pages weren't outlined. They were lived. They spilled out between dishes and tears, in the middle of sleepless nights, while my kids were laughing in the next room, while I was breaking open and piecing myself back together.

They don't sound perfect. They weren't meant to. Sometimes they came as whispers, sometimes as sobs, sometimes as sentences I barely managed to catch before they disappeared.

So if this book feels like a poem, that's because it is.

If it feels like a prayer, that's because I was praying.

If it feels like a conversation, that's because I was talking to myself, to the sky, to anyone who might understand.

You won't find tidy explanations here. You'll find pieces of a life, raw and unedited.

There's no table of contents to guide you. But maybe you'll find a piece of yourself tucked into the cracks.

This isn't the kind of book you finish and put back on a shelf.

It's more like a companion, a thread you follow, a breath you catch when you didn't realize you were holding your lungs too tight.

So let it sit beside you. In the messy kitchen. On the subway. In the quiet moments before sleep. Let it remind you that you don't need to be polished to matter, and you don't need to be perfect to be holy.

Let it breathe with you.

Interrupt you.

Nudge you.

Love you back to life.

– B.

CHAPTER ONE

The Fracturing—What Was Forgotten

I used to think the moment I forgot would be loud.
I imagined lightning tearing open the sky, glass shattering against tile, something sharp enough to split me into before and after. I thought there would be a sound I could point to later and whisper, *there... that's when I lost myself.*

But it wasn't like that.
It wasn't violent.
It was quiet. Almost unbearably quiet.

The forgetting came like fog rolling in at dawn, soft and steady, and I didn't notice until one day I woke up inside its weight, far from myself. It was the kind of losing you only recognize after it's happened—the kind where you touch your own face and realize you can't remember who's looking back.

Why didn't I notice sooner?

Because you didn't want to, love. Forgetting felt safer than remembering.

I breathe slowly, letting the truth of that land. Yes. I wanted the silence to shield me, to wrap itself around my ribs so I wouldn't have to feel what waited underneath. But my body...

She remembered.

She remembered everything I begged her to release.

Why her? Why couldn't she just let it go with me?

Because she loves you more fiercely than you've ever loved yourself. She is your archive, your living temple, your unbroken keeper. She held every fragment so you could keep moving, even when you thought you were falling apart.

I close my eyes and feel her there—my body, my witness, my oldest friend—and the tears rise unbidden because I realize now she's been carrying me longer than I've carried myself.

I used to call it the *fall*.
I used to believe I had fallen.

But the whisper comes, warm and steady beneath my ribs:
You didn't fall, love.

Then what happened to me?

You stepped away. That's all. You turned from the knowing, not because you were wrong, but because you thought you had to. You thought you couldn't survive seeing the fullness of yourself.

I let that move through me slowly, sinking deeper with every breath. And I know it's true.
I didn't fall from grace. I slipped only from the knowing of it.

One day I was weightless, resting inside that truth like sunlight rests on still water. And the next…

And the next, you woke here.

Here? In this life?

Yes. Inside time. Inside flesh that bruises and bleeds. Inside the roar of other people's truths, so loud they drowned out the hum of your own. Inside the silence where your voice once lived, waiting for you to come back.

That silence—I still remember its weight. It settled into my bones like stone in a riverbed, pressing down until even breathing felt like betrayal.

Was that the moment I disappeared?

Not disappeared. Hidden. That was when she—your body—began carrying what your spirit could not. That was when she became your witness, when survival began speaking louder than your voice.

In that quiet, survival became my first language. Forgetting became my sharpest tool.

I forgot the sound of my own voice until, the first time I heard it again, it scraped raw against my throat like something foreign.
I forgot the curve of my own power until my reflection blurred into the outline of a stranger.
I forgot I had ever been whole, because longing for it would have split me open.

Is that why I made myself small?

Yes. You thought smallness would save you.

I nod slowly, remembering how I wore the masks until they fused with my skin.
The good daughter.
The good lover.
The good light-worker who smiled when expected, softened where required, and gave until there was nothing left to give.

And they loved me for that, didn't they?

They loved the version of you that disappeared for them.

The words land heavy, but I can't deny them. And yet, even beneath the masks, something ancient pulsed on.

What was that ember I felt sometimes in my dreams?

That was you, love. The untamed you, untouched and unbroken, humming your name into your blood until you were ready to listen again.

Sometimes she slipped into dreams—temples, oceans, stardust clinging still to my skin, the memory of a love so vast it could never be broken, only buried beneath lifetimes of forgetting.

I used to think the ache was against me. That the pain was my enemy, the thing I had to outrun.

But the knowing comes now, slow and certain:
It was never the pain, love. The pain was never the enemy. The veil was.

I let that truth wash through me. Yes. The pain wasn't here to destroy me. It was pointing the way home.

Because when we forget who we are, we hand our names to others and let them carve us into shapes that do not fit.
We let shame write our stories in its sharp, unyielding tongue.
We turn our fractures into cages and then decorate the bars, convincing ourselves the prison is safety.

For years, I believed I was broken.
The world called it sensitivity, as though feeling deeply were something to hide.
I called it weakness, ashamed of the trembling, ashamed of the hunger, ashamed of the wild river inside me that refused to dry up.

But I wasn't broken, was I?

Never. What you carried was not fragility. It was a soul still singing the first songs it had ever known, refusing to quiet itself, no matter how many times you tried to bury it beneath the noise.

I let the words in. And suddenly, I understand: I wasn't losing myself. I was waiting for myself.

And then came the day I swallowed the No.

I was young then—not in years, but in voice. My throat was still fragile, unsteady, unsure of its own strength. I thought silence was safety, that belonging was worth more than breathing.

I can still see the room.
The way the light bent through the glassware.
The hum of voices meant to feel like home but never did.

The subtle pressure of unspoken rules.

I was surrounded by people I loved—or at least, people I'd been told I should. People whose approval I had been raised to crave. People whose validation I thought I needed to exist.

And then... something shifted. Someone crossed a boundary.

What was it?

I can't name it anymore. Maybe it was a joke sharpened just enough to cut. Maybe it was a lingering glance that stayed too long. Maybe it was the silence that followed my truth, heavy and unbroken.

But my body knew.

My womb clenched tight like a fist.
My throat sealed shut.
My chest rose to speak—and then collapsed, heavy with all the permission I didn't know how to claim.

I swallowed the No.

Why?

Because you believed keeping the peace would keep you safe. You thought bending was better than breaking, that silence was a softer wound than rejection.

I told myself it was fine, that it was easier this way. But deep down, I knew.
It wasn't preservation.
It was abandonment.

And it didn't stop there.

I swallowed that No again and again, in different rooms, beneath different lights. At gatherings where my soul begged me to stay home but I put on the dress anyway, painted on the smile, laughed at jokes that left bruises on my spirit.

I swallowed the No when unwanted guests filled my living room, sipping from cups I offered with polite hands, while my soul pressed itself into the farthest corner of the house, whispering for the space they had taken without asking.

Why didn't you ask them to leave?

Because you were taught that your comfort was expendable. That other people's ease mattered more than your belonging to yourself.

I swallowed the No when family wrapped their barbs in sugar and handed them to me as though sweetness softened cruelty.
The words still cut.
I smiled anyway.
They knew. I knew. And I buried it, because I had been raised to believe family peace— even a false one—was worth every wound it cost me.

I wore grace like a gown.
But grace without truth is just another mask.

My womb recorded every moment.
She whispered, Say something.
I whispered back, *It's not worth the fight.*

But beneath even that, softer, truer: *I don't believe I'm worth the disruption.*

And then comes the quietest reply, the one that still makes my breath tremble when I hear it:
You always were.

... and the reply arrives inside my ribs with the gentleness of a hand finding mine in the dark, you always were, and for a long, tender moment I just sit inside that sentence, feeling the way it widens the room and loosens the lock I once kept on my own mouth, until I can finally breathe a little deeper and admit to us both that it wasn't peace I kept all those years but a rehearsed stillness, a quiet pose that looked graceful from far away and yet scraped me raw from the inside.

What happens when I stop swallowing it? I ask, not defiant, not afraid, just tired of trading my name for safety, my breath for approval, my nights for their comfort.

When you stop swallowing betrayal, the voice answers, it doesn't explode your life the way you fear, it simply lays things back where they belong—your body in your body, your name in your mouth, your boundary on its feet like a gate that finally remembers which way it opens—and people who only loved the version of you that disappeared will drift, as shorelines do in the tide, while those who were always meant to love you in truth draw closer because there is finally something real to hold.

I let that future pass through me as if it's already here, the room brightening one quiet notch at a time, and I realize it has never been rage I needed, not even a speech, just a returning, which is how I come to this next truth, the one that writes itself on the back of my tongue like a vow I forgot to speak:

My No is holy, not a punishment but a prayer, not closure but covenant, the gatekeeper of my Yes, tending the small altar inside my chest where my life is allowed to burn at its own pace, and the longer I sit with this, the more I hear the older song beneath it— your No has always been a form of love, the voice murmurs, not a wall to keep the world out, but a threshold that teaches the world how to step in.

And Still I Loved

I want to tell you I didn't speak my No because I lacked courage, but the truer story is slower and more complicated, so I ask the question out loud the way a woman asks for water after a long walk through heat: *Was I a coward, or was I conditioned?*

You were devoted, the voice answers, and devotion is a beautiful thing until it is demanded by everything but your own truth; you had been taught that love was measured by how much you could swallow without complaint, that loyalty meant silence, that keeping the peace mattered more than keeping your soul whole, and for a long time you believed them because no one showed you a love that held you without asking you to vanish.

I feel the sting and the sweetness of that in equal measure, and it makes me want to gather the younger me into my lap, to smooth her hair and whisper apologies into the crown of her head for the years I chose harmony over honesty, until I hear the voice again, softer now, *forgive her, not for failing, but for surviving in the only language she knew*, and I do, right here, mid-sentence, forgiving all the versions of me who wore grace like a gown and called it love because the world applauded when I walked in quietly and left without leaving a ripple.

Then what do I call what I did? I ask, because the word love still tastes like a house I want to keep, even if I have to move the furniture.

Call it a first dialect, the voice says, a beginner's language for a body that had not yet learned to conjugate truth; you loved as best you could with the tools you had, and still you loved—yes, even then— but now you will love without erasing yourself, now your love will arrive with its full vocabulary, including the words that make the room grow quiet and the soul grow strong.

It feels like a benediction, and I bow my head to it without moving, a long, private nod no one sees, and in that small bow something reorganizes: I am not here to prove I am easy to love; I am here to love in a way that doesn't ask me to disappear.

Reflections on the Swallowed No

For years, I avoided the word betrayal, wrapped the whole thing in gentler names— patience, maturity, being the bigger person, spiritual kindness—and sometimes those were true, but often they were the lace draped over a blade, and my body kept the real record, because the body never signs false treaties and never edits the minutes of the meeting; she wrote it down as tension in the shoulders that would not drop, as a jaw that woke already clenched, as a heaviness low in the belly that no amount of water would wash away.

Is it only emotion I buried? I ask, tracing with my memory the map of ache she's been showing me for years.

Not only emotion, the voice says, but also instruction; truth refuses to die when you bury it, it grows restless instead, finds other ways to speak—through pain that lingers past its usefulness, through patterns that circle back like weather, through people who arrive as mirrors holding up the very edges you keep stepping over—and if you listen long enough, the body's symptoms begin sounding like verbs, not verdicts, impulses that want movement, not labels that require shame.

I think of the seasons when the anxiety hummed under my skin like a trapped insect, and how resentment simmered beneath the polite smile I wore at tables that asked me to cut my food into smaller bites than my hunger required, and how exhaustion pooled like standing water no sleep could drain, and I hear myself ask, almost in a whisper, *When does it change? When does the question stop being "Is it safe to be me?" and start being "Is it honest to be anything else?"*

It changes at the door, the voice answers, the one that looks at first like a keyhole and then like a window and then like a gate you can swing with a hand that is finally yours; it changes when you ask the small, fierce question you already know by heart—am I silencing my truth so someone else can stay comfortable?—and then you let the answer rearrange your furniture, your calendar, your guest list, your yes.

I breathe through that sentence the way a diver breathes before the plunge, and when I surface inside the next paragraph the light feels different, which is why I can say without flinching that the moment you stop swallowing your No, life begins to taste like itself again: you speak without apology, you say that doesn't work for me without a thesis of explanations, your boundaries become living gates, not fences—not walls—but thresholds that teach other people how to enter, and the world, like a crowd in a theater when the lights dim, shifts; some people leave, some resist, but the ones who remain stand closer and see you more clearly than they ever could when your outline was blurred by obedience.

And if they leave? I ask, because there is still a small ache that remembers the loneliness of empty chairs.

If they leave because you stayed, the voice says, then you did not lose them—you found yourself; when you stop betraying yourself you stop attracting those who ask you to, and the ones who love you in truth love you deeper for it, because at last the love has something honest to hold.

I do not argue with that, because my body has already said yes, and in this part of the story the body gets the deciding vote.

A Letter to the Woman Who Still Swallows Her No

I know the ache you carry, the way it gathers at the base of your throat like a held storm, how it makes a home beneath your collarbones and calls itself weight when what it really is—and always has been— is weather waiting to break; I know the tremble in your hands when you sit at a table that feels more like a stage than a sanctuary, the practiced smile that fits your face like a borrowed dress, the way your ribs feel like a shelf where you stack the words you will not say.

You weren't weak for wanting peace.

You were wise enough to want quiet.
You were simply never taught that quiet and silence are not the same prayer.

Tell her this gently, the voice breathes, *because she has punished herself long enough for surviving.*

You were surviving, love.
You swallowed your No because you thought it was the cost of being loved, because somewhere along the way you learned that your boundaries were negotiable but other people's comfort was sacred, because your body told you the truth in a language no one taught you to trust and your mind translated it into a sentence that began with *be good* and ended with *be small.*

This is not your failure; this is your map.

Each time you swallowed the word you needed, your body wrote the moment on the underside of your skin like a field note—a tightening here, a heaviness there, the hum beneath the smile—so that when you were ready, you could retrace yourself by touch.

Close your eyes with me now and step into the place that remembers you: the field at the edge of the town where your life learned its first letters, the grass tall enough to brush your knees, the air sweet with things that grow without asking permission, the sky that seems too open to hold and yet somehow holds you anyway; walk barefoot because you can, because you belong, because the ground knows your weight and calls it by your real name.

There—do you see her? The woman you are becoming has always been waiting here, not as a test but as a welcome, standing with her shoulders unafraid of their span, her spine telling the story of a thousand small choices to stay, her eyes unhurried, not begging to be seen because they know how to see; she is you, older in the way trees are older—rings hidden and rain remembered—and she is carrying something that glows like evening in her palms.

It is warm when she places it into your hands, warmer still as it spreads from skin to bone, a steady pulse as familiar as your first lullaby, and you understand without explanation that you are holding your truth—not a slogan, not a posture, but the original light you tucked under your ribs when you thought dimming would protect you.

Tell her what lives inside it, the voice suggests, and I do, because this is the part that cannot be rushed.

Inside this light are the No's you were never granted permission to say, the boundaries you were trained to barter for belonging, the questions you learned to leave unasked because they made the room go still, the laugh you swallowed because it arrived too loud for the moment, the tears you bit back because someone else's comfort was on the line; inside this light is your spine learning again what upright feels like, your breath remembering the path all the way down, your hands choosing when to open and when to rest.

Ask her the question she came for, the voice murmurs, and I do, because every return has a hinge.

When did I first forget?

Her hand—your own hand, older and steadier—comes to rest over your heart, and there is no impatience in her answer, no lecture, just the quiet certainty of someone who has walked your whole way beside you:

You never truly did; you dimmed your voice to survive a world that feared its sound, and dimming did its small job for a while, but you were not built for smallness and your body refused to sign the contract.

Then what do I do now?

Speak, she says—and the field seems to lean closer to hear it—speak even if your voice trembles, even if the room grows quiet, even if no one claps when you finish; speak because your truth is not a performance but a pulse, because every time you honor your No you bless your Yes, because every syllable you return to your mouth closes another hairline crack in the mirror you once mistook for your face.

Kneel if you need to.
Stand if you want to.
Either way, hold the light.

You have not missed yourself.
You are right on time for your own life.

And here the old voice—the one beneath your skin who has loved you through all your rehearsals and all your homecomings—leans in with that last, beloved sentence, the one that loosens the last knot and lets the breath move the whole way through:

Welcome home.

CHAPTER TWO

The Body is a Manuscript

A temple of memory. A living archive. A map back to wholeness.

The body is not a scroll you read once and set aside.
She is a living manuscript, inked in sensation, written beneath the skin in a language older than thought, older than prayer, older than even the first breath that carried me into this life. A temple of memory. A breathing archive. A map—not just back to wholeness, but into the places I have not yet dared to enter.

They told me healing was a matter of the mind. They said it as though they had memorized a rulebook carved in stone: Fix your thoughts, and the rest will follow. But my body disagreed.
She had her own knowing. Her own opinion.
Her own quiet rebellion.

— *I will not be rewritten by thought,* she whispers.
I carry what thought cannot hold.

She speaks in a dialect no one taught me to hear, yet one I have always known. It lives beneath language—in heat, in tremor, in weight and release. It is there in the way my chest tightens before my mind knows why, in the strange quiver in my belly when I betray myself, in the heat blooming along my skin when truth brushes close enough to touch me.

At first, I mistook her signals for defects.
I called her fragile. I called her too much.
I silenced the tremble in my voice, the pulsing in my throat, the goosebumps rising across my arms when something unseen entered the room.
I told myself: *Be composed. Be still. Be good.*

But my body has always had her own logic—wild, ungoverned, sovereign. She does not organize herself for other people's comfort. She does not care about the maps they handed me or the destinations they demanded I reach.
Her only allegiance is to survival, to memory, to keeping me alive when I have no idea how to hold myself intact.

— *I saved what you tried to leave behind,* she says softly.
I kept you when you could not keep yourself.

She has been writing my story in secret, storing entire chapters in bone and fascia and muscle, pressing each unsaid word and swallowed no into herself like petals pressed between living pages. Every silence I kept, she folded into her tissue. Every truth I swallowed, she carved into the hinge of my jaw, the slope of my shoulders, the curve of my spine.

And slowly—not with lightning, not with fireworks, but with the quiet repetition of waves against stone—I began to understand.

The understanding arrived in fragments:
My hand pressing hard against my sternum in the middle of a panic I couldn't name.

The warmth blooming low in my belly the first time I spoke a truth out loud and did not take it back.
The trembling release of my jaw when I finally whispered a no I had been holding for years.

The body is not just flesh.
She is history.
She is compass and cartographer, witness and altar.

She is scripture—but not the kind you read with your eyes.
This one you read with your breath, with your hands, with the unspoken way your spine straightens when you finally name what you have carried.

And she remembers everything.

Even the pieces I thought I had erased.

She remembers the nights I floated above myself to survive, watching the scene from the ceiling as though it belonged to someone else.
She remembers the afternoons I disappeared inside myself, becoming so still I almost vanished entirely.
She remembers the names I was called, how their syllables lodged like splinters in the softest parts of me.
She remembers the touch that wasn't safe, the way my skin learned to brace before I understood why.
She remembers the rage I swallowed before I even knew its name— how it pooled, hot and dense, in the pit of my stomach until I thought I would split from holding it.

— I did not forget, she says.
Even when you begged me to.

My skin remembers—not in quick flashes, but in waves that roll beneath awareness, holding every tremor I thought I buried. She remembers the nights I wanted to disappear, when my breath hid shallow at the top of my lungs, when silence felt safer than being seen. She remembers the afternoons I wore my smiles like armor, each one polished and practiced, hiding the quiet unraveling inside my chest.

— *I was with you there*, she whispers softly, like a hand resting against the back of my neck.
I carried the weight of what you would not name.

She remembers the names I was called and how their syllables sank deep, sticking to the tender walls of me, shaping how I learned to bend myself around other people's comfort.
She remembers the touch that wasn't safe, how my skin learned to brace before I understood why, how it flinched before my mind allowed the knowing to arrive.
She remembers the rage I swallowed, hot and endless, because I was too young to hold its fire and too afraid to let it out. It pooled inside me, molten and unmoving, waiting for the day I would allow its heat to burn clean.

— *I kept it for you*, she murmurs.
Every ember. Every tremor. Every truth you thought you buried.

My womb remembers too—the clench, sharp and sudden, when I crossed my own boundaries just to keep the peace, the way she pulsed warnings I ignored because I thought belonging mattered more than breath. And my spine remembers the days I bent too far for too long, contorting myself into shapes small enough to be loved, until the architecture of me began to ache beneath the weight of everyone else's needs.

Each vertebra a sentence.
Each curve an unsent letter.
Each misalignment a story paused mid-breath, waiting for my return.

This body—this soft, unyielding witness I once hid and criticized and compared until I could barely look at her—was never the problem. She was never the flaw. She was never too much or not enough.

She is the evidence.
She is the archive.
She is the one who remembered me when I forgot myself.

I used to think she was something to fix, as though she were glass shattered across tile, sharp and useless until gathered back into shape. But she was never broken. She was only carrying what I refused to hold, testifying beneath the surface in the only language I allowed her.

The tension in my shoulders is not random—it's the unspoken responsibilities stacked across bone and sinew, weight I inherited before I even knew its name.
The ache in my gut? It is not weakness. It is the words I did not say, the boundaries I never claimed, pressing forward, restless for air.
The fatigue behind my eyes is not failure—it is the cost of performing peace while my spirit kept screaming beneath the silence.

— *You thought these were flaws,* she says,
but these were my letters to you.
I was writing where you would listen.

The body doesn't lie.
Not once.
Not ever.

She stores every unprocessed moment as though tucking folded parchment into the hollow spaces of ribs and hips, waiting without rush for the day I would open her. And when I finally do, the ink is still fresh—the memory alive, untamed, unchanged, but no longer unapproachable.

— *I kept all of this for you,* she breathes.
There was never shame here. Only safekeeping.

Because the body doesn't just carry wounds.
She carries codes.
Blueprints of power and survival braided through lineage.

My mother's quiet strength.
My grandmother's silence like an unspoken vow.
My great-grandmother's songs humming in a language the world forgot, but my blood still knows.

She carries the codes of power too—not the kind given by titles or gates or laws, but the kind that hums in the marrow, in the steady rhythm of pulse beneath skin, in the wild, ungoverned memory of breath itself.

— *This power is yours,* she says.
It was always yours.

And beneath it all, she carries messages from places I thought were lost to me forever.
Buried deep, but never gone.

The womb.
The spine.
The breath.
They have been speaking longer than I have known how to listen.

The first time I truly heard her, there were no words at all—only waves.
Only the weeping that lived beneath language.

She wept through cramps that doubled me over, through migraines that arrived like storms breaking bone, through the quiet uprisings of my skin erupting in protest, through trembles and heat that came without explanation.

— *I wasn't punishing you,* she whispers.
I was asking you to come home.

I had mistaken numbness for strength.
I believed if I didn't feel it, I had conquered it.
I thought control was safety and silence was grace.

But she never stopped speaking.

The clenched jaw I called discipline was a warning.
The skipped breath I thought was normal was a signal.
The soft no blooming in my chest—the one I silenced over and over—was her voice, breaking through anyway.

I overrode her for years, forcing yes when my body begged me to stay, thinking self-betrayal was the price of belonging.
And still, she stayed.

She stayed through my dismissals.

She stayed through every apology I owed her.
She stayed when I silenced her.
She stayed when I forgot her name.

— *I waited*, she says simply,
not for your perfection,
but for your presence.

And now, I am here.
Not to fix her.
Not to master her.
Not to earn her forgiveness.

The Womb Oracle

The womb is not just an organ.
She is the first altar I ever carried, the silent oracle tucked beneath the navel, the deep-breathing chamber where memory, longing, and desire fold themselves into sensation, waiting patiently for the moment I remember how to ask her the right questions.

When I place my hand there, the warmth rises instantly—as though she has been listening for me longer than I have known how to listen for her.
"I'm here," I whisper, and before the words even finish leaving my lips, I feel her answer moving like current beneath my skin, pulsing softly into my ribs:

— *I never stopped speaking, love.*
You stopped hearing me.

Her voice is not sound; it arrives as knowing.
She shows me entire lineages at once—the thread of my mother's soft, unspilled tears; my grandmother's sealed silence, pressed flat beneath decades of endurance; the quiet ache of women who folded themselves smaller and smaller until their wildness lived only in their bones.

I tell her, "It feels so heavy here,"
and she hums through blood and memory:

— *You are carrying more than your own.*
This weight is not yours alone.
You took it because no one else could hold it.
But you do not have to keep it anymore.

Her words come like heat expanding from the center, and suddenly I know the weight beneath my ribs is not just mine—it is the ache of everything my lineage could not speak, the grief they wrapped in silence, the rage they feared would burn their lives to ash if they let it breathe.

She shows me fire—the wild heat I exiled for years because I was afraid of what would happen if I let it move through me.
I had mistaken it for danger, for chaos, for shame.
She corrects me softly, tender and unyielding at once:

— *This fire is holy.*
It was never meant to be extinguished.
Only understood.

I feel her power there, ancient and precise, and my chest tightens with the memory of how many times I abandoned her. I see the nights she bled without mercy, pouring out everything I refused to feel. I see the months she clenched in quiet protest when I said yes in places where my soul was screaming no, sending pain like thunderclaps through my body, not as punishment but as a final plea to listen.

— *I warned you every time,* she whispers.
You thought I was betraying you,
but I was protecting you from yourself.

I see, too, the seasons when she went silent—holding her breath deep within me because she knew I wasn't ready to hear her yet. And suddenly, I understand: her stillness was never indifference. It was devotion.

I close my eyes and apologize. For leaving her behind. For demanding her silence. For trading her knowing for belonging. And before I can finish forming the thought, she answers:

— *I was never angry, love.*
I waited.
I kept the keys.
I held the door until you remembered your way back.

I breathe her in, slow and deliberate, and she meets me there, pulsing once, twice, a rhythm that feels older than bone. I keep my hand against her and she softens under the weight of my palm, opening as though she has been waiting for this precise moment.

— *Come gently,* she says.
Come barefoot.
Come without apology.
This is not about fixing what you've carried.

It is about knowing you were never broken.

Her voice thickens here, rising like tidewater climbing stone, filling the hollowed-out spaces where I once stored my unspoken truths:

— Stay.
Stay when it hurts.
Stay when it opens.
Do not leave yourself again.
We stay until it opens.

And in that moment, I understand:
She is not asking me to heal her.
She is inviting me to remember her.

So I stay.
Breathing her rhythm.
Letting her speak the language I once forgot I knew.

The womb does not rush.
She will open when you do.

The Spine

The spine is the standing altar, the unbroken column of light and memory that keeps me upright even when my spirit bends. She is the ladder between worlds—root and crown, earth and sky—carrying the record of everything I have lived, everything I have avoided, and everything I came here to embody.

When I close my eyes and trace her length with my awareness, I feel her waiting. The hum is soft, deep, steady—like a river running beneath stone. I whisper, *Show me what you've kept*, and she opens slowly, vertebra by vertebra, offering her memories back to me like offerings retrieved from water.

At the base, in the sacrum, she holds the root—the quiet gravity that tethered spirit into flesh, the unbroken cord tying me to earth. There, beneath thought, beneath language, she carries the memory of my first belonging, the soft reminder of where I came from before I was named, before I was taught who I needed to be.

— *I anchored you here,* she murmurs, her voice low, ancient, steady.
So you would never forget where you came from.
Even when you wandered, you were held.

I climb a little higher, into the lumbar—the place of carrying.
Here, she holds the weight I agreed to shoulder before I even understood what it meant.
The responsibilities handed down without words.
The expectations I performed without question.
The grief passed from mother to daughter, absorbed like air, never named but always felt.

— *I have carried what they could not speak,* she whispers.
Your mother's swallowed truths,
your grandmother's sealed silences,
the quiet ache of women who learned to survive by disappearing.
I kept it here,
safe,
until you were ready to remember that you were born to put it down.

The breath deepens as I rise into the thoracic spine, the place where ribs cradle the heart.

Here, she holds every folding, every contraction, every time I curved inward to make myself smaller, believing that shrinking would keep me safe, believing that silencing my wildness would keep me loved.

I feel it as a subtle ache beneath my shoulder blades—the phantom shape of wings I once clipped to fit inside the rooms where my fullness was too much.

— *This is where longing lives*, she says, her voice softer now, almost tender.
The longing you called weakness.
The ache you mistook for shame.
It was never brokenness.
It was desire refusing to disappear,
refusing to let you abandon yourself completely.

I rise higher still, reaching the cervical spine, where the neck curves like a question.
Here, she has kept every word I swallowed, every no I muted before it touched the air, every truth I hid beneath politeness, beneath performance, beneath the practiced lightness of "I'm fine."

— *I kept them all for you,* she says.
Every syllable.
Every silence.
Every song you silenced before it reached your tongue.
I knew you would come back for them one day.

And then, at the crown, where bone meets breath, she speaks more quietly than before, but with a clarity that rings like bells carried by the wind:

— *You thought you were disconnected.*

But you were never apart.
Every prayer you thought no one heard has been stored here,
spiraling like light through your spine,
circling back to meet you now.

I rest my hand at the base of my neck and bow my head without moving, because I understand something I could not name before: this column has been holding me even when I thought I was falling.

I tell her I'm sorry for leaving her unacknowledged, for demanding her strength without offering her my presence. And she answers with the gentleness of an ancient witness,

— I was never impatient, love.
I have been waiting for you to remember:
You have always been upright,
even when you believed you had fallen.

And suddenly, I feel her—not as structure, but as song.
Not as bone, but as remembering.
Each vertebra a rung, each curve an invocation, each alignment a homecoming.

She is not asking me to climb her.
She is inviting me to listen.

When the Body Began to Speak Louder Than I Could

The more I listened, the more I realized: nothing inside me was random.

Every sensation was a sentence, every symptom a messenger, every ache a prayer disguised as pressure.

My gut wasn't failing me—she was carrying stories I hadn't dared to name, trying to digest betrayals I had never allowed myself to speak. My skin wasn't overreacting—she was pushing out energy I hadn't felt safe enough to voice, telling the truth through heat and eruption when my mouth stayed silent.
My heart wasn't weak—she was holding the grief I buried, waiting for me to unseal her.

The body is not inconvenient.
She is not dramatic.
She is not too much.

She is the quiet historian of everything the soul has lived,
and everything the soul still longs to embody.

She writes in a language beneath language, patient and unyielding, waiting for the moment I would stop treating her like a problem and begin to recognize her as my oldest witness.

— *I was never against you.*
I was always carrying what you could not bear to touch.

I did not let myself grieve when my father died. I told myself that strength looked like silence, that my worth was measured by how little I needed, that safety would come if I carried the weight without asking for help, and yet, beneath the surface of all that performance, something ancient and trembling inside me already knew the truth: I was not keeping myself safe by shutting it down, I was breaking myself apart one unspoken sorrow at a time.

I was six months pregnant with Maya then, her tiny body curled soft and unfinished inside me, her cells dividing in rhythm with my heartbeat, and I believed that every tear I shed might seep into her skin, that every tremor of grief might etch itself into her memory before she ever met the world. I imagined protecting her by refusing myself—so I swallowed the ache whole, pressing it down beneath breath and smile and spine, telling myself that there would be time later, always later, to fall apart.

But grief buried alive does not dissolve.
It lingers, heavy and quiet, waiting in the hidden corners until you are ready to meet it.
It curls itself into your bones, dense and silent as stone, shaping the way you hold your breath without knowing why.
It lives beneath the sternum where air struggles to reach.
It gathers in the spaces where joy is meant to move and makes a home there, patient and unyielding, until you finally turn toward it with both hands open.

After Zoe's birth, the waiting ended. The migraines arrived without mercy, waves breaking over my body with no shore in sight, forcing me to my knees again and again until I understood that these were not headaches but storms—vast, electric, unrelenting storms, carrying thunderclaps of everything I refused to feel, lightning bolts of memory I could no longer keep buried.

Warnings. Whispers. Roars.
All at once, until silence became impossible.

It was as if the quietest parts of me—the ones I had hidden beneath composure and performance—had grown restless from being ignored and had finally found a way to speak louder than my willpower could contain.

And still, I tried to outrun them.
I tried to be everything to everyone: the perfect mother, the devoted wife, the capable pharmacist, the reliable friend, the one who carried what no one else could, the one who smiled even when her mouth tasted of salt and metal, the one who disappeared so gracefully into usefulness that no one noticed she was vanishing at all.

Each title came with its own invisible contract—unspoken vows that my body signed without my consent, each one whispering the same quiet rule: Be less. Need less. Contain it all. I performed them so well I forgot there had ever been a me beneath the mask.

And my body noticed. She always notices.

She had been watching me abandon myself one small boundary at a time, watching as I folded myself into shapes too narrow to hold my breath, watching as I starved the wildness from my own veins just to belong to places that never wanted my fullness in the first place, and still she waited—patient, listening, silent—until the silence was no longer safe.

The migraines were the drumbeats. The first pounding signals that something inside me had cracked open, that the architecture I had built to contain my ache was splintering under the weight of all that had been denied.

But I didn't listen.

So she spoke louder.

My skin erupted in protest—psoriasis blooming across my scalp, eczema burning in patches like invisible fire, relentless itching that woke me in the middle of the night gasping for air. I coated myself in creams, whispered prayers into ointments, blamed the heat, the detergent, the stress, the hormones—but she said no, soft and steady beneath the noise:

— *This is not surface. This is signal.*
I am pushing out everything you refused to release.

And still, I kept pressing forward, determined to perform my way through exhaustion. I smiled at tables where my body begged me to stay home. I gave when I had nothing left to give. I held space for everyone else's chaos while mine screamed beneath my ribs, and I told myself I was strong, I was capable, I was built for this— but somewhere deep in the quietest folds of me, another voice whispered back: *This is not strength, love. This is erasure.*

Because somewhere along the way, I had learned the most dangerous lesson of all:
that to be loved, I must be empty.
That to be worthy, I must become what they needed.
That to be good, I must abandon myself entirely.

But love that costs your body, your breath, your belonging to yourself—that is not love.
It is erosion disguised as devotion.

And then came the rupture.

It happened beneath the heat of the Dominican sun, the air thick with salt and brightness, when a sudden pain split through sound itself, sharp enough to steal the entire world in an instant. One moment, the hum of life; the next, silence flooding like water. My eardrum had torn.

Two surgeries followed.
Recovery rooms. Cold light on white sheets. The antiseptic sting that clung to my skin like memory.
Each muffled sound afterward felt like losing another piece of the world—but beneath the fear, beneath the disorientation, something else moved like a quiet tide:

— *If you will not listen within, I will make it impossible to ignore.*

I hadn't been listening. Not to the whispers of my womb, not to the cries of my skin, not to the weight pressing against my chest every morning, not to the low hum of knowing that pulsed steady beneath every performance, whispering: You are not okay.

And my body, patient but relentless, answered in the only language I could no longer bypass:
— *Come back now, or we will sever this connection completely.*

Then came the cysts in my ovaries—tiny vaults of everything I had no place to put, sealed chambers of unlived dreams and unspoken rage, each one holding a promise I made to everyone but myself. They bloomed quietly, tenderly almost, where my boundaries had withered, carrying the weight of desires I kept trading away just to stay acceptable, just to stay loved.

There were precancerous moles carved from my skin—clean cuts, cold blades, the sharp scent of antiseptic still living somewhere in my memory—and I understood, without language, that what had grown in silence now needed to be cut away.

Then there were the cysts in my breasts, tender and aching, my body guarding the heart-space where I had over-given and under-received until my chest itself became swollen with withheld truths.

I had nourished everyone.
I had emptied myself to keep others fed.
And somewhere in the quiet collapse, I forgot to feed the one person I promised to protect: myself.

Not just with food, but with breath, with softness, with joy, with space to exist without being useful.

The exhaustion grew thick, sticky, unrelenting.
Brain fog arrived like weather I couldn't escape, draping itself over my thoughts until even the smallest decisions felt heavy, until language itself became slippery in my mouth, until silence became my only refuge. I blamed my hormones, my schedule, my roles, my restlessness, but the truth rose beneath all those stories, undeniable and wild:

— *You are carrying what was never yours.*

I had been holding the grief of others, the expectations of generations, the stories I inherited without consent, the weight of keeping peace no one else could name, and my body said no more.

The fatigue came next, deep and marrow-heavy, a kind of depletion no sleep could soothe, no vacation could erase, no quick fix could mend—because this was never about rest.
It was about returning.

My body wasn't trying to punish me.
She was trying to call me home.

And eventually, trembling, I came.
Not all at once, but slowly, breath by breath, truth by truth. I came through tears I could no longer postpone, through letting my hands fall open instead of clutching what was burning me, through unlearning the masks I had mistaken for my face, through softening into the places I once forced hard.

Every migraine.
Every eruption.
Every rupture.
Every ache.

A love letter written in discomfort.

Not to hurt me.
To deliver me back to myself.

And I hear her now, clearer than ever before, her voice spilling through my ribs, steady and unwavering, a vow etched into the softest part of me:

— *Feel everything. Stay with yourself when it burns. Do not decorate your pain to make it prettier for someone else. Do not trade your breath for belonging. Do not silence your soul to keep the peace. I am not breaking you, love. I am breaking the lie that your worth is earned by disappearing.*

And I stay here.
Hands over my heart, body against body, hearing what I spent a lifetime trying not to hear:
she has been on my side the entire time.

I Am Listening Now

Precious body, beloved keeper of my becoming, I am sorry I left you waiting so long. I see you now—the way you whispered through tremors and aches, the way you pulsed warnings into my womb, the way you sang through migraines and silence and storms just to call me back into myself. I see now that it was never weakness when you ached; it was wisdom. It was your palm pressed softly against the glass, mouthing the words I could not yet hear: You are not living in truth.

I forgive the silences I required of us.
I forgive the betrayals I dressed up as grace.
I forgive the way I praised sacrifice and called it virtue while your pain sat invisible at the edge of the table, waiting to be acknowledged.
I forgive the years I confused endurance for devotion, the way I demanded your patience while withholding my presence.

I didn't know how to stay with you, love. But I am here now.

I return to your rhythm—the ancient pulse beneath thought.
I return to your breath—the tide I once abandoned to perform composure.
I return to your truth—the knowing that lived beneath my rehearsals, beneath my masks, beneath every shallow inhale that stalled at the top of my lungs.

And when I finally arrive, when I let my palms rest against the altar of my ribs, you meet me without hesitation, as if no time has passed at all. Your voice comes—not as metaphor, not as idea, but as warmth threading through muscle and bone, loosening what I thought would never open:

— I was never your enemy, you murmur from somewhere inside me.
*I am the one who has kept what you could not carry. I am the tremor
in your womb when you step across your knowing; I am the weight in
your shoulders when you lift what was never yours; I am the locked
jaw guarding the power you've kept sealed behind your teeth.*

And then softer, like silk against skin:

*— I am also the warmth that returns when you allow yourself to be
real,*
*the fire that rises in your belly when you speak what you once silenced,
the softness that unfurls when you stop abandoning yourself for
belonging.*

I close my eyes and feel the depth of this, the truth of it humming
through the marrow, and I realize how long she has been waiting for
this—not for apologies, not for penance, but for presence.

— I have never asked for perfection, she says.
*Only your willingness to be here with me. I do not need you to fix me.
I need you to trust that I have always been sacred.*

Her words unravel something tight in my chest, and for the first
time in years, my breath moves all the way down, settling into the
root of me like water finding its depth.

I let the silence stretch wide enough to hold us both, and inside that
silence, I hear myself answer without effort, almost as if the body
has borrowed my mouth to speak her own vow back into being:

I am listening now.
I will not leave again.

And beneath those words, another knowing rises—softer than sound, deeper than thought—the recognition that this was never a return, not really, but a remembering of something that had been whole the entire time.

The distance dissolves.
The ache softens.
The river widens.

I rest my forehead against the place where ribs meet sternum and whisper once more, not as confession but as devotion:

I hear you.
I honor you.
I am here.

And for the first time, I feel her—not as symptom, not as story, but as presence.
The one who never left.
The one who carried me home even when I thought I was lost.

Preface to Chapter 3

For the One Unveiling with Me

This chapter is not a proclamation. It is not proof of having arrived or evidence of enlightenment, and it does not exist to lift me above you. It is a doorway. A threshold into a remembering older than thought, older than language, older even than flesh, and if you stand here long enough with me, if you breathe where the silence opens, you may feel something beneath your ribs begin to stir.

I do not write these words because I believe myself higher, holier, wiser, or more worthy than you. I write them because I, too, have walked barefoot through deserts that swallowed my name. I have knelt inside silence so deep it swallowed my voice whole. I have searched for pieces of myself inside the ruins of other people's stories and carried the ache of knowing there was more—always more—waiting just beyond the veil of what the world taught me to see.

What I offer here is not meant to be admired from a distance, as though I were holding something you could not touch. It is not performance, and it is not doctrine. It is an opening. A mirror. A sound beneath sound. Something inside these words belongs as much to you as it does to me, and if, as you read, your chest begins to tighten or your breath deepens without reason, if your palms tingle or your womb hums or your throat aches for no nameable cause, pause. Close your eyes. Feel. That sensation is not born from something foreign. It is not because this story is unfamiliar. It is because your body recognizes herself here.

You are not arriving for the first time.
You are returning.

And this is not a chapter about one woman rising, not a single awakening pressed between pages like a wildflower meant to be studied behind glass. This is the living invitation to all of us—to step closer to the thread that has been tugging at us since before our first breath, the one that refuses to be silenced, the one that sings our real name into the marrow even when we have forgotten how to listen.

May these words meet you gently.
Not as a sermon delivered from a pulpit, not as a teaching meant to instruct, but as the sound of a song you once knew by heart—the kind of song you hear carried on the wind, soft at first, and then suddenly you are weeping without knowing why.

This is that song. This is the edge of the veil. Step closer.

CHAPTER THREE

Priestess of the Veils

The soul does not become divine. She unveils that she always was.

There are parts of me I haven't met in this lifetime, and yet I've felt them for as long as I can remember. You know that feeling—when something brushes against you in a way you can't explain, when you're standing in the middle of your own kitchen and suddenly you're somewhere else entirely, pulled into a memory that doesn't belong to this life but lives in you anyway.

Sometimes it comes in dreams that stay with me for days, dreams that don't feel imagined but recovered, like I'm walking back into a room I left lifetimes ago. Sometimes it's the way my hands start moving in shapes I don't understand—tracing symbols in the air as though my fingers remember an alphabet my mind forgot. Sometimes it's the tears that come out of nowhere when I hear a certain chant, a single vibration, a sound I've never learned but know deep down in my body.

You've always known, the voice whispers, soft as breath against the skin.

And I sit there in the quiet, shaking my head, trying to laugh it off, trying to talk myself out of it like I always do: *you're making this up, you're reaching, you just want it to mean something so badly.*

But wanting doesn't explain why my whole chest aches when I hear those sounds.
Wanting doesn't make my palms burn like they've held light before. Wanting doesn't make my breath catch in the middle of folding laundry because suddenly, out of nowhere, my body remembers something my mind can't name.

This isn't your imagination, she says again, steady now.
It's memory. Let it come.

I tried to dismiss it for years, but the threads kept finding me, tugging softly, patiently, like they knew I'd try to turn away and loved me enough to circle back again and again until I finally stopped running.

And here's the thing—in this life, I've worn so many names. Daughter. Lover. Mother. Friend. Each one carving something new into me, some soft, some brutal, some that cracked me open so wide I thought I wouldn't survive it. But underneath all of them, there's always been something untouched. Something older. Something truer than anything I've been taught to be.

It's hard to explain, but there are nights when I can *feel* the temples even if I can't see them.
I close my eyes and I'm there. My bare feet on cool stone, a silence so alive it hums against the skin, incense in the back of my throat though there's none burning here. My hands start to ache like they remember pouring water from star-marked vessels, like they remember calling light into form, opening gates with sound, touching what was once too holy to name.

Because you have, she whispers, right on the edge of my breath. *You've done this before.*

And I believe her. God, I do.

There are lifetimes folded into my marrow—lifetimes where devotion wasn't taught, it was breathed, lifetimes where I would have laid my body down to protect what was sacred, lifetimes where my voice wasn't language but vibration, where touch was ceremony, where remembering wasn't something you tried to do but something you couldn't forget.

And yet, I buried it once.
I had to.

You know how the world can be.
You learn to tuck the wild parts away just to survive it.
I learned to soften my edges, smooth the sharpness, swallow the knowing so I could pass through unnoticed.

But buried isn't gone.
Buried is only waiting.

And now... now it rises again.

Not like an explosion.
Not like lightning.
More like embers, curling smoke from a fire that never died, soft and steady, steady enough that this time, I know I won't turn away.

We never left you, the voice murmurs, so quiet I almost miss it. *We've been waiting for you to turn back toward us.*

The veils began to lift when I stopped asking *is this real?* and started asking the better question—*then why does it feel so much like home?*

And that's when it hit me.
I didn't invent any of this.
I carried it here.

I have walked these paths before.
I have sung these songs before.
And this lifetime, I am choosing to open them instead of hiding.

And maybe that's all it ever was—this whole journey of remembering. You don't become her.

You finally remember you've been her all along.

That's why the word *priestess* lands in the body before the mind can catch up. Why it stirs something deep and nameless you can't explain, why it makes the ribs ache with a kind of recognition no language can hold. It isn't performance. It isn't curated ritual or perfect robes or incense arranged just so for someone else's gaze.

It's the echo.
The bone-deep yes.
The soft hum moving through the marrow.

The body always remembers, she says, and I believe her now.

This isn't awakening.
This is return.

Mary Magdalene—Gatekeeper of This Passage

I didn't see her at first. There was no blinding light, no cinematic beam from the heavens, nothing anyone else would have noticed. But something shifted—the air thickened, like the way a room feels just before a summer storm—and before my mind could name it, my body knew. My ribs tightened, my palms tingled, and there was this deep, low ache beneath my sternum like something ancient had just stepped forward.

"Is this you?" I whispered, though I wasn't sure I wanted the answer.

You already know, she said—not in sound, but in that place under the skin where knowing lives.

I froze, breath caught halfway. And then it came—the same quiet fear I've carried for years, the one I almost hate admitting out loud:

"What if I'm too much?"
A pause, then softer:
"...or not enough?"

The words left me fragile, ridiculous even, and I laughed nervously as I said them, like maybe humor would make them less true.

And yet she didn't flinch. I felt her there— close, closer than anyone ever has been—and if a silence could hold someone, hers did.

Then came this warmth, low and steady, and I swear I could feel her smile before I could believe it:
Sweetheart, she murmured, *you've been trying to manage the shape of your soul for so long, it forgot what it's like to just be wild.*

I groaned and covered my face with my hands. "Great. Roasted by a saint. That's exactly what I needed today."

I could feel her laugh ripple through me, quiet and knowing, the kind that doesn't sound cruel but carries the kind of affection only someone who's walked the same road can hold.

You've been bending yourself into versions of yourself that will be accepted, she said gently. But love, your soul was never designed to be bite-sized.

I exhaled hard, leaning forward, elbows on my knees, and whispered, "...It's exhausting."

I know, she said simply. I know, because I've lived it too.

And that's when I felt it—her weight in the room. Not lofty, not untouchable. She didn't hover above me in a halo of light; she sat cross-legged right there on the floor beside me like a sister who wasn't leaving, no matter how messy it got.

They called me names, too, she said after a long silence, her voice low and unshaken. *Sinner. Whore. Fallen. They rewrote my devotion into desperation, twisted my power into shame, turned my name into something I didn't recognize.*

Her words vibrated in my bones, not because they were new, but because they were familiar.

I know what it is to be misnamed, she went on, her voice trembling with something stronger than pain. *To hear a story about yourself told so many times that even you start to question your own knowing. To feel the weight of their projection until it sinks into your skin.*

I swallowed hard, eyes fixed on a knot in the wooden floor beneath me. "...Sometimes I believe them," I admitted, barely audible. "The names. The stories. The things they decided I was."

For a moment, the air went impossibly still, like even the earth was listening.

Then I felt it—her hand over mine. Not literal, but real in the way the ocean is real when you're standing at its edge.

You are not the wound they named you after, she said, slow and steady, each word deliberate, like stones laid carefully along a path. *You are the pulse beneath it. You are the river that refuses to dry. You are the part they cannot touch.*

Something inside me cracked at those words, sharp and soft at once, like glass splintering under heat. I laughed through wet cheeks, shaking my head. "...God, it's so hard to hold that some days."

I know, she said again, quieter this time, like someone stroking your hair after you've collapsed into their lap. *But listen to me. Being misunderstood does not mean you are mistaken.*

I sat there for a long time, letting the truth of it seep into the places I had abandoned.

Finally, I asked the question I've whispered to the dark for years, the one that lives under my tongue no matter how many times I try to swallow it:

"And what if I forget?"

She didn't hesitate.
Oh, love. You will forget.

I looked up, startled, almost offended. "...Wait, excuse me?"

You'll forget, she repeated, but there was laughter in her tone this time—that soft, knowing kind that holds no judgment at all. *You'll doubt. You'll bend. You'll swallow your own voice when the room gets loud. You'll shrink when your truth feels too big to carry. Of course you will.*

I leaned back against the wall, groaning dramatically. "Great pep talk, thanks."

Her laughter rolled through me like warm water against cold skin. *But I'll remind you,* she said, voice steady now, almost like a vow. *I'll remind you ten times, a hundred times, a thousand times if I have to. That's what sisters do.*

I pressed my palms against my cheeks, still damp, and let the smallest, truest smile rise through me. "...Even when I make a mess of it?"

Especially then, she said without missing a beat.

Something loosened in my chest, subtle but certain, like an old lock clicking open. I breathed deeper, steadier, and for the first time in a long time, I believed her.

She didn't need me to be perfect.
She just needed me to keep listening.

Mother Mary—The Holding Field

She didn't come in visions or revelations.
She came in silence.

Not the kind of silence that feels like absence—but the kind that softens the edges of the room, the kind where even your own breath sounds different, like it's landing in a deeper place.

The first time I felt her, I almost didn't notice. It was so quiet. No words, no instructions, no holy proclamations—just this sudden, gentle weight in the air, as though something unseen had already decided to love me without waiting for me to earn it.

It's hard to describe, because she didn't arrive with answers. She arrived the way light spills across a floor without asking permission, the way warmth moves through a blanket before you even realize you're cold. It wasn't about doing anything. It was about being held.

I think that's the thing about her presence—it bypasses the mind entirely. One moment, I was holding myself together with both hands, trying to manage the mess, trying to manage *me*. And the next, my shoulders softened without my permission. My breath dropped lower into my body. The ache in my chest eased, just a little, the way water finally finds a hollow to rest in.

She didn't speak, but I understood her anyway.

I had been so busy performing strength, performing healing, performing okay-ness, and she just... refused to meet me there. She didn't ask for explanations. She didn't need my composure. She wasn't interested in my "I'm fine." She slipped right past the story and went straight to the part of me that had no words left.

She wrapped herself around the unraveling—not to stop it, but to give it somewhere safe to land.

I remember sitting there, hands limp in my lap, realizing how long I'd been holding myself rigid against everything I couldn't control. And for the first time in what felt like years, my body stopped bracing. My breath widened. The ground beneath me felt... softer somehow.

It was like she was reminding me, without saying it, "*You don't have to hold it all right now.*"

And God, I didn't realize how much I needed to hear that—not from anyone else, but from inside the quiet of my own ribs.

I felt my chest tremble before I realized I was crying, and then I started laughing because of course I was—of course the moment someone shows up and says nothing, I fall apart completely.

There you are, she said—not with sound, but with something older, softer, a warmth blooming right behind the ribs.

I pressed my palms to my face. "I was fine five minutes ago," I muttered into my hands, already knowing she wasn't buying it.

Sweetheart, the voice brushed through me like breath, *you haven't been fine for a while. You've just gotten very good at performing it.*

And I laughed, wet-faced, because she was right and we both knew it.

Because the truth is, I had forgotten how to be held. I had forgotten how to let the weight drop without explaining why it was heavy. I'd forgotten how to rest without apologizing for it.

Mother Mary brought that back to me—not by telling me to trust, but by giving me a space where I didn't have to. A space where the air itself carried the message: *You don't have to earn this.*

She didn't rush me toward hope. She didn't try to fix the ache. She didn't make the silence into something it wasn't. She just stayed— in the warmth of the sunlight falling across the floor, in the steady rhythm of my own breath, in the way the room held me like it had been waiting for me to stop running.

And maybe that's her gift.

Not miracles.
Not instructions.
Not grand revelations.

Just presence.

The kind that steadies your shaking hands when you've run out of words. The kind that reminds you healing isn't always about rising; sometimes it's about pausing long enough to remember you're allowed to belong to yourself again.

Mother Mary doesn't ask me to lead.
She invites me to rest.
To loosen my grip on all the ways I try to hold the world together.
To let my chest rise and fall without negotiating for the space to breathe.

Sometimes I think her entire message is contained in one breath, one line she never speaks but somehow I hear anyway:

"You can let go now, love. You are already held."

—

Isis—The Invocation of Power

She didn't come gently.
Not with silence, not with the soft weight of comfort, not like Mary does when she folds the room into stillness. Isis doesn't arrive with lullabies. She arrives with pulse.

I felt her before I knew her name—the way you feel heat before you see the fire. It was in my palms first, this faint trembling I couldn't explain, and then behind my ribs, like something older than thought was pushing to the surface.

I didn't ask her to come. Honestly, I was just trying to survive the day—moving through the hours like a vessel on autopilot, answering phone calls, arranging details, keeping the mask steady so no one would see how close I was to breaking. It was the day my father died.

Six months pregnant with Maya, holding life in my womb and loss in my lungs, I moved like someone underwater. Everything was muffled: voices, footsteps, even my own heart. And beneath it all, a quiet terror I couldn't name—that somehow, if I let myself *feel* any of it, I wouldn't make it through.

So I held it in.
I told myself I was protecting her—the tiny body growing inside me, listening to everything I couldn't speak. I thought if I swallowed my grief, she would be spared it. I thought if I kept my chest steady and my breath even, she would never know the storm.

I was wrong.

Grief doesn't disappear because we hide it. It lives in the body, folded deep into bone and blood, waiting. My silence didn't protect her; it just buried everything inside me until my body started to ache from the weight of what I refused to name.

And that's when she came.

I felt her standing behind me before I dared to turn inward.
And then I heard it, soft but unshakable:

"What if this pain has a purpose?"

I actually laughed out loud—wet-faced, breathless, almost hysterical. "I beg your pardon?"

But she stayed, quiet, steady, not asking me to stop crying, not asking me to stand up, not telling me to move on. She just waited.

And when the silence stretched long enough for me to hear myself breathe again, I felt her lean in closer, and somehow it was both fierce and tender when she said:
"Let it open you."

I shook my head. "That sounds... wildly inconvenient."

And she laughed—not in mockery, but the way someone who loves you laughs when they already know the ending and you don't.

I didn't know to call her Isis then. But my body did. My blood did. Some part of me that has walked this earth far longer than this lifetime recognized her before my mind ever could.

She came with neither rescue nor permission. She stood in the place no one else could reach—not because they didn't love me, but because some griefs live in chambers where only the soul can enter. And in that chamber, she didn't soothe. She witnessed.

That was the moment I understood what power feels like. It isn't loud. It isn't performative. It doesn't demand. It doesn't even ask. It *reminds*.

She reminded me of every lifetime I had forgotten:
Lifetimes where I sang gates open and poured water across temple stones carved with star-etched markings.
Lifetimes where my hands called light into form, where breath itself was ceremony.
Lifetimes where I carried codes I couldn't yet name, where my devotion was not performance but pulse.

And then she reminded me of something even deeper:
This is not the first time I have lost and rebuilt.

I have died before. Not in body, but in the vanishing of self—the girl who gave until nothing remained, the woman who swallowed her voice to keep others comfortable, the one who stayed silent when her whole body was begging her to speak. I buried her so many times, thinking she would stay gone, and yet... here she was. Here I was.

Isis didn't hand me a ladder out of the dark. She sat with me in it until I could see there was gold down here—that my breaking was not punishment, it was initiation. That the ache was not a wound, it was a doorway.

She didn't tell me to rise for anyone else. She asked me to gather myself—the silence, the fire, the longing, the loss, all of it—and bring it back into my own hands. Not flawless. Not fixed. Just whole.

And as I sat there, palms resting on my belly, something in me rearranged. The grief didn't leave. The ache didn't soften. But the fear... the fear loosened its grip. My breath dropped lower into my body. For the first time in days, I felt space open behind my ribs.

This is the thing about Isis: she doesn't come to take the pain away. She comes to awaken the part of you who can walk with it, the part who knows she has done this before and will do it again, the part of you that does not break when the world says you should.

She comes to remind you of the heat you carry.
She comes to put your name back in your own mouth.
She comes so you stop mistaking survival for living.

Isis brings you back to the wild, breathing center of yourself—the place where you are still untouched, still untamed, still yours.

—

Hathor—The Return of the Body

I would think she would come with incense or chanting or hours of preparation.
In contrary, she came back with my hips.

Not in a temple. Not in a carefully staged ritual.
In my kitchen.
Dinner halfway burned, kids yelling in the background, music playing low from some random playlist I hadn't touched in months.

It wasn't supposed to be sacred.
But that's the thing about Hathor—she never waits for "perfect timing." She sneaks in sideways when the mind is distracted, when

the heart has stopped trying so hard, when your body is too tired to argue with itself.

That day, the light hit the floor just right, warm and soft against my bare feet. I was standing there, spoon in one hand, half-focused on some to-do list that felt endless, when suddenly something in me loosened. A note in the song landed in a place I hadn't opened in years, and before I even realized what was happening, my hips… moved.

Just a little sway at first. Hesitant.
Like testing the water before you dive.

And then more—a curve, a circle, a rhythm older than thought.
And then, oh, there she was.

I didn't plan it. I didn't "decide" to invite Hathor back in. My body did it for me. Somewhere between the garlic and the rising heat of the stove, something ancient cracked open, and this low, quiet laughter bubbled up from my belly—not from my mouth, but from deep inside my womb.

That's how Hathor enters: not like lightning, not like fire.
Like honey spilling without asking permission.

I'd forgotten what it felt like to enjoy my own weight, to feel my softness without apology. I had spent so long holding, bracing, carrying everyone else's needs that I had turned my own body into a container instead of a home.

And she—oh, she was not having it.

I could almost hear her whisper:

"Enough surviving, love. You were built for more than holding it all together."

Hathor didn't come to remind me of discipline or devotion. Isis brings heat; Magdalene brings truth. But Hathor? She brings pleasure. Permission. Play.

And not the curated, Instagram-ready version of pleasure that smells like expensive candles and looks like a goddess retreat. I'm talking about the barefoot, half-sweaty, laughing-alone-in-your-kitchen kind. The one that makes your kids peek around the corner and ask, *"Mom, are you okay?"* and all you can say is, *"Better than okay, actually."*

That's her medicine. She doesn't care if the house is a mess, if the dishes are piled, if the to-do list is laughing at you from the counter. She just wants your body back in motion. She wants the hips to circle, the breath to deepen, the shoulders to shake off everything you've been holding.

Hathor came to remind me that joy is not something you "earn" after the work is done. Joy is the work. Pleasure is not a distraction from the path—it is a way home.

Sometimes priestesshood looks like temple floors and chants that rise like prayers.
But sometimes it looks like this:
Moving in your kitchen, sweat on your skin, dinner on the stove, singing half-wrong lyrics into a wooden spoon because the song hits different tonight and for no reason at all, you let yourself feel good again.

And I swear, when my hips found that rhythm, something unclenched inside me that had been holding its breath for years. My whole body exhaled.

That's when I knew Hathor wasn't just returning.
She was reminding me:

"You don't have to wait to live, love. You get to taste it now."

—

Inanna—The Descent and the Climb

There is a version of me buried beneath everything I gave away.

She's been down there for years, under the polished yeses and careful smiles, beneath every moment I dimmed my edges so no one else would have to adjust theirs. She's under the dinners I cooked while quietly starving, the laughter I performed while something in me was splintering, the long list of sacrifices I made because I thought that's what love was supposed to look like.

She waited in the dark.
Not shattered. Not gone. Just... holding her breath until I was ready to come for her.

And one day, I finally heard the call.

It didn't come as thunder, no lightning tearing through the sky, no loud, cinematic unraveling. It was quieter than that. It sounded like exhaustion so deep I couldn't fake another smile. It tasted like rage I could no longer dress up with spiritual language. It felt like the slow, aching thought at the back of my mind: *"I don't know how much longer I can keep doing this."*

And suddenly, there it was—the edge I had been circling for years without realizing it.

This was the descent.

And listen, it wasn't poetic. It wasn't graceful. It wasn't bathed in candlelight and chants. It was messy. It was scrolling my phone at 2 a.m. trying to outrun my own thoughts. It was crying quietly in the shower so no one could hear me. It was snapping at the people I loved most and hating myself five minutes later. It was lying awake replaying conversations in my head, whispering to the ceiling, *"Maybe it's me. Maybe I'm the problem."*

It was quiet, and it was brutal.

I didn't lose everything. But I came close to losing me.

That's when she came.
Inanna.

The priestess of sacred undoing.

She didn't rush in like a savior. No ladder. No instant relief. She came and sat next to me in the dark—not above me, not ahead of me—and said without saying, *"I won't pull you out. But I'll help you find what's down here."*

At first, I didn't believe her. I thought descent meant failing, meant falling apart, meant proof that I wasn't "doing the work" well enough. But Inanna kept leaning in closer until I finally felt it: this wasn't punishment. This was initiation.

She showed me the hidden gold in the place I had avoided for so long—the wisdom under the weight, the pulse under the ache, the raw self I had buried just to survive.

And she was right.

Because when I finally stopped trying to climb my way out, when I let myself sink lower, I found her—the version of me I'd left behind.

She wasn't angry. She wasn't bitter. She was just... waiting.
Arms crossed, a little annoyed maybe, but mostly patient, like:
"Finally. Took you long enough."

That was the first time I laughed down there.
The first time the heaviness cracked.

I didn't come back carrying everything I thought I'd lost. I came back carrying essence. My voice was scratchy, my hands were dirty from the digging, but they were mine.

And when I climbed, I climbed differently.
Slower. Truer. Less concerned with being good, more committed to being real.

This is what Inanna teaches:
You don't rise by bypassing the descent.
You rise because of it.

I didn't come back polished.
I didn't come back "healed."
I came back alive.

And alive, I've learned, is better than perfect.

—

The Forgotten Priestess—The Confession

There was a time when I translated my power into politeness.
I didn't mean to. It just... happened slowly, the way waves carve stone without meaning to change its shape.

I took the raw pulse of my truth and sanded it down until it was smooth enough for everyone to swallow.
I dressed my fire in soft fabrics so it wouldn't scorch anyone.
I smiled when I wanted to scream.
I said "it's fine" when my whole body was begging me to tell the truth.

And for a while, I believed that was love. That was grace. That was goodness.
That if I could just be soft enough, easy enough, small enough, maybe—finally—someone would stay.

It wasn't weakness. It was fear.
Fear of being too much.
Fear of shaking the room.
Fear of what would happen if I let the full weight of my voice land, unedited.

And if I'm honest, I became very good at it—at shaping myself into something people could manage, something they could love without having to stretch.
I made myself smooth where I was meant to have edges.
I made myself quiet where I was built to roar.

But here's the thing no one tells you: you can disappear without ever leaving.
You can lose yourself by degrees, smiling the whole way down.

And one day, I realized I was exhausted.
Not the kind of tired that a nap fixes.
The kind of tired where you want to crawl out of your own skin just to stop performing inside it.

That was when she came—the part of me I had buried so deep I'd almost forgotten her name.
The priestess who refused to shrink. The one who wouldn't trade her fire for belonging. The one who could walk into a room and be without apology.

She stood there in the doorway of my own remembering, arms crossed like she'd been waiting for this conversation for years, and said—
"You're kidding, right? We softened our edges for this?"

I laughed. Out loud. Alone in my kitchen.
Because, God, she was right.

I had been bending myself into shapes that didn't fit, trading truth for acceptance and calling it devotion.
I was exhausted from holding the middle, from managing everyone's comfort, from contorting myself into someone easier to love.

So I confessed to myself the thing I had been avoiding:
I wasn't being honest.
Not with them.
And definitely not with me.

And once you tell the truth—really tell it—you can't go back.

I don't want to be easy to digest.
I don't want to dress my words in soft cotton just to protect someone else from their own discomfort.
I don't want to apologize for my edges when they were the very things meant to carve a path forward.

Because the world doesn't need another carefully curated, perfectly-lit, spiritually-branded version of the truth.
It doesn't need another woman dimming herself to fit into a frame someone else is holding up.

It needs the wild ones.
The untamed ones.
The women who speak from the marrow, even when their voice shakes.
The ones who let their words rumble through the room and rearrange the furniture if they have to.
The ones who laugh too loudly, love too deeply, and refuse to sand down their edges just to make everyone comfortable.

And I've decided—I'm going to be one of them.

Not the performance of power. Not the aesthetic of freedom.
The real thing.
Messy. Alive. Unapologetically here.
I am done asking permission to exist. I am done trimming my truth into bite-sized pieces so it's easier to swallow. I am done mistaking being liked for being free. I want the kind of belonging that doesn't require me to disappear. I want the kind of love that can stand in the heat of my full fire and stay anyway.

If my voice shakes, then let it. If the sound of me unsettles someone, I trust that the discomfort is theirs to hold, not mine to fix. If my light lands too bright for someone still hiding in the shadows, then I bless them –but I will not dim. I will not make myself smaller so someone else can feel safe inside their cages.

Because here is what I know now, what I had to walk all the way down into the dark to find:
I was never too much. Not once.
I was never too loud, too soft, too emotional, too wild, too knowing. None of those names ever belonged to me.

I was only ever misplaced.
And the thing about finding yourself again—really finding yourself— is that once you've touched that pulse, you can't unknow it. You can't go back to sanding yourself down just to fit.

Now, I will live unhidden.
Now, I will speak the words my bones have been storing for lifetimes.
Now, I will rise—not as someone new, but as the woman I refused to leave behind.

The priestess they forgot has returned.

—

The Black Madonna—The Final Flame

This was never going to be a soft chapter.
I knew it the moment she came— not as light, not as comfort, but as heat.
The kind of heat that doesn't ask if you're ready.

She arrived when I was holding too much again, pretending I was fine, smiling like I wasn't quietly fraying at the edges. And listen, she didn't knock. She didn't send a polite warning. The Black Madonna never does. She showed up like someone walking into your house, taking one look at the mess, and saying: *"Alright. We're burning this down."*

This is her gift.
She does not negotiate with illusions.
She doesn't stroke your hair and promise it'll be okay.
She points at everything you've been protecting, everything you've been polishing, and whispers, *"That goes."*

And she's not cruel. She's honest. Sometimes the honesty just feels cruel because we've built entire identities out of what was never ours to begin with.

She is the keeper of thresholds—the guardian of the exact moment when the life you've outgrown can no longer hold you. She doesn't wait for your permission to do her work. She asks one question only:

"Are you ready to stop pretending?"

And God, I wanted to say yes. But the truth is, there was a part of me still trying to hold it all together—the part that believed I could carefully edit my way into freedom. I wanted transformation to be tidy, aesthetic even. You know, candles lit, playlist curated, incense burning. But she just laughed—this deep, holy laugh that shook right through me—and said,

"Baby, you don't get to feng shui the fire."

That was the moment I surrendered.

This is not a gentle unraveling. This is the stripping. The burning. The unmaking. And yes, it's uncomfortable. It's the part where you feel the walls closing in, where your excuses sound thin even to your own ears, where the version of you that played small realizes she's out of time.

And yet—beneath the terror, there is relief.

Because here's the truth no one tells you: the fire doesn't take you. It takes everything that isn't you.
It burns the false names, the masks, the careful performances. It melts the cages you built out of old stories. And underneath all of it, you're still here—raw, steady, alive in a way you forgot you could be.

The Black Madonna isn't here to make you fearless.
She's here to make you faithful—to your own becoming, to the deeper pulse beneath your resistance, to the knowing that you will not burn away. Only the lies will.

You will try to bargain with her. Everyone does.
You will try to save the old life, salvage the old patterns, hold on to one last version of who you thought you had to be.
And she'll let you try—she's patient like that—but eventually, she'll lean in close and whisper,
"You already know it's over."

And she's right.

Because by the time she comes, the burning has already begun. The leaving has already started inside your bones. You can pretend you don't feel it, but your body knows. The part of you that aches in the quiet knows.

This is the threshold where the air feels different.
Where you can't unknow what you know.
Where you can't go back, even if you want to, because the old self no longer fits—like trying to zip up a dress three sizes too small and wondering why you can't breathe.

I used to think I had to earn my way into this fire, prove I was ready for it, gather enough courage to deserve the transformation. But she taught me something else entirely:

You don't step into the fire because you're fearless.
You step into it because staying where you are has finally become unbearable.

And when you do—when you let yourself walk straight into the blaze—you realize the thing you were most afraid of losing was never you.

You emerge stripped, yes. But also whole.
You emerge carrying the pulse you buried beneath obedience.
You emerge knowing that you will never, ever again trade your wildness for safety.

She is the final flame, the last gatekeeper, the one who does not flinch when you set down the last of who you thought you were.

And when it's done—when the heat has passed through you and you stand barefoot in the ash of everything you used to carry—there is no applause, no lightning cracking open the sky, no voice booming, *"You've arrived."*

Just silence.
Breath.

A ground that feels different beneath your feet.

And the knowing, deep in your ribs, that the fire was never here to destroy you.
It was here to set you free.

—

I sit in the hush after everything, my hands resting on my thighs, my breath unspooling slow enough to finally hear what's underneath it.

"Is it over?" I ask, though I already know the answer.

No, she says, her voice more vibration than sound. *This part is just beginning.*

I groan softly and tilt my head back like maybe the ceiling has a better plan than she does.
"Of course it is. God forbid we ever just... rest."

I swear I feel her laugh, low and warm, the kind that hums through your ribs instead of in your ears.
Rest will come, she says. *But not the kind you think. Not the nap-you-out-of-it kind. The kind where you finally stop fighting yourself and the quiet stops being so loud.*

I sigh, sliding my palms together, half-prayer, half-resignation. "I don't know if I'm ready."

You were never meant to feel ready, she murmurs, soft but unflinching. *You were meant to be real.*

I blink at the floor, then squint suspiciously into the air like she can actually see me.

"You love dropping cryptic one-liners and then disappearing, don't you?"

This time, her laugh is louder, shaking the space between my lungs. *Oh, sweetheart, if I gave you all the answers right now, you'd find a way to organize them into a spreadsheet and ruin the entire point.*

I press a hand to my chest, pretending to be offended. "Rude. Accurate... but rude."

Silence again. But it's a different silence this time. Not the heavy kind I used to get lost in— this one feels like being held.

"So," I whisper after a moment, softer now. "What happens next?"

Next, she says, and I can feel the words settling into my bones, *you stop performing sacredness and start living it.*

I breathe that in and feel something loosen deep inside m, a place I didn't know I had been holding on so tightly. But before I can stop myself, the question slips out anyway, carried on the edge of breath: "And what if I lose it again?"

She's quiet long enough for my doubt to rise, and then –
Oh, love. You will lose it again. No doubt you will. That's part of being here.
A pause, so tender I feel it in my throat.
And I will come for you as many times as it takes. I will call you home until you remember the sound of your own name.

Something catches behind my ribs, but I manage a shaky laugh. "You make it sound like I'm a lot of work."

You are, she say, but I can feel the smile in it. *But you're worth every reminder.*

I swallow hard, staring at the pattern of light across the floor. "...And you'll stay?"

Always.

There is no lightning, no trumpet announcing I've arrived, no voice from the clouds declaring me whole.
Just this: me, here, breathing.

I close my eyes, press my palm against the thrum beneath my sternum, and whisper back to her:

"I'm listening now."

And for the first time in a long time, I feel her smile inside me— that soft, knowing one that says without saying:

Good. Don't stop.

And maybe that's the thing.
This isn't an ending.
It never was.

It's the quietest beginning,
and it's already here.

CHAPTER FOUR

The Sacred Mirror—Love as Alchemy, Union as Catalyst

Opening Reflection—Love Didn't Save Me, It Initiated Me

I didn't fall in love with him then.
Not at fifteen.
Not even close.

We weren't lovers.
We weren't even circling the idea.

We were just... two people quietly orbiting each other's worlds, drawn into the same spaces without knowing why, curious in that soft, unspoken way you can't explain to anyone else. That first connection wasn't grand or obvious— it was subtle, like catching the faintest scent of something familiar on a stranger's sweater, something that pulls at a place in you that you didn't know was paying attention.

Back then, we were friends—loose, undefined, still unshaped by expectation. We traded glances that didn't seem to carry weight at the time, made jokes that weren't actually that funny but somehow always ended in laughter anyway, and sat in silences that weren't heavy yet, just unformed—the kind of quiet that lets you breathe deeper without realizing it.

I didn't name it.
I didn't analyze it.
I just let it exist, the way you let the tide touch your toes without questioning where it came from.

And then there was distance. Years of it.

Continents stretched between us, life folding and unfolding across separate paths. Time zones layered over time zones, messages that sometimes made it across oceans and sometimes didn't, seasons piling into years while we built separate lives that somehow kept brushing against each other, even from far away.

That distance—it was a wall, yes. But walls have their own strange kindness sometimes. Looking back now, I think space protected us from burning through something before we understood what we were holding. From far away, you can't rush it. You can't ruin it. You can't set fire to something too soon and watch it turn to ash before it's had time to grow roots.

All you can do is carry it quietly, deep in your pocket, uncertain whether it's even yours to keep—and yet somehow, without trying, it stays.

Because something in me carried him anyway.
Not as longing.
Not as fantasy.
But as a thread that refused to dissolve.

A recognition that didn't need words, didn't need explanations. My body knew it before my mind could ever name it.

And then, one day, we were in the same place again.

After years of living whole lives apart, we stood on the same ground, and yet—it wasn't cinematic. There were no fireworks, no swelling music, no sudden realization of love like in the movies. If anything, it was quieter than I expected. Softer.

It was more like... an exhale I didn't know I'd been holding for years. Like walking into a room I didn't even realize I'd left, and seeing that my fingerprints were still on the walls.

There was a steadiness to it, like time itself had been waiting for us to arrive here—and yet there was no rush, no pressure to name anything or make it more than it was in that moment. It didn't feel like falling in love. It felt like remembering the sound of my own name after forgetting it for a while.

And still—he watched me.

Even when I didn't know it.

Not in the sharp, heavy way that makes you feel like you need to shrink yourself, but in the quiet way someone watches the horizon just before sunrise—like he was waiting for something he didn't even know he was missing. His attention was soft but steady, the kind you only notice when you're still enough to feel it.

And sometimes, he told stories.
Not lies—not the kind meant to wound or deceive—but little edits, playful twists on details, like he was testing me without meaning to.

Will you catch it?
Will you notice if I'm hiding?

And I always did.

Not because I was clever or suspicious, but because my body had already learned his unspoken language. There was something about him my senses tuned into without trying—
I could feel the outline of what wasn't said, the quiet places where words failed but energy leaked through anyway. I noticed when the smile came half a beat too late, when the voice didn't quite match the story, when the light in his eyes didn't line up with the sound of his laugh.

I don't think he expected me to catch him.
But I think, somewhere deep down, he wanted me to.

And the day he realized I could see through him—not past his walls, but beneath them—something in him softened. Something small but unmistakable... exhaled.

She sees me.

Not the mask.
Not the bravado.
Not the carefully arranged edges.
Me.

The boy beneath the man.
The tenderness beneath the armor.
The one who'd been waiting to be met without having to hand someone a manual on how to love him.

That was the mirror.

It wasn't when he told me I was beautiful—he didn't.
He never said the words, and somehow that made it matter more.

It was the night when everything was quiet and the air felt heavier
than usual, like the world was holding its breath around us.
He looked at me, not the way people look when they want something,
but the way someone looks when they finally see.
And he said it. Softly.
"You're powerful."

The words didn't crash into me. They sank.
Slow. Certain.
Like a stone finding the bottom of a river that had been waiting for
it all along.

"You're capable of more than you've ever let yourself imagine," he
said, and it wasn't a compliment—a breaking-open.

Something inside me shifted without warning, like the first crack of
light in a sealed room.
I didn't answer, but I felt it.
Felt the heat in my chest rise, felt the quiet ache of all the years I had
hidden, folded, shrunk myself just to fit where I was never meant to
belong.

And for the first time, I understood—
It had never been about being beautiful.
It had never been about being chosen.
It had never been about being enough for anyone else.

It was about the wildfire sleeping beneath my skin, waiting for someone, anyone, to point to it and say:
There. That's yours. Stop pretending it isn't.

I didn't thank him.
I couldn't.
Some moments are too holy for language, and this was one of them.

Because in that quiet,
I realized he hadn't given me anything at all.
He had only mirrored back what had always been mine.

He didn't try to shape me into what he needed me to be.
Didn't ask me to shrink.
Didn't try to make me softer where I was sharp, or quieter where I was loud, or safer where I was wild. He simply held up the reflection of who I already was beneath all the noise.

And that reflection... it changes you.

Not into someone new.
But into someone real.
Someone closer to the bone of who you've always been, even before you could name her.

He believed in a future I couldn't see yet.
He whispered dreams into my path before I had language for my own worth.
He lent me his faith when all I carried was doubt—the kind so heavy you don't even realize you're dragging it until someone gently reaches down and lifts just enough of it to remind you how light you were meant to feel.

That's where it began.

Not with desire.
Not with fireworks.
But with resonance.
The quiet hum of recognition.
The sense of home that doesn't demand you move in right away, but leaves the door unlocked in case you ever do.

I didn't know it then.
I didn't know this was the fire that would one day remake me—that love, when it finally arrived in full, wouldn't come carrying comfort at all.
It would come carrying truth.

I didn't know it would ask me to unearth every buried part of myself I had tucked away just to be loved.
Didn't know it would demand my undoing before offering my becoming.

I know now.

Love didn't come to save me.
It came to initiate me.

The Early Mirror—When Love Saw Me Before I Did

I moved in with him before I turned eighteen, still more girl than woman, still learning how to carry the weight of my own feelings— the kind that rose up in unpredictable waves— while stepping into a home already heavy with its own quiet, unspoken tension. It wasn't the kind of silence that gave you rest; it was the kind that made you hyperaware of your every move, the kind where you'd sit on the couch and immediately wonder if you should have chosen the chair instead, because suddenly you're convinced there's a family seating hierarchy you were never informed about.

No one said anything unkind, and there were no dramatic scenes to point to, no slammed doors or shouting matches. It was quieter than that, subtler than that—a glance that lingered just long enough to make your skin warm, a half-finished sentence that stopped when you walked into the room, a sudden stillness where the walls themselves seemed to carry opinions they weren't sharing with you. I found myself learning how to fold my presence into smaller, softer shapes, like maybe if I took up less space I'd belong more fully.

So I taught myself to enter rooms gently, to measure my voice before it left my mouth, to find ways to be useful before daring to be joyful. I didn't make these choices consciously; my body simply knew how to adapt. There was something in the air that said, *You can stay, but only if you don't ask for too much*, and I listened.

And so I stayed kind, I stayed helpful, and when I couldn't stay soft, I stayed small—a survival skill I didn't have a name for back then, though looking back, I probably could have written the manual on "How to Become Practically Invisible Without Leaving the Room."

All of this was happening while I was carrying a full course load in pharmacy school—long lectures and longer labs, evenings spent bent over clinical notes that blurred together under tired eyes— and somehow, alongside all of that, I was caring for someone I loved dearly: his mother, whose body was growing more fragile with each passing week.

I learned her rhythms until they lived inside me, the way her lips would press together just before a wave of pain crested, the way her eyes searched mine for reassurance she couldn't bring herself to ask for, the way her breath would slow when my hand found hers and stayed there. I went with her to appointments, sat through treatments, brewed tea she could actually stomach, and leaned close enough that she didn't have to endure any of it alone.

She trusted my hands more than I trusted myself back then. When the fear rose, when the pain came, when the silence between us got too thick, she'd call for me—and I came. Always. I didn't pause to think about what I was giving or what it was costing me. I simply gave. Not because I was trying to be a savior or earn anyone's praise, but because I didn't know how not to show up for someone who needed me. There's a kind of love that bypasses thought, that moves before you have time to weigh it; that's what this was.

Meanwhile, he was working three jobs, doing whatever he could to hold everything together. We were so young—carrying more than our years could explain, quietly exhausted but unwilling to admit it. There wasn't much space for self-reflection then, no time to process how much was falling on our shoulders. We just kept going. We woke up, worked, studied, cared, collapsed, and then woke up again. There was no other option, so we didn't look for one.

And yet somehow, in the middle of all that survival, he saw me. Not the surface version of me—not the girl with her endless lists, holding everyone else's schedules, managing tears she didn't have time to cry—but the woman inside all of that, the quiet light still flickering beneath exhaustion and duty and growing pains.

He saw how hard I was trying, even when I felt invisible. He knew the house didn't feel like mine, that I moved through its rooms like a guest inside someone else's story, and he also knew that despite it all, I kept showing up as though it did.

One night, he said something I've never forgotten. He looked at me like he was seeing the version of me I couldn't yet see for myself and said softly, "You don't know who you are yet. But one day, you will. And I'll still be here when you do."

He didn't try to fix me, didn't try to make the heaviness easier, didn't wrap it up in speeches about strength or faith or perspective. He didn't need to. He simply named what was true and left space for me to grow into it.

And maybe that was the real gift of those years—that even when I couldn't find my own reflection, he became the mirror I couldn't yet hold. Even when I doubted my belonging, even when I felt unseen, he found quiet, steady ways to remind me: *You are not invisible.*

The Grief and the Womb—Becoming Mother in the Fire

I was in my final year of pharmacy school when she died.
His mother.
The woman I had been caring for—not just on the hard days, but on all the endless, ordinary ones that blurred into each other. Days that stretched longer than they had any right to. Nights folding into more nights.

By then, I knew her body better than I knew my own. I knew the way her shoulders shifted when the pain was starting to build, the subtle crease between her brows when she tried to hide it, the soft sigh that escaped her chest when my hand found hers.

We went to appointments together—endless hospital corridors that smelled faintly of bleach and something metallic, the kind of smell that clings no matter how many showers you take. We sat in waiting rooms where time warped and slowed, where you could almost taste the mix of fear and hope tangled thick in the air.

Her silences were never empty. They were layered with unspoken things—stories she never told me but that lived in the way she gazed out the window, searching the clouds like someone trying to remember where they'd left a piece of themselves.

Somewhere along the way, she became like a child to me—not because she was helpless, but because she trusted me in that raw, childlike way, as though my presence could somehow protect her from what was coming. She called for me when the pain rose, when fear crept in, when she needed someone who could sit beside her without rushing her to "be brave."

And I gave everything I had.
Every ounce of steadiness I could gather.
Every skill I had learned and every instinct I didn't know I had until the moment demanded it.
Every drop of tenderness I could still find in my body after twelve-hour days on my feet.

Not because I was trying to be extraordinary. Not because I expected anyone to remember. But because sometimes love is wordless like that—you pour because someone is empty, you hold because someone is slipping, and you stay even when your own roots are barely holding you upright.

When she passed, something inside me collapsed, too.

It didn't happen loudly. There were no plates shattering on the floor, no screaming into the night, no obvious undoing. From the outside, I still looked intact. But inside, a quiet implosion—a pillar within me gave out, and I had to pretend the building was still standing.

I was supposed to be graduating, smiling for pictures, celebrating "the start of my life," like everyone kept saying. But all I could feel was the hollow space where she had been, the weight of absence pressing heavier than the milestones around me.

And then came the questions I didn't know how to answer:
What now? Who am I if I'm not needed? Who am I if I'm not holding someone else together?

And just as I was asking those questions, life moved.
It always moves, whether we're ready or not.

I became pregnant.

Maya came quickly. Her presence didn't feel planned; it felt inevitable—like sunlight touching skin that had been cold for months. It wasn't a choice we made so much as something larger whispering *yes* before I had time to catch my breath.

But even as her heartbeat began inside me, another life was ending.

My father.
Colon cancer.
Fast.
Aggressive.
Final.

There was no slow goodbye. No easing into it. One week I was carrying life; the next, I was watching life leave.

He died before Maya was born.
Six months into carrying her, and already she was holding my grief in her waters, floating inside the weight of everything I couldn't bring myself to release.

I remember sitting on the edge of my bed, one hand resting over the curve of my belly, feeling the slow, steady rhythm of her heartbeat pulsing beneath my palm. The house was quiet, but inside me there was a storm, a weight pressing against my ribs that had nowhere to go. I kept thinking the same thought over and over, like a whisper I couldn't silence:
I can't fall apart. I can't let this reach her.

Because what if it did?
What if the heaviness made its way into her tiny, perfect waters – what if she absorbed it before she even had the chance to take her first breath?

So I began tucking the grief into the hidden corners of my body, folding it into places I thought she couldn't touch. I pressed it down into the spaces between my ribs, behind my lungs, deep into the marrow of my bones—anywhere I could store it without breaking. I convinced myself I was strong enough to contain it. I told myself that was what mothers do: protect, even from ourselves.

But holding it was not gentle. It wasn't soft. It was effort layered over effort, my chest tightening with each breath until it felt like the air itself was growing thinner. I swallowed the wail each time it rose up my throat, forcing it back down like something dangerous, like a tide I couldn't afford to let break.

I did it for her—for the small, fragile heartbeat floating in my waters, for the promise I hadn't yet spoken but had already made. I did it for everyone who was watching me, for the family that needed me steady, for the unspoken expectation that I could keep it together when everything around me was unraveling. And maybe, if I'm honest, I did it for myself— because some part of me believed that if I let the ache move, if I really let it move, it would swallow me whole.

So I buried it.
I folded every sharp edge and aching memory into silence.
I locked the door on my own sorrow and stood in the hallway pretending the house was still intact.
But grief buried alive doesn't vanish.
It waits.
It lives beneath the surface, patient and unrelenting, until one day it finds its way out.

Two days before Maya arrived, we moved into our new home. It wasn't ready—half-build furniture, boxes stacked in corners, spaces still carrying the breath of the people who lived there before us. Some rooms felt unsettled, like they were holding their own secrets. Some corners made my shoulders tense when I walked past them.

There were eyes in that house—not literal ones, but the kind you feel. Conversations lingering in the walls, fragments of lives left behind, whispers half-heard but impossible to place.

And then... she came.

She didn't just arrive quietly, like another moment passing on a calendar;
she entered like breath after being underwater too long,
like light suddenly spilling into a room I hadn't realized was so dark.

Her birth wasn't just the start of her life—it was the soft, trembling restart of mine.
Because the truth is, I was unraveling by then.
I was split open by grief I hadn't had the time or permission to name.
I didn't know who I was anymore, only that the person I had been was dissolving—
and then she appeared, pulling me back into my body,
anchoring me to the earth at the exact moment I thought I might float away.

She didn't just come into the world;
she came *into me*.
Into the hollow, into the ache, into the space where the woman I had been used to stand.
And somehow, just by existing, she became the reminder that life was still moving,
still choosing me,
still finding ways to rise inside me
even when I couldn't find the strength myself.

Because now there was someone watching me.
Learning me.
Studying the way I breathed, the way I moved, the way I carried the day.

And so I rose.
Not all at once.
Just slowly. Layer by layer. Step by step.

I didn't know who I was anymore.
But I knew I had to become her—the mother, the protector, the anchor.

For her.
And, eventually... for me.

The Breath Between Storms—A Moment of Light

There were nights I didn't sleep, and not for the reasons people like to warn you about. It wasn't Maya. It wasn't the midnight feedings or the bleary-eyed diaper changes or any of the clichés people like to package into neat little warnings about motherhood. It was something heavier, quieter—a stone I carried in my chest that no one else could see, but I could feel pressing down on me every time the house went still.

Grief doesn't leave just because there's a new heartbeat in the room. It lingers—patient, persistent—like a shadow that knows all your hiding places. It lived in the corners where I didn't let myself cry, tucked itself into my muscles, my jaw, my breath. It followed me from room to room, silent but present, asking to be witnessed even when I couldn't bear to look at it directly.

And yet, life kept pulling me forward. There was always something waiting for me: a bottle that needed washing, a tiny body that needed feeding, a floor that somehow managed to gather crumbs no matter how many times I swept. I kept moving because life left no space to pause, no place to crawl under the covers and stay curled there, no matter how much my spirit longed for it.

But then—without warning, without invitation—the light would find me.

It came in small, almost unremarkable ways. The kind of moments you don't think to write down because they seem too ordinary—until they split something open inside you.

Like the way she'd fall asleep on my chest, her small breaths syncing perfectly with mine until I could feel her warmth settling into me, loosening my shoulders, softening places I hadn't realized were clenched. Skin to skin, as if my body was still the only home she trusted, the only place where her world made sense.

Or the way Oerti would look at her, then look at me—his eyes soft, full in a way words would only cheapen. There was something ancient in those moments, like an unspoken vow passing between us: *We're in this together. We may not know what "this" is supposed to look like, but we'll figure it out.*

Or the mornings when sunlight spilled across the kitchen counter, grazing the fruit bowl, the unwashed mugs, the pile of unopened mail we kept meaning to deal with. Somehow, the light touched everything—even the mess—and for a breath, it all felt holy, as if the universe had paused just to remind me that beauty doesn't wait for things to be perfect.

Or her laugh—that wild, untamed, unexpected baby laugh that cracked open the silence and spilled across the room. It would crash into me like a wave, and suddenly I'd find myself laughing, too, without thinking, without effort—like my body remembered joy before my mind did.

One morning, I caught myself smiling. Not because I told myself to, not because I thought, *Okay, it's time to be happy again*, but because it happened on its own—a small curve at the corners of my mouth, unforced and honest. And for the first time in months, I felt something loosen, something return.

It was a reminder: *You're still here.*

Still breathing.
Still loving.
Still capable of feeling wonder, even after everything that's been taken.

It wasn't a roaring fire of joy—just a flicker, fragile but real.
And sometimes, one flicker is enough. Enough to keep going. Enough to believe there might be more light ahead. Enough to remember that not everything inside me had been broken.

Some part of me—quiet, steady, waiting—was still intact.
Still mine.
Still ready to be found when I was ready to open the door again.

What I Thought Love Would Be

I used to think love would feel like safety—like finally walking into a room where my shoulders could drop, where my body could exhale without having to ask permission first. I thought it would be soft and steady, like a warm blanket pulled around me at the end of a long day. I imagined it as a kind of homecoming, where I could walk barefoot without worrying that something sharp was hiding under the rug, waiting to catch me by surprise.

I thought love would take things away.
The fear.
The pressure.
The endless weight of carrying everything on my own. In my mind, it was going to be this gentle hand at the small of my back, steering me away from all the hard edges, whispering, *"Here, let me make this lighter for you."*

I thought love would be the reward for everything I had endured. That once it arrived, the heavy would finally lift. That the grief would soften. That the ache would be replaced by mornings full of sunlight and coffee and laughter—the kind of laughter that makes your stomach ache in the good way. I thought all those nights of swallowing tears in silence would somehow balance out, as if life were keeping receipts, as if someone somewhere was tracking it and would send me joy like a refund check in the mail.

But love didn't erase anything.
It revealed it.

It turned the lights on in rooms I'd avoided for years—the ones I thought I'd permanently locked. And there I was, standing in doorways I didn't want to open, watching the dust floating in the air, realizing how much I had left unswept. Love doesn't politely wait outside. It walks right in and sits down in the messiest corner of the room, crossing its arms like, *"Alright, let's talk about this one."*

And no, I did not appreciate it at first.

Love didn't come to hand me answers wrapped in silk. It came carrying better questions, the kind I'd spent years outrunning. The kind that peel away the masks I didn't even know I was still wearing—masks I thought had fused to my skin, masks I believed were *me*.

And suddenly, the life I'd built to feel safe didn't feel safe anymore. Love didn't make it easier. It made everything more alive, which meant it made everything louder. My voice shook the first time I spoke truths I had never dared to say out loud. The walls I'd built to keep everything contained grew thinner, and every echo came back sharper, clearer, impossible to ignore.

Love didn't take away my pain.
It walked me straight into it.
It sat me down in front of every old wound I'd carefully tucked out of sight, handed me the mirror I'd avoided, and said, *"Here. Look."*

And I hated it, even as I needed it.

Because here's the thing no one tells you about love: it refuses to let you perform forever. It shines a light into the places you've been hiding, the small beliefs that still live like whispers in your bones— the ones that say you have to earn affection, the ones that make you flinch when someone gets too close, the ones that leave you suspicious of tenderness like it must secretly be a setup.

There were days I wanted him to save me. I wanted him to see the exhaustion written all over me, to lift the weight from my chest and say, *"I've got this. Rest now."* I wanted him to meet my silence with the exact softness I didn't know how to ask for.

And he didn't.

Not because he didn't love me.
Because he couldn't.

Because love is not rescue.
Love is revelation.

And the truth was, I didn't even know how to receive what I thought I was longing for. I said I wanted tenderness, but when it arrived, I stiffened like it was a test I was about to fail. I said I wanted to be seen, but I had built entire masks designed to keep me invisible. I said I wanted partnership, but deep down, I was still rehearsing worthiness like there was an audition happening that I hadn't been told I'd already passed.

Love didn't come to fix me.
It came to free me.

But freedom, I learned, isn't soft in the beginning. First, it dismantles you. It shows you the walls you've built and the ways you've shrunk yourself to fit inside them. It makes you see all the places where you've chosen to make yourself palatable, small, acceptable to everyone except the parts of you that ache to feel fully alive.

And then it waits.
It doesn't push.
It doesn't shame.
It doesn't rush.
It just waits.

It comes with eyes that don't look away when you unravel.
With hands that don't reach to fix you, but stay close enough to steady you when you're ready.
With a presence that lingers in the quiet, saying without words: *I'm still here. I can hold all of this. Even the parts you think make you unlovable.*

And maybe that's what real love does.
Not sweep you off your feet,
but plant them firmly on the ground.
Not carry you away from yourself,
but invite you home to the places inside you you've been avoiding.

It doesn't free you from the fire.
It teaches you that you've always belonged to it.

How Love Showed Up (Even When I Didn't Know It Was Love)

It didn't look the way I thought it would.
It didn't come with roses on the doorstep or dramatic declarations in the rain, no cinematic speeches where someone yells *"Don't go!"* just before the credits roll.

Most of the time, it came quietly—so quietly I almost missed it.

It was less fireworks, more sunlight. The slow kind.
The kind that spills across the living room floor in the late afternoon, warming up your skin without asking for attention—until one day you realize the light has already seeped in.
It lived in the smallest, most ordinary things.
The ones you don't think to take pictures of.
The ones no one writes poems about. The ones you only realize mattered years later.

Like the way he came home at night, the faint smell of car engine exhaust and work still clinging to his shirt, shoulders carrying the weight of the day.
He'd set his keys on the counter with a soft clink, glance at me from across the room—not a long look, but enough for me to feel the quiet question in it: *Are you okay?* He didn't say it out lout, but somehow, I always heard it.

It was in the pauses.
In the way he'd just be near me when I was too tired to speak, our silence finding its own rhythm until our breaths synced without us trying. A small, secret vow between us, as if the air itself was saying: *I'm not leaving.*

It was in the way his hands kept moving, fixing things that needed mending, building what needed building. Paying attention to anything that had been worn down, as though holding the outside world intact might make it easier for me to hold myself together on the inside.

And still there were days I swore I wasn't loved enough.
Days when I thought, *If he really saw me, he'd know exactly what to do. He'd know exactly what to say.* I wanted him to read the ache in me like a book and respond with the perfect chapter.

But now, looking back through clearer eyes, I see that love was already there—just wearing a different face than the one I had imagined.

It was in the way he worked three jobs, burning himself down to two hours of sleep, so we could stay afloat.
It was in the way he didn't ask questions when I fell asleep at six in the evening, my back to him, the tears still drying on my cheeks. He just let me rest.

It was in the way he'd reach across the car to hold my hand, even if I was turned toward the window, pretending to be interested in the blur of trees and streetlights because I didn't have the words yet for what was hurting.
Sometimes his palm felt rough, calloused from days that demanded more from him than he had to give—but his grip was steady. And sometimes steadiness is everything.

It was in the way he'd stop at the gas station and come out with my favorite drink, never asking if I wanted it, just placing it in the cup holder like it belonged there.

Or how he'd push the last bite of something across the table toward me, pretending not to watch, but always waiting to see if I'd take it.

It was in the way he celebrated my smallest victories as if they were the whole point of life—a good grade, a passed exam, finally finishing a paper or a speech I swore was impossible.
The way his eyes would light when I entered the room, even in the seasons when I felt dull and faded, when I had convinced myself there was nothing left in me worth looking at.

I had been waiting for love to swoop in and lift the weight from my shoulders.
To carry me when I didn't have the strength to stand.

But love wasn't offering to carry me. Because real love wasn't saying, *"I'll carry you."*
Real love was saying, *"I will walk beside you until you remember how to carry yourself."*

That was his way.
Not polished.
Not poetic.
But constant.

Even when my reflection felt like a stranger.
Even when the fog between us was heavy enough to choke on.
Even when I didn't reach for him.

He stayed.

I remember one night in particular.
The rain had been falling all day, a slow, steady drizzle that made the air smell like wet earth. We were in the car, the heater humming

softly, the windshield wipers moving too slow to keep up. I was staring out the window, my thoughts heavy and miles away.

He didn't say anything, just reached over, found my hand, and kept it there.

I don't even think I looked at him. But I felt it—the quiet kind of love that doesn't ask for attention, the kind that doesn't need to be named to be real.

He didn't always know what to say.
He didn't always know how to meet me in my storms.
But he stayed through them.

Even when I was hard to love.
Even when the silence between us felt endless.
Even when I didn't reach back.

He stayed.

And maybe that's what love really is. Not the grand speeches, not the flowers—even though I do love the flowers he gets me just because, for no occasion and no expectations,
the ones he shrugs off like it's nothing,
while I secretly save the petals like its everything.

But the person who is still there when the storm is over, when the quiet feels heavier than the noise, and when you can't remember who you were before all of this.

The one who stays, not because it's easy, but because it's you.

Three Lights, One River

Maya was the first light.
The one who opened the door I didn't even know was waiting for me.
The moment she came, the entire shape of my life shifted, even if I didn't yet understand just how much.

I still remember the first time I heard her heartbeat—that tiny, steady rhythm that somehow rearranged me completely, like the air around me suddenly knew I wasn't just mine anymore. She came at a time when I was still learning who I was, when I was still holding questions about belonging and love, and somehow she chose me anyway.

Her energy was different from what would come later.
Where Zoe would bring sparks and Bliss would carry medicine, Maya arrived with roots. A quiet anchoring. A soft gravity. A presence that whispered rather than demanded, as though she had been watching me from somewhere just beyond the veil and finally decided it was safe enough to step through.

When she came earthside, she didn't feel small to me, even though she was. She felt vast— like she carried an entire story folded inside her tiny body. The first time our eyes met, there was no searching, no hesitation. She found me instantly, like she'd been memorizing me long before we arrived here together.

Maya didn't crash into my life with noise or demand; she slipped in like a knowing. There was a steadiness to her, even as a newborn— this grounded presence that felt older than time. I swear the room felt different when she was near, like she had shifted the atmosphere without anyone noticing.

And she cracked me open in ways I didn't expect.

Before her, I thought I understood love. I thought it would feel like safety, like something familiar and soft. But Maya showed me something deeper—a love that asks you to become more than you ever believed you could be. The nights were long, the exhaustion bone-deep, but in the quiet between the chaos, there was this unspoken vow between us: *we'll figure this out together.*

I remember one night in the half-dark, her tiny body curled against my chest, the room hushed except for the rhythm of our breathing. Outside, the world felt impossibly big— deadlines, decisions, responsibilities waiting at the edge of dawn—but inside that moment, it was just us. Her breath, my heartbeat, and the soft weight of her teaching me to stay, to be still, to breathe even when everything in me wanted to keep running.

Maya made me a mother, yes.
But more than that, she made me more myself.
She arrived carrying a grace I didn't know I needed, a steady light that rooted instead of burned, a reminder that life didn't always need chasing—sometimes, it only needed holding.

She opened the door.
She made space in me for everyone who came after.
She taught me how to listen when words weren't there, how to feel the unspoken currents beneath the noise, how to hold an entire world in my arms without collapsing under the weight.

Even now, there's something in her presence that feels like the pause between breaths—grounding, luminous, unshakable in its quietness. She taught me early that sometimes the deepest kind of power doesn't announce itself. It just arrives, rests, and changes everything without needing to be named.

After Maya, life began expanding in ways I couldn't have predicted—messy, beautiful, exhausting, holy.

And then came Zoe.

Where Maya brought roots, Zoe arrived carrying wild motion. From the beginning, she had this spark threaded into her, a quick, untamed energy that rippled through the house like sunlight dancing on water. You could feel her before she spoke, before she smiled—an aliveness that belonged only to her.

She carried curiosity like a birthright. Always watching, always moving, laughing as if she had an inside joke with the universe itself. Her laughter came before language, those wild, unexpected bursts that arrived like tiny bells, shaking something loose in the air.

Zoe shifted us without trying to. She tilted the balance of our family just enough to wake us up, to remind us there were still corners of life left unlit, unplanned, beautifully unpredictable. She wasn't here to ground us; she was here to make sure we didn't stay too grounded.

She reached for me in those early days before I even knew how to reach back—her small, impossibly soft fingers curling into the fabric of my shirt, holding on like she already knew some secret truth: *you're mine.*

With Zoe, the air moved differently.
She carried us forward.
She stirred us alive.

The air felt fuller somehow, like every corner had been asked to hold more—more warmth, more sound, more life spilling into places that had once been quiet. There was this low, humming undercurrent to everything, not chaotic but charged, like the world inside these walls had taken a deeper inhale.

And yet, inside that light, something in me began to dim.
I kept moving—because mothers do. Nursing and rocking, answering questions I didn't remember hearing, stacking folded laundry into neat little towers that would collapse before sunrise, and wiping counters that would mysteriously self-destruct again within the hour. At one point, I swear the socks were multiplying when I wasn't looking, possibly breeding somewhere in the dryer just to test my will.

My body was present, endlessly doing, but a part of me hovered somewhere just outside myself, watching the woman in the scene like she was playing me instead of being me.

I didn't call it postpartum depression. I told myself I was just tired. Overwhelmed. Adjusting. I gave it names that felt manageable, names that made me believe I could still muscle through. But the truth was simpler and sharper: I was disappearing. Quietly, invisibly. Smiling when my body wanted to scream. Saying I was fine when the closest thing to rest I'd had that week was hiding in the pantry for seven silent minutes with my forehead against the door.

And him—
he was building.

The dealership had just opened, and Oerti threw himself into it with the kind of focus that doesn't leave much room for detours. He was carrying dreams on his shoulders, balancing deadlines and risk and responsibility, pushing himself past exhaustion to build something better for us. And I loved him for it. I admired his discipline, his fire, his refusal to let go of a vision he believed in.

But building doesn't leave much space for being.
His body came home, but his mind stayed tethered to the weight of everything he couldn't drop. I felt it in the small things—the way his keys landed harder on the counter at night, the way his shoulders didn't fully lower even when he laughed, the way his jaw stayed set like he was holding his breath too.

And me?
I was stretched too, but from the opposite direction.

I was carrying the inside—the meals, the moods, the midnight wakes, the quiet emotional currents no one else named. I had become the unofficial keeper of the atmosphere, making sure the air stayed soft enough for everyone else to breathe, even if it meant holding my own breath so long I occasionally wondered if I was accidentally training for competitive freediving.

Some days, it felt like I was mothering alone—not because there wasn't love, but because the space between us was thick with everything unsaid. Present, but not always met. Tended to, but not always touched.

I told myself to be patient.
To remember the weight he was carrying.
To meet his silences with softness.

And most days, I could.
But some nights, the ache didn't listen to reason.

Because the truth was, I missed him.

I missed the ease between us, the way our bodies used to lean toward each other without thinking, the small collisions in the kitchen, the secret glance across a crowded room that said everything without needing a single word. I missed his palm on my back—not as reassurance, not as ritual, but as instinct, as if his body simply knew where to find me.

Now, his presence carried a different weight. Not gone, but thinned somehow. I could feel the static in his nervous system even when he swore he was fine. I heard it in his breathing. Saw it in his clenched jaw, in the way his shoulders never really dropped, even when he pretended he was resting.

We were loving each other the best way we knew how, but we weren't moving together. It was like we were dancing to the same song at slightly different tempos—connected, but off-beat. Sharing rooms but not always moments. Breathing the same air but carrying different weather in our lungs.

The love hadn't left us; it had simply drifted to a softer, steadier place—like a song humming low in another room, the one we kept promising to turn up again when there was finally more time. But time kept running, faster than our bodies, faster than our hands could hold it, and I found myself longing for pause. For presence. For one deep, unbroken exhale where we could find each other again, stripped of the roles, the deadlines, the endless expectations.

We hadn't lost each other,
but the distance between us had shape now.
And beneath all the movement, a quiet question began rising in me, steady and insistent:

Can we find our way back?
Not just to the love,
but to the us inside it.

And then came Bliss.

Even before she came earthside, I felt her like a gentle current under the chaos, something ancient threading its way toward us. Her name wasn't just an idea we chose; it was the sound of her frequency, the soft hum she carried with her—a promise whispered long before we could hear her voice.

She came into a world tangled in fear, headlines, masks, and uncertainty—and yet her presence was untouched by it. She carried her own weather. It felt like she brought a pocket of another sky with her, one where everything was softer, slower, steadier. The first time I held her, there was this deep stillness, the kind that settles into your chest and rearranges everything without asking permission.

And oh, her laugh—wild and unexpected, like a string of bells spilling across a quiet room, cutting through the heaviness without denying it existed. It carried this brightness that didn't try to soothe; it simply reminded you of something your body had forgotten: joy lives here, too.

I remember sitting on the edge of the bed one night, exhausted and half-convinced I'd never sleep again, and she let out this ridiculous, squeaky newborn sound—somewhere between a giggle and a hiccup—and I laughed so hard I startled myself. I thought, *Okay. I can do this. Maybe we'll survive after all.* Bliss had this way of cracking the edges just enough for the light to sneak back in.

Her gaze... it was steady in a way I still don't have language for. Those wide, blue eyes, unblinking, as if she knew something I didn't yet. There was no performance in it, no strain, just this quiet, ancient knowing—like she had come carrying instructions we didn't even know we'd need.

She didn't come to fix us—but she changed the temperature of the whole house.

She brought warmth into rooms that had been filled with obligation, shifting the energy without asking anyone to notice. She made time bend in ways I didn't understand—whole hours vanished with her asleep on my chest, her breath syncing with mine, my hands tracing the edges of her tiny fingers as if I could memorize them before she grew.

Bliss cracked something open inside us.
Not to heal it.
Not to solve it.
But to remind us it was still alive.

And yet, even with all their light, we kept moving in the old ways. We kept saying yes when our bodies were begging for pause. We kept helping, giving, hosting, holding—trying to be the steady ones for everyone else when, in truth, we were barely steady ourselves.

Even after the world stopped, we didn't.

We gave time, money, shelter, energy.
We carried people who had no intention of carrying themselves.
We opened our doors, our wallets, our calendars, our hearts, and called it generosity, when in reality it was a kind of beautiful, exhausting self-abandonment we were too tired to name.

We told ourselves, *They need us.*
We told ourselves, *This is who we are.*
We told ourselves, *This is love.*

But underneath all that giving, something else was slowly unraveling.

Our peace.
Our clarity.
Our bond.

We weren't fighting.
We weren't breaking.
We were just... leaking.

Little bits of truth we didn't say out loud.
Little hesitations we pretended we didn't notice.
Tiny aches we kept promising we'd tend to later.

But the later never came.
And eventually, the fire did.

And here's the thing:
The fire didn't start with the trial.
It didn't begin in courtrooms or accusations or whispers passed hand to hand.

The fire began with our tiredness.
With the weight we kept dismissing.
With the way we kept stretching beyond our edges until we couldn't remember what our edges even were.
With the quiet betrayals of our own needs, one "yes" at a time.

The fire came to show us the cost of forgetting ourselves.

And it came to teach us what we were no longer willing to lose.

The Reckoning—When Fire Became the Teacher

We thought we were being kind.
We thought saying yes was love.
We thought holding everyone else up was what good people do—
and for a long time, it felt holy.

At first, giving was easy. It was light spilling from a cup so full it couldn't help but overflow. It felt effortless, almost romantic, like we were participating in some secret exchange with the universe: "We'll hold the fire for others, and when we need it, they'll hold it for us." Our home felt like a harbor back then—doors open, lights on, food always ready, no invitation required.

And for a while, it worked.
The laughter was real.
The meals were shared.
We believed the love coming in matched the love going out.

But generosity, when it doesn't have roots, eventually turns into erosion. And it happens slowly—so slowly you convince yourself it's nothing. You keep saying yes because that's what love does, right? You tell yourself it's fine, we can handle it, we always do.

We gave and gave.
To friends.
To family.
To people with stories that hooked right into our softest places.

Some arrived carrying goodness.
Some arrived carrying shadows.

Some brought truth.
And others... oh, they came carrying stories dressed up in tenderness, carefully folded lies tied with the prettiest little bows of need.

And still, we said yes.
Yes, even when our bodies said no.
Yes, when my chest tightened the moment their names lit up my phone.
Yes, when the house got heavier just by them stepping inside.

We told ourselves we were strong enough to hold it all. That kindness meant being available. That real love stretched without breaking. That we were somehow built for this— the helpers, the holders, the ones with endless hands and bottomless cups.

But the thing about constantly pouring yourself out is... at some point, you forget to notice when you've been emptied.

And somewhere in there, without even meaning to, we stopped hearing ourselves. Stopped noticing the quieter truths. Stopped closing the door when our bodies whispered to.

Truth didn't kick the door down.
It started soft, inconvenient, like a knowing you try to smother under endless to-do lists and late-night laundry and one more round of saying yes. At first, I thought I was imagining it. Thought I was tired. Thought I was being dramatic.

But the body always knows.

I started noticing the way the air shifted after certain conversations— like something sour lingering in the corners long after the voices had gone quiet. I noticed the way I held my breath when certain people walked in. The way my ribcage pulled tight when their stories didn't match their eyes.

I ignored it. Of course I did. I told myself, "Don't be paranoid, this is what love looks like. You don't scan your friends. You trust them."

But the shadows... they had shape. And they had already started moving.

And then came the trial.

I wish I could tell you it all made sense right away, but it didn't. At first, it was just a few whispers—the kind you hear thirdhand, the kind that make your stomach drop even when you don't have the details yet. Then came the accusations, carefully rehearsed to sound like concern, delivered with soft tones and tilted heads and that unbearable, syrupy faux-compassion that makes you want to laugh and throw up at the same time.

People we had loved. People we had fed, prayed with, wept with, given our couch and our time and our table to—suddenly speaking about us like we were an idea instead of human. Like we were a story they could edit. No, worse than strangers—at least strangers can't weaponize your tenderness.

And still, for a moment, we tried to give them grace. Told ourselves, *"They must be hurt. They must be confused. They must still love us somewhere underneath all this."* We wanted to believe that, because believing anything else felt unbearable.

But then the pattern began to show itself, slow and sharp, like film soaking in a darkroom.

This wasn't confusion.
It was choreography.

The planning.
The positioning.
The "innocent" questions asked months before, filed away like evidence.
The smiles that lasted just a little too long.
The hugs you realize, in hindsight, were surveillance more than love.

Once you see it, you can't unsee it.
The veil drops, and the air changes.
Even the light in our home looked different.

That's when the grief really began.
Because the betrayal wasn't sudden.
It had been growing in the walls, in the wiring, the whole time.

We had been living beside something that had never loved us at all.

It tolerated us while we were useful.
It studied us while we thought we were sharing.
It memorized our rhythms—not to join them, but to learn the weak points.

And when the time came, it struck.

Not openly, but in the way cowards strike—with paperwork and gossip disguised as warnings, with half-truths sharpened into knives, with stories rehearsed just close enough to sound plausible if you didn't know better.

There were nights we sat across from each other at the kitchen table, papers spread between us, staring like strangers, asking out loud if maybe we had imagined the life we thought we were living. Because honestly—who does this? Who gets close just to take?

And then came the absurd moments. You know, the kind of things you wish you could make up. Hearing accusations so wild I actually laughed, out loud, ugly-snorted, in the middle of tears, because what? Some of it was so petty, so manufactured, so performative it could have won an Emmy if betrayal came with trophies. There were entire nights Oerti and I sat there shaking our heads, going, *"Really? That's the story you're going with? That's the villain they cast me as?"*

But the body always knows.
Energy doesn't lie.

And underneath the shock, the nausea, and even the dark humor, there was a deeper ache— because the thing about betrayal is that it breaks you twice. First in the moment you realize what was taken. And again when you realize they were never who you thought they were at all.

And this is where we chose differently.

We didn't run.
We didn't numb out.
We didn't hand our story over to anyone else to rewrite.

We walked into the fire together.

No music.
No heroics.

No grand speeches.

Just two exhausted people, cross-legged on the kitchen floor at 2 a.m., surrounded by papers and shattered expectations, looking at each other with swollen eyes and saying the same thing without saying it:

"If we lose everything else, we don't lose us."

Some nights, we screamed. We cursed. We hit walls we had spent years keeping pristine. And then we collapsed into each other like survivors of the same wreck, laughing mid-sob at the absurdity of it all, because what else do you do when the people you once prayed with are now inventing scripts about you like they're auditioning for a drama you didn't sign up for?

Other nights, we just sat in silence—opposite ends of the couch, breathing the same air until the weight lifted enough to move closer, to remember that we were still here, still us, underneath all the noise.

And somewhere in the middle of the wreckage, we remembered.
Not the polished version of us.
The real one.
The one from before the yeses that cost us our edges, before the open doors we forgot to close, before the spell broke.

"This was never about them," we said.
"This was always about us."

We let it burn.

We let it burn until the walls we built for safety fell.

Until the versions of ourselves we'd outgrown turned to ash.
Until, through the smoke, we finally saw the outlines of the life we
were always meant to live.

We weren't destroyed.
We were remade.

And there's something holy about that.
Something unpolished, feral, and alive.
Something that doesn't need anyone else to name it to know it's real.

Closing Reflection—The Mirror and the Fire

Real love doesn't always arrive like a soft landing.
Sometimes it comes as a confrontation—not the kind with shouting
or slammed doors, but the quiet kind that presses against your
chest and steals your breath. It's a mirror so clear you can no longer
pretend you don't see yourself. A gaze that strips away the makeup
you didn't even know you were wearing, leaving you bare and
blinking under light you can't turn away from.

It doesn't always feel safe. Sometimes it feels like being split open in
the presence of someone who refuses to look away—who loves you
enough not to collude with the performance you didn't even know
you were still giving. There's no room for half-truths, no space for
rehearsed smiles. Their eyes hold steady on yours, not because they
want to hurt you, but because they believe you can bear to be fully
seen.

And that's the thing about real love—it holds you while everything
false falls apart.
It keeps its hand at the base of your spine when your knees threaten
to give out.

It stays in the room when your voice shakes, when your pulse races, when your entire body wants to turn away.

It shows you the masks you didn't know you were still wearing and says,

You don't have to keep performing. You don't have to earn me. I'm still here.

When the mirror cracked—when our stories were questioned, our names distorted, our belonging put on trial—we had a choice.

We could keep pretending.

Keep playing the part.

Keep swallowing the words we wanted to scream, just to keep the peace.

Or we could burn it down.

Not in anger,

but in reverence.

Reverence for what was real.

For what we wanted to keep.

For what was finally ready to rise from the ashes of pretending.

We chose the fire.

And it wasn't elegant.

It wasn't soft.

It was messy and holy and relentless, the kind of transformation you don't walk through with dry hands and clean faces.

We didn't just survive it—we let it undo us.

We let it strip away every performance: the polite nods, the too-tight smiles, the small-talk dinners where our insides screamed louder than our voices ever dared. We let it take the guilt, the shame, the compulsive way we kept bending ourselves into shapes that would make other people comfortable. We let it burn away the habit of shrinking so someone else wouldn't feel small.

We let it turn to ash the lie that love is earned through exhaustion— that saying yes to everything is the way to be worthy.

And when the flames settled, what remained was honest.
Unadorned.
Rooted.
Sacred.

We became more sovereign.
More awake.
More whole.

He didn't save me.
I didn't save him.
But we stood in the wreckage side by side, breathing the same heavy air, choosing, over and over, to keep meeting each other there—not through fantasy, not through the version of us we performed for everyone else, but in the rawness of what remained when there was nowhere left to hide.

I think about the quiet mornings when we'd steal a moment over coffee, his hand brushing mine as if to say without words, *I see you.* I think about Zoe's laugh spilling through the hallway like sunlight we couldn't contain, how her brightness insisted on reminding us that joy refuses to be extinguished.

I think about Bliss curled against my chest during the pandemic, both of us floating inside her tiny, perfect breath—her presence somehow whispering life goes on, even when the whole world felt paused in fear.

I think about Maya, my steady one, the first light—her loyalty, her fierce, protective love for her sisters, her sharp, quiet watching. How she held more than she should have had to, and somehow, she became an anchor in the storm without even trying.

I think about the trial, too—the way our hands clasped under the table when the air was thick with accusations, when people we once fed and prayed with turned their backs while wearing practiced smiles. I think about sitting there, heart pounding, whispering to myself, *We may lose everything, but we don't lose us.*

This was never a fairytale.
It was a forge.

And a mirror.

For anyone who has ever loved so deeply you lost yourself inside it, only to discover that what cracked you open wasn't breaking you— it was remaking you into something truer.

So may every relationship that scorched you teach you the difference between burning out and burning clean.

May every mirror, no matter how painful, teach you to see yourself more clearly.

And may every time you thought you were lost become the exact place where you finally came home.

CHAPTER FIVE

The Voice Returns—Reclaiming Self After Silence

"There was a sound I used to swallow.
I can't anymore.
It's rising now—not to explain, not to be praised—but to be free."

There was this quiet, steady feeling I couldn't name yet, something whispering *there has to be more than this*. It is the kind of longing you try to reason with while folding laundry or writing the grocery lists.
I had started meditating by then. Not because I was trying to be spiritual, but because I was tired of feeling like I was drowning.

Not in the literal cinematic drowning where someone jumps in and saves you, but the quiet kind, where you don't even realize you're underwater until you're sitting in the car in a grocery store parking lot wondering why it feels like your lungs forgot how to work.

I was moving through my life on autopilot, folding tiny socks, memorizing pharmacy protocols, keeping thirty-seven lists in my head at once while forgetting to drink water— and somehow still feeling like I was failing at everything.

So one night, when the house was finally still and no one needed anything from me, I sat on the floor.

I didn't know what I was doing.
I just knew I couldn't keep doing what I was doing.

The carpet had that slightly scratchy feel that makes you instantly question all your choices. I pulled my legs into what I thought was a cross-legged position but was definitely closer to a tangled pile of limbs. My back was already aching before I even closed my eyes.

I lit a candle. Then immediately blew it out because I didn't trust myself not to fall asleep and burn the place down.

And I sat there, in the half-dark, trying to remember how to breathe.

Breathe in for four. Hold for seven. Out for eight.
The app had such confidence in me.
Meanwhile, my mind had other plans:

Did I pay the water bill?
I definitely didn't.
What if socks actually do disappear into another dimension and I've been blaming the dryer this whole time?
Did I leave the dryer on?
It wasn't holy. It wasn't peaceful. Mostly, it was me thinking about laundry.

And yet, I kept showing up.

Sometimes I lasted twelve minutes.
Sometimes three.

And yes, most nights, I fell asleep upright like some exhausted baby Buddha, drooling slightly, neck bent at a 90-degree angle that my chiropractor would absolutely disapprove of.

I used to feel guilty about it—like I was failing at enlightenment. But eventually, I realized maybe the falling asleep was part of it. Maybe my body was smarter than me, whispering, *Honey, we're starting with rest. The divine will wait until you're horizontal.*

—

I didn't have any lightning bolts. No angel choirs. No downloads from the cosmos announcing my grand awakening.

What I had were these slow, awkward, ordinary nights where I was sitting in silence long enough to finally hear myself again.

And then, somewhere in the middle of one of those evenings where the whole house seemed to hold its breath, something shifted.

It was subtle, at first—the air thickened, the way it does before a storm, and time stretched in this strange, syrupy way where I could actually hear the sound of my own inhale. That small, delicate rise of air.

And beneath it, something else.

Something older than me.

Not words. Not thought. Just... presence.

She was there.

The part of me I had left behind somewhere between keeping everyone else comfortable and forgetting my own name.
The one who used to trust her knowing without explanation.
The one who waited patiently while I swallowed myself to keep the peace.

She didn't come back soft.

She came back like heat under ice, like honey hitting the back of your throat, like something ancient and certain waking up in a body that had been holding its breath for too long.

And she didn't hand me a long sermon.
She didn't explain.
She just offered one sentence, quiet but steady enough to rearrange me:

"Your paycheck is not your provision. God is."

I laughed. Out loud. Alone in the room.

Not a delicate, enlightened laugh—one of those sharp, single-breath bursts where even your own body seems surprised by the sound.
I thought, Yeah, okay. Sure. Tell that to the electric bill.

But she didn't argue.
She just stayed, pulsing underneath everything, waiting.

I didn't stop after that night.
I kept sitting.
I kept falling asleep.
I kept half-praying, half-dozing, half-ignoring the laundry I still hadn't folded.

And the voice kept waiting.
Patient. Certain.
Like a friend who refuses to rush you, who leans against the doorway with her arms folded, smirking, knowing eventually you're going to see what she sees.

And I did.

It didn't happen overnight. It wasn't one big, brave decision.
It was hundreds of tiny ones—choosing to pause when I wanted to sprint, choosing to listen when I wanted to numb, choosing to stay long enough in the quiet to feel the ache instead of explain it away.

And then, three years later, standing under fluorescent lights in the pharmacy, counting pills into tiny amber bottles while the air smelled like alcohol swabs and cardboard, I heard her again.

Only this time, she wasn't waiting.
She wasn't whispering.
She was humming through my ribs like a current I couldn't ignore anymore.

And I knew, before my mind could even catch up,
it was time.
The pharmacy smelled like alcohol swabs and cardboard, that faint metallic tang that seeps into your clothes, into your hair, into your skin until you can't tell where you end and the sterile air begins. The lights hummed overhead, a constant, low electric note that made time feel slow and flat, like sunlight was just a rumor people talked about but no one had seen in years.

I was six months pregnant, belly pressed against the counter, counting tiny white pills into amber bottles, five by five. My fingers moved like they belonged to someone else: count, click, slide, seal, repeat.

Beside me, the charts piled up. Each one a name. A story. A whole human being reduced to paper and protocol.

And God—they got to me. Every single one of them.

Each one was a story, but none of them got told. Rows and rows of diagnoses, refill notes, insurance codes—all neat little boxes pretending this was care. And behind every label, a human carrying something too big to fit into a line of protocol.

I'd glance at a name and feel the weight of what wasn't being said— the mother with migraines that were really grief, the man whose insomnia came from heartbreak, the teenager on anxiety meds whose body was just begging for someone to sit still and see her. We were handing out bottles to silence symptoms, but I could feel it in my bones: the body wasn't broken. The system was.

A system that didn't see any of that.

They saw dosages. I saw despair.
They saw numbers. I saw names.
They handed me labels. I held stories no one asked me about.

The protocol told me to count, to fill, to label, to seal.
It didn't tell me what to do with the hollow look in a patient's eyes when they asked quietly, "Do I really need this forever?"
And it sure as hell didn't prepare me for the weight in my chest every time I realized the answer I had to give them—bound by policy, by liability—wasn't the whole truth.

I'd smile softly, give instructions, reassure them we were "managing it." But inside, my body rebelled. My pulse would kick up, heat crawling up my neck, this quiet, feral knowing pressing against my ribs:

This isn't what healing looks like.

And that day, as the amber bottles clicked and the overhead lights hummed, something inside me cracked.

The hum started deep—low, steady, impossible to ignore. It rose behind my ribs and caught in my throat until I could feel my heartbeat everywhere at once. I froze mid-verification, prescription bag in one hand and the bottle in the other, and just stood there staring at my hands like maybe it knew what I was supposed to do.

The baby moved then—a soft, deliberate nudge beneath my ribs, like she'd been waiting for me to notice. It felt like agreement. Like she knew before I did.

I set the bottle down gently, palms flat against the counter, holding on like the earth had tilted beneath me. My breath caught and stayed there, suspended, as the knowing rose higher:

We can't stay here.

That night, I carried it home in my chest, heavy and alive.

He was sitting down in our bed, one hand his folder with car lists, other hand calculator and pen, watching me with that quiet, steady patience that somehow reads me better than I read myself.

"I think..." I hesitated, which annoyed me, because I wanted to sound certain and cool and untouchable, but my voice cracked anyway. "I think I want to leave the pharmacy."

I expected questions. Logistics. Bills. Maternity leave. Reality. I expected him to remind me that we had another baby coming, that now wasn't the time, that safe was better than free.

But he didn't.

He tilted his head slightly, his gaze steady and confident, and then said the thing that rearranged my entire nervous system:

"Jump."

One word. No hesitation.
Then softer, like an anchor dropping right into my bones:
"I'll be right here."

That was it. No speeches. No "what ifs." No spreadsheets. Just faith.

I stepped into him then, letting my forehead fall against his collarbone, and he slid his hand up the back of my neck, warm and grounding. I could feel his breath against my temple, steady and certain, and thought, *Okay then. We're doing this.*

Two days later, I walked into the back office at the pharmacy.

The hum overhead seemed louder now, the sterile air sharper, almost like the place knew I was leaving it behind. My manager looked up from his desk, distracted at first, then confused when he saw my face.

"I need to put in my notice," I said, my voice steadier than I expected.

He blinked slowly, leaning back in his chair like he needed a moment to process.
"Besi... you're six months pregnant."

I nodded. "I know."

"You need this job."

I smiled faintly, not out of rebellion but out of relief.
"Exactly."

He stared at me like I had just announced I was leaving to start a cult in the Alps, then muttered something about maternity benefits that I absolutely did not stay to hear.

I walked out into the Florida heat, the air thick and wet and buzzing with summer. It clung to my skin like it wanted to know who I was becoming now. I sat in the car with my hands on the steering wheel, laughing under my breath, not because anything was funny but because everything suddenly felt absurd and terrifying and wide open at once.

I didn't know what came next. I didn't know how we'd pay the bills or what kind of mother I'd have to become to carry this leap.

But for the first time in years, the hum inside me was quiet—not because it had disappeared, but because I had finally said yes.

I looked down at the curve of my belly, pressed my hand there, and whispered,

"Okay, baby. We jumped."

And she kicked, sharp and certain, like, *"Finally."*

—

Walking away didn't make the guilt vanish overnight. It lived in my ribs, quiet but persistent—for every bedtime I'd missed, every kiss on autopilot, every time I'd hugged Maya and Zoe while my mind was still in the pharmacy aisles.

I'd picture it without meaning to—Zoe in her pink pajamas, curls sticking up like she'd been climbing invisible mountains, holding her blanket in one hand, asking if I was coming home soon. I'd hear Maya's soft, just-woken voice through the phone, her tiny inhale before she said "Goodnight, Mommy" while my hands kept moving through muscle memory, counting pills for someone else's story while I wasn't there for my own.

I remember the sound of my keys hitting the counter, soft but heavy, the little thud of my bag sliding down onto the kitchen floor like it was exhaling for both of us. And before I could even take my shoes off, Zoe and Maya's footsteps would come thundering down the stairs, small sticky hands already reaching for mine, trying to pull me back into the world I kept leaving behind.

I'd kneel down and hold them, inhaling the scent of peanut butter, crayons, and the faint sweetness of whatever snack had been smuggled past dinner rules. Zoe would be mid-sentence before I even said hello, talking so fast my brain had to run to keep up, while Maya would lean in quietly, pressing her cheek against my shoulder like she'd been saving that spot for me all day.

And I'd smile. Always smile. Always bend low and make it seem soft, easy, fine.
But inside, my chest ached with this quiet panic: *Was this enough? Was I enough?*

Later, after they were asleep, the house breathing quiet, I'd sit on the edge of the bed with my head in my hands, exhausted and pretending it was just the long day catching up to me. But the truth was simpler and sharper: I was afraid they'd grow up remembering a mother who was always near but not always there.

I told myself I was doing what good mothers do—working, providing, wearing my exhaustion like a badge of honor. But sometimes, walking down those pharmacy aisles late at night, I'd catch my reflection in the mirrored doors and barely recognize her. She looked like someone who'd been misplaced inside her own life.

And when I left the pharmacy, the guilt began to lift slowly, the way fog rolls back after rain—not all at once, not clean, but enough to see the ground again.

The mornings slowed down in ways my nervous system didn't know how to trust at first. For years, my days began in fluorescent light, the soft click of pill bottles replacing the sound of my own breath. Now, the light was different. It came in slanting through the blinds, soft and golden, landing on the counter like a quiet offering I almost didn't know how to touch.

The house smelled like cinnamon rolls and yesterday's coffee—that deep, slightly bitter note still clinging to the air—and for the first time in a long time, I wasn't already running before my feet hit the ground.

Zoe was always the first one in, bursting into the kitchen like her thoughts had been lined up overnight, ready to launch at full speed. She'd lean against the fridge, hair tangled and unbrushed, talking faster than I could follow, her hands painting the air with details I couldn't possibly catch.

"Mom—so Maya said there's this girl at school who –"

"No, wait, before that, you have to hear what happened in art class –"

"Actually, you know what, I'm just gonna start from this morning –"

And I'd just stand there, coffee in hand, smiling into my mug, pretending I was following, because interrupting Zoe mid-story is like throwing yourself in front of a train.

Sometimes, halfway through her monologue, she'd stop suddenly, gasp, and whisper dramatically, "Oh my God, I forgot to match Olivia's (the doll) dress with mine, I'll be right back..." before running off down the hallway like she was managing a full ranch operation on the side.

I'd sip my coffee—cold, always cold by the time I actually remembered to drink it—and think, I would have missed this.

Maya wandered in next, quiet where Zoe was wild. Always soft in the mornings, still half-dreaming, carrying that gentle magic threaded through her. She'd curl into the kitchen chair, one sock missing as usual, holding her favorite stuffed animal and a book she hadn't finished reading yet.

"Did you know," she'd start softly, like she was giving me a secret, "that if we were on Saturn, a day would last only ten hours?"

She always came with facts like gifts—quiet little offerings that opened new corners of the universe for me before I'd even finished my first sip of caffeine. I'd tuck a strand of hair behind her ear and hum, pretending to understand Saturn time, while secretly just marveling at how she always seemed older than the day she was in.

And then Bliss.

Bliss arrived like a prayer you forgot you whispered, padding into the kitchen in her footie pajamas, cheeks flushed, curls wild, dragging her favorite stuffed bunny by the ear like it had survived some kind of epic battle in her dreams. She'd climb straight into my lap without a word, her tiny fingers finding a strand of my hair and twisting it absentmindedly while her warm little body melted against mine.

And that was it. That was the whole sermon.

The weight of her in my arms. The hum of Zoe talking in the background. Maya humming softly under her breath while flipping pages she wasn't reading. The clink of spoons against bowls. The dishwasher running its steady rhythm.

Life wasn't quiet, but I was.
Finally, finally quiet on the inside.

And then Oerti would come through, half-dressed, one hand on his phone, the other brushing across my back as he passed behind me. It was barely a touch, a soft graze of fingertips just at the curve of my spine, but it said everything it needed to: *I see you. I'm here.*

Sometimes he'd set a fresh cup of coffee in front of me without saying a word, knowing full well I was going to get distracted and let it go cold anyway. He'd smirk when I'd take one sip and forget about it all over again. That was our little ritual. Him pretending to save me from myself. Me pretending I'd do better tomorrow.

It wasn't glamorous. It wasn't curated. But God, it was holy.

I'd stand there some mornings, just leaning against the counter, soaking it all in. Oerti brushing his hand along my back as he passed, sunlight spilling all over the kitchen counter, my daughters filling the air with giggles and questions, and I would think:

This is why.
This is the life I was killing myself for and missing entirely. This is the medicine.

Because if I had stayed, I would have missed this.
The sound of them. The weight of them. The wild, ordinary sacredness of it all.

And the truth was, it wasn't just about leaving the pharmacy.
It was about finally choosing my own life.
Choosing mornings like this one—chaotic and tender and full—over fluorescent lights and sealed bottles.

It wasn't the escape.
It was the return.

When My Body Started Speaking

But freedom asks for more than leaving.

It asks for listening.

Before my voice came back, my body started talking.
It wasn't loud at first, not shouts, not sirens, just little murmurs I kept brushing aside, like background noise I didn't want to tune into.

It began with the fatigue. Not normal tiredness, but the kind that seeped into my bones, the kind that made sitting upright at 3 p.m. feel like climbing Everest. I'd laugh it off when anyone asked, telling them it was just motherhood, just "life," just too many nights up late folding laundry and pretending I was going to drink the cold coffee Oerti kept reheating for me. But inside, I knew it was different.

Then the migraines—sudden, sharp, rolling in without warning like thunderstorms, blotting out whole afternoons I didn't have time to lose. And the brain fog, so thick I'd walk into a room and forget what I came for, end up staring at the refrigerator like it held the answer to all my life's problems. Sometimes I'd just make a snack and call it fate.

And my skin—God, my skin. It flared without reason, red, hot, burning like it was carrying something my words hadn't been able to.

I kept moving anyway. Mothers do.
You wipe the counters, return the texts, drive the carpools, pay the bills.
You tell yourself, *This is fine, this is normal, this is just what it looks like to hold it all.*

But my womb wasn't buying it.

She spoke the loudest.
She pulsed with a rhythm I couldn't ignore, holding cysts and memories I hadn't made space to feel, storing the exact places where I'd swallowed myself. Every "yes" when I meant "no." Every truth I'd tucked beneath the need to be liked, needed, praised. Every moment I'd chosen peace on the surface and paid for it inside my own tissues.

I used to think symptoms were something to fight, but now I see they were love letters written in a language my mind had forgotten but my body still spoke fluently.

The migraines were where I'd silenced my knowing.
The skin was where I'd stored the heat of unspoken anger.
The exhaustion was where I kept bending beyond my edges until I couldn't find them anymore.
And the womb... the womb was the vault, keeping all the moments I didn't have space to grieve yet.

It was her way of saying:
"This is where you stopped choosing yourself."
"This is where you swallowed the words."
"This is where you put yourself last."

The fire hadn't left me. It had only moved inward.
It became heat. Inflammation. Tension. Symptom.
Code.

And finally, when I sat still long enough—when the girls were asleep, when the dishes were done, when the house breathed quiet and I was too tired to perform—I heard her clearly for the first time.

You're not broken, she said.
You're birthing.

I wanted to believe her, but God, there were nights I doubted. Nights when my chest felt tight and the to-do lists multiplied like rogue rabbits and I'd whisper into the dark, "I can't hold all of this anymore."

And still, she'd answer, patient and steady:

Then stop holding what isn't yours.

That was the truth my mind didn't want to touch.
I wasn't tired because of the weight in my hands –
I was tired because of the weight I kept picking up that was never mine to carry.
People's stories, people's crises, people's comfort.
The endless yeses that had drained me dry.

And slowly, she taught me to speak differently.
Not to explain.
Not to apologize.

She asked me to write from the place where my truth trembled instead of where it had already been polished.
She asked me to leave space for grief without needing to wrap it in a bow.
She asked me to let myself be messy, human, holy—without packaging it to be consumed.

And the more I listened, the louder she became.
She told me: *Stop bleeding for their comfort.*
Stop editing the fire out of your own words.
Stop asking permission to be what you already are.

The voice that came back wasn't neat or gentle.
It rose from my belly, raw and unfiltered, carrying the heat of every swallowed no, every silenced knowing, every piece of myself I'd handed away too cheaply.

It didn't ask if it was safe anymore.
It became the safety.

This wasn't about becoming louder.
It was about becoming whole.

That's when I realized the voice wasn't returning to be liked.
It wasn't returning to be tidy.
It wasn't returning to fit neatly inside anyone else's expectations.

It came back to pierce illusions.
To stir what was sleeping.
To speak like a drumbeat.
To write like a flame.
To mother like a priestess.
To live like a woman who remembers.

And I could feel it everywhere now—in the quiet mornings with the girls, in the kitchen where Oerti brushed his hand across my back, in the laughter spilling into hallways, in the storms that had cracked us open, in the hum of life I almost missed but didn't.

Because once you give the body a voice, it doesn't go quiet again.

Where the Silence Taught Me

I used to think finding my voice would mean becoming louder.
Like I'd walk into rooms with words sharp enough to part the air, ready to finally be heard.

But that's not how it came back.

It didn't return as a roar.

It came back like water, slow, steady, reshaping me from the inside. And before the words returned, there was silence. Long, aching silence.

This was not silence born from fear, but from knowing.

Because there are rooms that cannot hold your truth, and wasting breath in them is its own kind of violence against the self. I used to think speaking was always power—that telling my story in full, every time, everywhere, meant reclaiming it. But some truths are too sacred to lay bare in front of the wrong eyes. Some fires are not meant for small rooms.

So yes, there were days I went quiet.
Not because I didn't know what to say, but because I finally understood that speaking would have cost me more than silence ever could.

That isn't self-betrayal.
It's self-preservation.
And it took me years to learn the difference.

But even in that quiet, something was stirring.
The faint and unrelenting hum beneath my ribs of the reminder that my voice wasn't gone. It was gathering strength. It was waiting for me to come back to myself.

And without warning, the mornings began to hold me.

Our days were not calm, but they were alive. Zoe doing her flips and handstands right on the kitchen wall, halfway through a story she'd started three sentences ago, words tumbling faster than my coffee could cool. Maya playing with her soccer ball in the living room, barefoot as always, socks always mysteriously missing (I'm convinced there's a portal in our dryer). She'd pretend to be playing, but I'd catch her stealing glances at Zoe's dramatics, secretly amused. Bliss perched on my hip, her tiny fingers tangled in my hair, giving one of those deep, content sighs that made my entire nervous system unclench without permission.

And Oerti moving through the kitchen like his own gravitational field, quiet, steady, pretending to be invisible but somehow orchestrating the entire morning. He'd pass behind me, sneak in a kiss in my shoulder, and without a single word, I'd feel it: *I see you. I love you.*

Thirty seconds later, of course, he'd be at the dishwasher, wielding a spatula like a microphone, announcing to the household that he was "the best houseman in world" and demanding a standing ovation for his "45-degree cup-stacking technique for optimal airflow." Zoe would groan, Maya would mutter, "Here we go again," and Bliss—his one loyal fan—would belly-laugh so hard she'd nearly topple over.

Then came the chaos: Maya chasing Zoe around the house, Zoe shrieking with laughter, Bliss clapping from her throne on my lap like she was watching a Netflix comedy special. Someone's toy inevitably landed in my coffee, the dishwasher hummed like background applause, and Oerti shouted from the refrigerator that, once again, "we're completely out of eggs."

It was messy. It was loud. It was ours.

And inside these unpolished, unplanned, imperfect mornings, I began to return to myself. Not because everything was healed, but because I finally understood: this was the life I had once prayed for in the silence of fluorescent-lit pharmacies, stacking pill bottles like tiny, desperate prayers.

This was the place where all the missing pieces of me slowly walked back home.

And now, when I speak, it's not to be heard.
It's not to prove that I belong.

I speak for alignment and for truth.
For the three lights watching me from across this kitchen—
Zoe, wild and untamed, already bartering with the universe in her laughter.
Maya, steady and unshakable, with a depth that holds oceans beneath her quiet.
Bliss, soft joy in motion, carrying an ancient song disguised as a giggle, the kind of sound that stitches broken places without even trying.

I speak for them,
and I speak for the girl I once was.
The one who thought her voice was too much for this world and swallowed entire galaxies to make herself smaller.

I speak so they know.
I speak so they never forget.

That no table,
no title,
no system,
no silence,
no story built by someone else's hands has the power to decide their worth.

That their wildness is welcome and celebrated like the very thing that makes them closest to God.

That their edges are holy—the parts of them the world may call "too much" are the exact places where their power lives.
That they never, ever have to make themselves smaller to be loved, to be chosen and to be kept.

That they do not have to fold themselves into polite little shapes just to fit into rooms unworthy of their magic.

That their "no" carries the same sacred weight as their "yes".
That their softness is not weakness.
That their fire is not too much,
That they are allowed to be both the storm and the stillness,
the howl and the hymn,
all in the same breath.

That there will be people who cannot hold them, and that this is not proof that they are unlovable—it is proof that they are vast.
That they are galaxies,
and not everyone is meant to map their stars.

I want them to know what I had to remember the hard way:
that their voice is not something to earn.
That they came here carrying it.
That they were born belonging.

And if there are rooms that cannot hold their truth,
they are free to leave those rooms
with their heads high,
their laughter intact,
and their magic untouched.

Because I have learned that you do not dim for love.
You do not disappear to keep the peace.

And you surely do not trade your fire for proximity to anyone who fears its heat.

This voice didn't return so I could be loud.
It returned so I could be whole.
So I could mother them from fullness, not from fracture.
So I could show them, not tell them,
what it looks like when a woman roots into herself and refuses to move.

I want them to remember,
when the world tries to make them small,
that they are uncontainable.
That they are allowed to take up space without apology.
That the life they are building is theirs alone to claim,
and they never, not once,
have to trade their truth to belong to someone else's story.

And standing there, in the middle of my kitchen with coffee gone cold, toys floating in mugs, Oerti smirking against the counter like he has choreographed the whole circus,
I felt it in my bones:

The crown was never given back to me.
It was never lost.
It was always mine.

And when my daughters read these words one day,
I want them to feel the inheritance rising in their own bodies.

I want them to know the voice they carry
was never meant to sound like mine.
It was always meant to sound like *theirs*.

CHAPTER SIX

The Night the Rain Remembered Me

The baptism that needed no church—the night the elements returned me to myself.

We were already outside when it began. No grand announcement. No holy man raising his hands to the sky. No music cued up behind us, promising redemption. Just the ordinary air of an evening we thought would end quietly—dinner, a walk, maybe a conversation meandering softly into night.

And then the sky shifted.

That hush came—the one the earth always gives you right before it delivers something bigger than you thought you were ready for. The sound of the world paused, holding its breath. The air thickened, still and charged, and then the first drop found me.

One. Then two. Then three. Cool against my skin, quick as a secret being passed, like the sky leaning down to whisper, Pay attention.

And then the rain came.

Not the kind of rain that sprinkles gently, asking permission to land.

This rain had intentions.

It came fast and hard, like it had been storing itself for lifetimes, hoarding weight in the clouds until it finally couldn't hold it anymore. The first drops hit warm, then cold, sliding down my neck, clinging to my spine. I gasped, out loud—which the rain absolutely did not care about, by the way—and I swear I heard that quiet inner hum chuckle:

Relax. You asked for this, remember?

"I did not ask for hypothermia," I muttered under my breath.

Not hypothermia, it teased back, *initiation*.

And so we kept walking.

We didn't run for cover the way everyone else might, ducking under awnings or scrambling toward car doors. We didn't look for a shortcut home. We didn't argue with the weather app about how this wasn't in the forecast. We just kept moving, step by drenched step, as if something deep in our bones already knew this storm wasn't meant to be avoided—it was meant to be received.

Thunder cracked in the distance, low and ancient, like the earth clearing its throat. A branch snapped off a tree ahead, sudden and sharp, crashing onto the soaked earth like an offering no one had asked for but was suddenly needed.

Still, we didn't stop. Didn't back off. Didn't even look for another path. The rain was guiding us. And somehow—and I can't explain how I knew this, only that I did—we were meant to be here, in this exact storm, on this exact night.

I glanced over at Oerti. His shirt clung to his chest, his hair plastered to his forehead, his jaw set in that calm way of his. I raised an eyebrow like, *Are we really doing this?* He gave me the smallest shrug, the kind that said, *Apparently, yes. Apparently, we're the people who walk into storms on purpose now.*

And that's when I felt it—words rising between us, not spoken out loud, but humming just beneath the sound of rain:

Let it fall.
Let it clear.
What doesn't belong anymore is leaving.

The water soaked everything. My shirt plastered to my body, fabric glued to my arms and ribs until there was no separation between me and the storm. It pooled at my collar, slipped down my spine, crept into the places where warmth usually hides. And somehow, instead of discomfort, I felt reverence.

It was baptism without an altar.

Not the kind someone invites you into. Not the kind with a priest, or candles, or choirs. This was a blessing older than all of that—a prayer I didn't know I had whispered, arriving straight from the earth herself.

And here's the strangest part: I wasn't afraid. Not even a little.

I was claimed.

It didn't feel like the rain was falling on me; it felt like it was falling for me. As if the sky had been saving this particular storm, this particular weight, until I was steady enough to receive it.

Beside me, Oerti walked step for step, stride for stride. He didn't move ahead. He didn't trail behind. He didn't break the spell with unnecessary words or try to throw his jacket over my head like some tragic movie cliché. He just stayed. Completely with me. In it.

And somehow, that—that—was the truest kind of love: not the one that protects you from the storm, but the one that refuses to leave your side while you're inside it.

By then, the night was speaking its own scripture:

Let it wash what isn't true.
Let it strip what isn't you.
Let it bless what remains.

And so it did.

That night, the rain remembered me.

And in its remembering, I remembered myself.

I remembered the one who does not apologize for intensity.
The one who trusts her wildness more than her plan.
The one who can walk fully clothed into a storm and not shrink, not apologize, not break stride.

The one who looks up into the chaos, dripping, laughing, heart pounding, and whispers into the soaked night sky:

"Yes. This is my temple too."

I Came Home to Her

Something in me died that night.

And it didn't happen with screaming, or collapsing, or lightning bolts of revelation. From the outside, I probably looked... fine. Just a woman walking in the rain beside a man she loves, soaked to the bone, silent except for the sound of her breath.

Inside, though? My entire life tilted.

I felt it before I understood it—like a thread loosening quietly in the dark. That version of me, the one who had bent herself into a thousand shapes so nobody else would feel afraid of her edges, finally... stopped holding on. She had been performing softness for so long she had forgotten the sound of her own wild. And that night, she just... let go.

I didn't try to catch her.
Didn't gather her pieces.
Didn't bargain or negotiate with the part of me unraveling in my hands.

I just stood there.
Breathing.
Letting the rain take her where she needed to go.

And then, somewhere between the thunder and the sound of my heart pounding in my ears, came this quiet, steady nudge inside me:

"There you are."

Me: "Excuse me?"

"You've been circling. Leaving yourself. Trying on masks that don't fit. You can put them down now."

I swallowed hard. My hair was plastered to my cheeks, my shirt clinging to my skin, the water running straight down my spine like a warning shot.

"I'm not ready," I muttered, half to myself, half to whatever was happening in my chest.

"Yes, you are."

That was the whole dialogue. That was the funeral and the birth. Two sentences.

I used to think transformation would arrive with trumpets, chanting, angelic lights, secret codes whispered in the dark. But this wasn't that. There was no ritual. No guru on a mountain. Just me, drenched and shivering, standing in the middle of my own undoing while the rain washed the story off my skin.

And then, something else happened.

She came back.

Not the mystical priestess I had been chasing in books and prayers for the longest time. I thought of her as a myth, ancient and untouchable. Like a story I carried in my chest but never quite in my hands.

I imagined her the way children imagine seashells hold entire oceans. If I pressed my ear close enough, maybe I'd catch her song. Maybe I'd hear echoes of who I used to be, lifetimes ago, when my hands knew how to pray in ways no book could teach me.

I used to think she was just behind me, breathing against my shoulder but never stepping in. A silhouette in the corner of my awareness, half-dream, half-memory. I studied her like she was someone outside of me, reading books, scribbling prayers in margins, longing for her like a lover across lifetimes.

I thought she was something to become. Someone I had to reach. A threshold I had to cross before I'd be worthy of carrying her name. But that night, in the rain, everything shifted.

She didn't descend from some higher plane; she slipped in through my breath.
She was already here. She always had been. She wasn't robed, crowned or distant. She didn't look like an oracle or a painting on the walls of ancient temples. She didn't speak in prophecy. She spoke like an old friend who'd been waiting at the kitchen table this whole time, sipping rea, tapping her fingers, smiling knowingly when I finally noticed her.

And she was... funny.

"You've been treating me like I'm a myth," she teased.
"Like I'm locked behind some temple door you haven't earned the key for."

Me, defensive: "Well, excuse me for respecting the lineage."

"Respect is fine," she said, *"but stop acting like I live anywhere but here. I'm in your spine when you stop curling in. I'm in your throat when you finally say the thing. I'm in your legs when you stand still instead of running. Stop outsourcing what's been yours this whole time."*

I laughed—in the middle of the street, soaked and trembling and probably looking slightly unhinged to anyone watching from a window. Oerti glanced at me again, eyebrows raised. I shook my head, unable to explain it in that moment, but he smiled anyway, that small, knowing smile he gets when he senses something's shifting. He didn't need to ask. He just… stayed.

But it was funny. Because she was right.

I had spent years imagining her as a woman behind me—whispering, waiting, holding secrets I wasn't ready to hold yet. But that night, under the weight of thunder and wet earth, I finally understood:

She was never behind me.
She was me.

Not the perfected, curated, high-vibration version. The messy, loud, alive one. The one with wet socks squishing with every step, dripping mascara probably making me look like a raccoon in mourning, muttering curses into the wind. The one who loved fiercely and sometimes too much. The one who had been here the whole damn time, watching me audition for my own life and waiting for me to stop.

It wasn't that I had to become her.
I just had to stop abandoning myself long enough to remember she was already here.
I saw her in the smallest gestures—the way I walked back into my home not just because but to truly arrive. The way I poured coffee slowly instead of rushing through the next task. The way I held my daughters when they cried, not to fix them but to let their grief be witnessed like sacred medicine.

I felt her when I stopped filling the silence with explanations. When I spoke only when truth was present, and when I stayed quiet even when silence made other people uncomfortable.

It wasn't about summoning anything ancient.

It was about inhabiting.

The priestess wasn't waiting outside the door.
She had been sitting with me this entire time, patient and steady, waiting for me to stop acting and start being her.

And when I finally let her, the weight of it broke me open.
The way relief does when you didn't realize you'd been holding yourself up by sheer force.
She whispered, soft but certain:

"Stop trying to deserve me.
I was always yours."

And for the first time in years, I believed her.

I Lit the Temple, And Then It Sealed Itself

Even after the rain stopped, something inside me kept moving.

It wasn't thought. It wasn't emotion. It was deeper than that—a vibration, a soundless hum in my womb, a trembling in my chest that felt like earth herself had reached inside me and whispered, *"Wake up. You're still here."* And suddenly, I was. Alive. Not just breathing, not just surviving—but alive in a way I hadn't touched in years.

It was the same kind of vastness I used to feel after hours of meditation, back when silence wrapped itself around me like a soft blanket of light and I actually believed I was "doing it right." Back when the air between my breaths felt like a prayer, and the smallest pause carried holiness. Those were the days I thought I was enlightened because I could sit for two hours without yelling at anyone. Spoiler: I wasn't enlightened. I was just very good at pretending my legs didn't hurt.

But the practice slipped away from me. Slowly, quietly, like sand sliding through my fingers. Weeks turned into months, maybe longer, since I had been able to sit in silence without it turning on me. What once steadied me began pressing on me instead, like a well-meaning friend saying, *"Relax"* when you're clearly on the edge of screaming. The cushion that once carried me became a place I could no longer rest, and every time I avoided it, I felt that familiar sting of guilt rise in my chest: *failure.*

It felt like I had outgrown one temple but had no idea how to find another.

And then this night came.
The storm.
The drenched, unapologetic baptism.

It gave me something stillness never could. It didn't ask me to rise above anything. It didn't ask me to "visualize the light" or "breathe through the discomfort" or any of the other lines I used to give myself when I was trying very hard to be calm while secretly unraveling. It didn't ask me to reach for God. It didn't ask me to climb out of my body to find peace. It dragged me straight into it. Into the ache, the breath. Into the sound of water pounding the earth and my skin until I couldn't tell where the store ended and I began.

It didn't feel transcendent. It felt human—wet, messy, ridiculous human.

This was not stillness the way I had once imagined it, sitting cross-legged on a cushion, palms open like I had life all figured out. No. This was wild stillness. It roared and hummed and cracked open the air, and somehow, instead of drowning in it, I dissolved into it.

For years, I thought healing would come when I finally mastered quiet. When I learned how to disappear in the hum of my own breath. But this storm reminded me that the point was never to escape this body. The point was to inhabit it. To let the heartbeat, the tremor, the breath, the soaking-wet skin all belong.

In that moment, standing there, drenched and shivering and more alive than I had been in years, I thought "So this is it. This is presence. Turns out God doesn't care if I'm centered—just if I'm here."

—

After the rain, after the ache, after laying down the version of myself who had spent years managing life like a checklist of survival, I came home—not to a house, not to a practice, but to the quiet, trembling space inside my own skin. The place I had mistaken for a burden. The place I had been abandoning for years while chasing the safety I thought lived everywhere but here.

At first, stepping back inside felt strange, almost too intimate, like walking into a room where I had once wept but never cleaned the floor, the air still holding the ghost of everything I had refused to feel. The silence pressed against me, thick and alive, as if it was leaning close, asking without words: *Are you really staying this time?*

I hesitated, my palms resting on my thighs like anchors, whispering softly into the hush, "I want to." And somewhere deep inside, I swear I felt her—my body, my knowing—leaning back with a sigh so old it carried lifetimes, and in her half-amused, half-weary way, she murmured, *Mmm. We'll see.*

I laughed quietly, shaking my head. "You're still mad at me," I whispered.

Mad? she teased, voice rich with something like mischief. *Darling, you left me on read for a decade.*

That was fair.

I didn't bargain this time. I didn't fill the air with promises I wasn't sure I could keep. I didn't apologize for showing up late, empty-handed. I just stayed—messy, trembling, imperfect, but present.

And slowly, almost shyly, she let me in.

It began with my breath, shaky and uneven, catching halfway as though my ribs were still deciding whether they could trust me to make space for myself again. It wasn't the cinematic inhale you read about in meditation books. It was the breath of a woman returning after years of leaving. But even in its clumsiness, it was holy—the sound of air finally flowing into a place that had been holding itself tight for too long.

Then I felt it in my belly. My soft, tender belly—the one I had spent years criticizing, covering, silencing. The place that had carried both life and loss, desire and intuition, a thousand quiet truths I had tucked away for safekeeping. When I placed my palm there, it was like touching an old friend who had waited by the door, arms crossed, leaning on one hip. And I swear she sighed beneath my hand, slow and deliberate, like she was saying: *Finally. Took you long enough.*

I smiled through tears, whispering, "I know, I know. I'm here now."

We'll see, she hummed again, softer this time, and I could feel the tiniest loosening in my hips, the faintest shift, like ice melting under the first light of spring. My body was negotiating with me, testing me, leaning in the way you lean toward someone who's left too many times but might—just might—stay this time.

There was no altar, no ritual, no chants to mark this moment. There was just me, barefoot on the floor, rainwater still clinging to my hair, my breath unsteady but present, my heart pounding against silence that finally felt big enough to hold me. That's when it hit me—not gently, but all at once, like something ancient breaking open under my ribs: my body was never where I carried the damage. My body was where I carried God.

I hadn't been banished from the temple. I had just been too afraid to walk through its doors.

And the second I finally crossed that threshold, she exhaled in a soft, relieved whisper that carried more knowing than a thousand sermons: *There you are.*

I pressed my palm deeper into my belly and whispered back, "Don't gloat."

She ignored me entirely. Typical.

And then the inevitable happened. The sealing. It wasn't given to me. It wasn't earned or announced. It arrived quietly, as though something ancient inside me had finally stopped searching for permission and clicked back into place.

And here's the thing no one ever says: sealing doesn't feel like floating upward into light. It feels like dropping down. It feels like gravity claiming you again after years of hovering just above your own life. It feels like your bones taking back their weight, your breath sinking into deeper soil, your voice steadying without effort because it no longer trembles for someone else's comfort.

I didn't feel new. I felt real. And God, real was enough.

Now, I can feel it everywhere—in the way I move barefoot through my kitchen on cool tile, in the silence I carry into rooms where I once felt the need to over-explain, in the soft steadiness of my gaze when I no longer wait for permission to belong.

I'm not performing presence anymore.
I'm inhabiting it.

And inhabiting it—finally, fully—was always the point.

The Lies That Tried to Rewrite My Life

They didn't just speak about me. They spoke for me. They carried my name in their mouths as if it were theirs to define, telling my story with a tone that never belonged to my voice. They used my truth—truth I had placed in their hands with reverence, truth that was sacred, raw, whispered in trust—as material for their own performance.

And the deepest cut was never what they said. It was who said it.

The ones I once let into my softest places. The ones I prayed with, shoulder to shoulder, our voices braided into the same song. The ones I cried beside when the night was heavy. The ones who once sat at my table, their plates filled with my food, their presence received as if they came carrying reverence in their hands.

And then—one day—they turned. My vulnerability became their ammunition. My sacred was turned into storyline. They passed my name around as if it were currency, trading it for ego, for proximity, for control.

It is its own kind of heartbreak when those you once believed were safe turn your intimacy into spectacle, when the prayers you shared in holy hush are carried as whispers for their convenience.

Not romantic betrayal. Soul betrayal. The erosion of bonds you believed were built on truth. The collapse of spaces you once called holy, now revealed as hollow.

Because the thing about distortion is this—it doesn't just sting. It unravels. It leaves you doubting your own sight. Questioning your own discernment. Wondering if the intuition you trusted, the sacred yes you once placed in their direction, had been foolish all along.

I stood in the fire of falsehood and felt the room around me go quiet. Their version of my life grew louder than my name. Their echo carried further than my truth.

And then I realized: they didn't care if it was true. They only cared if it served a role. They needed hierarchy. They needed a stage. They needed a place to stand taller than me, so they could point downward and call themselves wise. They needed to root their identity in the illusion that I had fallen. That I was less. That they were above the fire I was walking through.

I remember sitting in our bed late one night, my head in my hands, papers spread across the comforter like a battlefield. Oerti leaned against the pillow, silent, watching me read the latest filing. At one point, I muttered without looking up,
"Apparently, I'm the villain in their story this week."

He raised an eyebrow, deadpan.
"Only this week? Amateur work."

I laughed—sharp, hollow at first—then softer, because that's what saved us sometimes. The absurdity of it. How ridiculous it all was. The way people could rewrite an entire life from the outside and call it fact.

And if you've lived this too, I know you still carry the echo in your chest.
So hear me:

There are people who will only love you if you remain beneath them. Not beneath in power, but beneath in presence. In radiance. In truth. The moment you rise—clear, unshaken, embodied—they panic. Not because they hate your light, but because they need the world to feel safe again. And your light undoes the illusion they built for safety.

They were never afraid of your failure. They rehearsed it. They anticipated it. They counted on it. It was the story they held in their pocket for the day your truth grew too real to ignore.

Your collapse would have comforted them. It would have said: "See? She was never that whole. She was never that clear." Your falling apart would have soothed them, because it would have kept their shadows unchallenged. Failure would have returned the world to the order they knew.

But sovereignty? That terrified them.

They could handle your silence, as long as it leaned toward them for approval. They could tolerate your strength, as long as it bent when they pressed against it. But when you stopped bending, when your truth stopped waiting for permission, their comfort began to unravel.

They were not afraid of your voice. They were afraid that your voice no longer needed their echo. Afraid that your clarity no longer required a panel of opinions. Afraid that your prayers no longer carried apology in their seams.

They were afraid of the way you spoke without flinching. The way you chose who had access, not out of fear, but out of love. The way you didn't ask to be seen anymore, because you had already seen yourself, and it was enough.

They were afraid that grief hadn't shattered you. That distortion hadn't defined you. That you could still offer love, but this time, not for acceptance—only because it was who you were.

They were afraid that joy came back. That softness remained. That your power returned braided with discernment.

They were afraid that, no matter what they twisted, you rose anyway.

And when you did, your radiance became a mirror to their avoidance. Not the radiance that seeks attention, but the kind that rises quietly after you have walked through fire, held your own ashes in your hands, and still chose to bless the day.

Your clarity didn't argue. It didn't defend. It simply existed. And in its existence, it unsettled those still performing alignment. Your wholeness made their performance unravel—not because you exposed them, but because you stopped playing along.

This was never revenge. It was the peace of no longer asking to be believed.

And that kind of peace terrifies those who build safety on control. Because you become unmanageable. Uneditable.

That betrayal taught me what love is not. And it taught me this:

Not everyone who sits at your table came to feed you. Some came to study you. To imitate your warmth. To take your words and drape them across their mouths as if they were their own. Some came to be close enough to say they knew you, but never close enough to truly see you. Some came to gather your softness, only to spit it out when it no longer served their story.

They will use your name for proximity. They will carry your offerings like props. And when you stop giving, they will say you changed.

But you didn't change. You only stopped bleeding for those who mistook your lifeforce as a favor. You stopped handing out light to those who only came to measure their shadows against it. And when they realized they could no longer source themselves through your flame, they tried to discredit the fire.

But the fire never belonged to them.

Your fire doesn't need their belief. Your wholeness doesn't require agreement. Your truth isn't waiting for permission to burn bright.

And so I did not defend myself. Not because I couldn't. Not because I lacked words. But because I finally understood: the moment you try to prove what is sacred to those who only came to misunderstand it, you have already left yourself.

I didn't need to convince anyone. I didn't need to fix perception. I didn't need to spend one more breath in the courtroom of people who had already decided what version of me kept them most comfortable.

I was done explaining to ears that weren't listening. Done softening sharp edges to be allowed back into rooms I had already outgrown. Done translating my clarity into tones that made others feel safer.

Because truth doesn't explain itself. It lives. It breathes. It endures.

It speaks in the way my body moves now. In the silences I no longer rush to fill. In the gaze I meet without apology. In the space I take up without shrinking.

I became selective. Sacred. Sharp.

Not bitter—rooted.

Not guarded—clear.

Because not everyone who smiles at your softness knows how to hold your power. Not everyone who asks for your story has earned the right to witness your truth.

This is how discernment is born. Not from shutting down, but from waking up. Not from bitterness, but from betrayal.

It is born when you realize that not everyone who sat at your table came to eat with you. Some came to feed on you. To study you. To extract what they could not cultivate within themselves. To copy your becoming without ever tasting the fire that forged it.

They borrowed your language but not your integrity. They admired your glow but not your grieving. They quoted your prayers but never lived their own.

And so discernment sharpened in me. Proximity no longer equaled loyalty. Shared tears no longer guaranteed shared values. Spiritual language no longer disguised spiritual immaturity.

And I drew the line. Not with fury, but with finality. Not because I was above them, but because I was no longer beneath myself.

The ache became clarity. The rupture became boundary. The silence became wisdom.

And my truth? It became untouchable.

Because now it belongs only to me. Not to the crowd. Not to the gossip. Not to those who tried to reshape it with their fear.

I carry it differently now. Closer to the bone.

Deeper in the body. Not to defend. But to live.

The Fire of Falsehood—And the Truth That Held Me Anyway

There was a season when deception walked into our lives wearing the mask of law. When the story I had lived—carried in my breath and in my bones—was suddenly rewritten without my consent. What I had walked, what I had touched with my own hands, what I had poured my devotion into... reshaped by others into something unrecognizable. It didn't arrive like chaos, didn't scream its way into the room. No. It came with the cold certainty of a verdict already written. A play staged before the actors even stepped onto the floor. Evidence arranged like theater props to match the ending they wanted. Papers filed. Stories spun. Shadows dressed as evidence.

It was never about justice; it was about theft. A scheme designed to drain us, corner us, dismantle what we had built with our hands and our hearts.

We weren't accused of wrongdoing. We were hunted. Preyed upon. The trial became the stage they needed to make their lies look legitimate. Those deposition rooms felt like war disguised in paperwork. Every page they slid across the table stitched with intention: confuse her, exhaust her, make her question her own ground.

This is not truth.
I know.
Then why does it feel like quicksand?
Because distortion always tries to seduce you into doubting what you lived. Keep breathing. Stay here.

I sat there as fabricated images were placed before us—screens glowing with distortions polished into something that resembled proof. Timelines bent into cages. Facts stripped of soul and rearranged into a narrative I did not recognize but was expected to live inside of. It wasn't sloppy. It was precise. Calculated. A dismantling designed to unravel me from the inside out.

And for a moment, I almost let it. My hands trembled as I tried to steady my breath, my chest tightening as though I were the one on trial for a crime I had never committed, in a house I had helped to build, with fingerprints they had invented for me. That's the danger of distortion—it doesn't storm the gates; it whispers. It leans close, slides into your ear, makes you question your memory, your sight, your sanity.

Maybe I imagined it.
No. You were there. You lived it. Trust that.
But they sound so sure.
So does theater. That doesn't make it real.

That was the moment I learned that spiritual attack doesn't always arrive with rage. Sometimes it dresses itself in paperwork, logic, and perfectly curated sentences. It wears a suit. It calls itself reasonable. It arrives with graphs, screenshots, videos—a gallery of certainty arranged to look impenetrable. But none of it carried the vibration of truth, and my body knew. Deep in my womb, deep in my bones, something ancient hummed: *Do not leave yourself here.*

But still—I had no proof that would satisfy them. Every photograph we offered was met with a doctored one. Every timeline we laid down was buried beneath another manipulated screenshot. It wasn't the absence of truth that crushed me—it was watching them bury it alive. Watching them stack illusion on top of illusion until the weight of lies tried to smother the reality I had breathed with my own lungs.

So I stopped. I stopped pleading. Stopped trying to explain the vibration in my chest to people trained to worship documents over presence. Instead, I turned. I rested my head on his chest, listening for what no counterfeit could mimic:
the steady rhythm of his heart, the way his arms didn't falter when the whole world tried to burn down around us, the sound of our daughters' laughter in the other room cutting through the heaviness like sunlight breaking through storm clouds.
That was the evidence that mattered. That was the truth no courtroom could hold.

The months leading up to the trial felt like living inside a storm someone else had summoned. Papers landed at our door like weapons—legal letters sealed with precision, accusations wrapped in polite language but sharpened to cut. Each one designed not to reveal truth, but to wear us down. I'd open an envelope and feel it immediately: exhaust her, confuse her, make her question the ground she stands on.

It was never about justice. It was a scam from the start—a performance staged by people hoping the audience wouldn't notice the script was nothing but smoke. Greed draped itself in law, hunger dressed itself in righteousness, and they expected us to bow.

That morning, I stood in front of the mirror longer than usual. Not for vanity—for steadiness. I chose my clothes like armor, not flashy, not trying to impress, just something that made me feel like myself. Neutral. Clean. Unshakable. The fabric settled across my shoulders, and I breathed into one thought: *Whatever happens today, I walk in whole.*

And if they throw fire?
Then we don't burn. We walk through.
Promise?
Always.

The drive to the courthouse was quiet, the kind of quiet where words are too small for what rises in the body. Oerti kept his hand on the gearshift, close enough for mine to find it. Every few minutes, our fingers brushed—tiny lifelines we didn't name out loud. Outside, the world kept turning like nothing was happening. Gas stations. School buses. The sun climbing casually into the sky, unaware that we were walking into a storm.

We arrived early, though time didn't care. Time moved differently inside a courthouse, like the air had been pressed between too many histories, too many secrets. The walls carried weight. We walked through metal detectors, handed over our belongings, passed officers who looked through us instead of at us. My chest tightened under the hum of it—but beneath it all, something steady whispered: *They can't take what isn't theirs.* My heels clicked against the polished floors, louder than I wanted them to, like a reminder: *You belong here too.*

The courtroom was cold—not just the air, but the energy. Sterile in a way that tried to strip you of your softness. We sat side by side at the table, Oerti's hand brushing against mine beneath the wood, quiet, deliberate. Across the aisle, they were already waiting. Shoulders squared. Faces composed. Lips curved into easy smiles that had nothing to do with peace and everything to do with hunger. They looked like people arriving at a banquet, not a hearing. It wasn't guiltless confidence. It was arrogance rehearsed into performance. They looked proud of themselves, like actors who'd memorized their lines so well they believed them now.

Greed does that to a face. It gives it a certain glow, the kind of shine you can mistake for confidence if you're not paying attention. But I was paying attention. I saw the hunger pulsing beneath every calculated gesture, the arrogance in the slow swing of a crossed leg, the flick of a shoe keeping rhythm like they were dancing to their own performance.

One of them smirked when our eyes met. That mocking little curl, sharp and deliberate, like they wanted me to flinch first.

I didn't.

Don't give them the blink, something steady whispered inside me, so calm it startled me. *Stay here. In your breath. In your body. Don't look away.*

So I didn't. I held the gaze, unbroken, until their smirk faltered just slightly—a hairline crack they probably didn't even know they gave away. I looked at Oerti out of the corner of my eye and felt him exhale. He didn't move, didn't need to, but I knew he felt it too— the tiny shift in the room when you stop playing the part they've scripted for you.

Then the lawyers began. Papers shuffled, voices lifted into tones trained to sound neutral, rational, factual—except they weren't. They pointed at dates, waved photographs stripped of soul, stacked distortion on distortion until it looked like evidence, rehearsed so well it almost passed for truth.

I could feel my jaw tighten as they spoke, my chest heavy with the kind of restraint that makes your ribs ache. I wanted to say, *That's not what happened. That's not who we are.* I wanted to stand and name the game they were playing, rip the mask off the theater they had built. But instead, I breathed.

Not yet, the voice said again, low and certain. *Let them build their tower. Truth doesn't compete. It waits. And it outlives them all.*

They're lying.
I know.
Then why are they winning the room?
Because shadows always dance loudest before the light cuts through.

I felt my pulse steady. Even as they layered lie on lie, even as they paraded manipulated screenshots and timelines folded into cages, even as they slid photos across the table they had doctored into weapons—I stayed. I listened. I let the quiet speak louder than anything I could have said.

Across from us, their smiles widened when they thought a point had landed. They leaned into each other with little nods, pleased with their choreography. It was almost beautiful, in a way—how hard they were working to make illusion believable. But beauty built on falseness always collapses. You can feel it when you're close enough. And I was close enough to hear it in the pause between their sentences—that faint, frantic hum of people afraid of being exposed, dressing their panic in confidence.

I glanced at Oerti again. His jaw was locked tight, but his thumb traced slow, steady circles over my palm beneath the table. *I'm here*, it said, without sound. One quiet promise between us: *They can twist the story, but they can't touch what we've built.*

One of them smirked when our eyes met. I didn't look away. Neither did he. And in that moment, something clicked: we weren't battling truth against truth—we were standing in truth against appetite. And appetite always underestimates the ones who stay.

The judge listened, unmoving, his expression carved from years of neutrality. But then... a flicker. He raised his eyes from the stack of files, looked at them, then at us, then back at the papers. And in that pause, I felt it—he smelled it. The performance. The overpolish. The story that tried too hard to be perfect. Something inside him stirred, and I could feel it from across the room.
He was measuring the gap between their smiles and their souls, the weight between their tones and their truths. I swear I saw him inhale differently, as if even his body could smell the falseness in the air.

And for the first time since walking into that room, I felt something unclench in my chest.

Stay steady, the voice hummed again. *We're almost there.*

The ruling came faster than I expected.
No grand speech. No thunder of gavels. No cinematic pause for justice to descend from the heavens. Just a few quiet sentences, spoken in a tone so even it almost sounded like nothing at all— except everything shifted on the inside of those words.

The scheme collapsed under the weight of its own falseness.
The theater unraveled.
And the truth—the one they had tried to bury under paper and performance—didn't need to prove itself. It simply remained.

For a moment, I didn't move. I just stared at the desk in front of me, my breath caught in the back of my throat, and felt the tension I'd been carrying for months start to slip—not all at once, but in quiet waves, like silk falling from my shoulders.

I looked at Oerti.
He didn't look at them.
He looked at me.

And in his eyes, there was no victory dance, no "we won," no gloating, no vindication. Just that steady, grounding gaze I've known for half my life—the one that has always said without needing words: *I'm here. I stayed.*

I don't know how long we sat there after the ruling. Time bent. The edges blurred. Across the aisle, the smiles stayed plastered on their faces, but now I could see it—the brittleness beneath, the cracks showing where greed had overpromised and reality came to collect. They looked smaller somehow, not because we had "won," but because I finally saw through the entire performance.

And somewhere in the silence between us, that quiet presence stirred—the same one that's been with me in the rain, in the storms, in the long nights when I thought I wouldn't make it through.

See? it whispered. *You thought the fire would take you. But love... love made you unburnable.*

I closed my eyes for a moment and let the words land in my body.

Because the truth is, this was never really about the court. It wasn't about paper or signatures or property or even the schemes that brought us here. It was always about our foundation. About the love they tried to fracture and the family they thought they could undo.

They underestimated the quietest thing about us:
We don't break.
We bend, we bleed, we scream, we tremble—but we don't break.

When we finally walked out of that courthouse, the sun was sitting low and gold on the horizon, and for the first time in months, the air didn't feel like it was pressing against my chest. My heels clicked on the concrete, and I swear even the ground sounded different, like it had been holding its breath with us all this time and was finally exhaling.

I stepped outside, and the light hit my face. It was warm. Unexpectedly soft. Oerti's hand found mine, not with urgency but with the same quiet steadiness that's carried us through every storm we've walked.

And then I heard them—our daughters.
Their laughter spilled out of the car, Bliss's tiny giggles tangled with Zoe's dramatic retelling of some story only half-finished, Maya rolling her eyes but laughing anyway. And that sound—that bright, wild, uncontainable sound—sliced straight through everything that had been heavy and anchored me back where I belonged.

That was the moment I understood it:
This was never about winning or losing.
This was about keeping what was already ours.
The warmth of his hand.
The breath of our girls.
The pulse of a life built on love deeper than the reach of anyone's performance.

I leaned into his shoulder, let my forehead rest there for one stolen second, and whispered— not for him, but for us both:
"We made it."

And in the smallest grin, without even looking at me, he whispered back:
"We were always going to."

I laughed. Not a soft, cinematic laugh—an actual, shaky, exhausted laugh, the kind that leaks out when your body realizes it's allowed to rest for the first time in forever. He looked down at me like I was ridiculous, which I probably was, and I said under my breath, "Can we never do this again?"

And for the first time in months, he smiled.
"Deal."

We stood there for a while, arms wrapped around each other, the courthouse shrinking behind us, the sky splitting open above us— not with thunder this time, but with light.

And I realized: this... this is what had always been on trial.
Not money.
Not property.
Not even reputation.

It was love.

And love endured.
Love endured every paper, every whisper, every lie dressed as evidence.
Love endured when exhaustion pulled me to the floor and his hands pulled me back up.

Love endured when the world tilted sideways and the system tried to swallow us whole.

And maybe that's what I want you to know, if you're holding this book in your hands and your own fire feels endless:

You can walk through what you think will undo you.
You can lose almost everything they try to take—and still rise carrying more than you had before.

Because no verdict decides your wholeness.
No distortion can touch what is built in truth.
And no courtroom on earth has the power to undo what was sealed in love.

And that is enough.
More than enough.

Storyline

If you gave someone your truth and they turned it into a rumor, it does not mean you failed. I know it feels like failure at first, like you must have been reckless with your softness or naïve with your trust. *"I should have known better,"* you tell yourself, rehearsing every moment, every word you offered them. But you were not wrong. You were simply honest in a world that bows to appearances, and honesty will always look too raw for those who are still polishing their masks.

You were not too open. You were not too naïve. You were real in a place that could not carry reality. Your honesty was never the problem—it was the container you offered it to that was too small, too fragile, too unready. They could not meet you there. Not because you asked for too much, but because in that moment, their own soul was too brittle to hold what was living in yours.

You were not wrong for trusting. Trust is never the mistake. The mistake is theirs, for treating trust as if it were weakness instead of the crown jewel it truly is. You were the one who dared to stay sincere when the world around you was rehearsing connection. You handed them something holy, and they thought it was theirs to own.

You are not what they said about you. You never were. You are not a character in their narrative, no matter how many times they repeat the story. You are not the rumor, the echo, or the shadow. You are a living grace, a flame lit by the divine, and they mistook your sacredness for something they could trade like currency.

So let them go. Let them decorate their distortions. Let them invent the versions of you they need to soothe their shame. That is their business, not yours.
Your business now is the silence you choose instead.

And hear me: silence is not retreat. Silence is not weakness. Silence is the quiet that knows. It is the sovereignty of a woman who no longer needs to shout her truth into ears that were never listening. *"But won't they think they've won?"* Let them. Silence is not surrender. Silence is how she clears the room of those who no longer deserve front-row access to her becoming.

You are not too much. You are not hard to love. You are not broken for being sincere in a place that only knew how to perform connection. And those who are truly worthy of your presence—they will never distort your softness just to justify their distance. They will know how to hold you, and they will want to.

Because you were never meant to be tolerable. You were meant to be whole. And your wholeness is not a debate—it is your birthright.

So let them perform their distance. Let them whisper their justifications. *"But I want them to know the truth."* They won't. And that's okay. You already know: anyone who turns your tenderness into spectacle has shown you the limits of their own capacity. Believe what they've shown you. Believe it, and rise anyway.

Because the ones who tried to rewrite me didn't know what they were awakening.
They thought they were breaking me open. But really, they were leading me into the fire—the one they summoned, the one I survived, the one that tempered me into something they could never touch again.

CHAPTER SEVEN

The Myth of the Fully Healed Woman

Why we don't have to be perfect to be loved.
Why some of our deepest healing begins inside love itself.

I was seventeen when I fell in love with him.

It wasn't planned. It wasn't perfect. There were no signs in the sky, no whispered omens, no divine scroll announcing his arrival. It was just him—this boy who somehow felt like home before I even had words for what home meant.

I can still feel it if I close my eyes: the way the world blurred a little when he looked at me, like time tilted on its side and gravity shifted just enough to let me fall without noticing. I wasn't thinking about forever. I wasn't thinking about destiny or soul contracts or healing. I wasn't even thinking about love, not really. I was just seventeen—all skin and nerves, still growing into myself, still figuring out where I ended and the world began.

And yet, when it came to him, there was no hesitation. No weighing of pros and cons. No inner debate. My body knew before my mind did. There was an ease to it, a quiet yes lodged so deep inside my chest I didn't need to explain it to anyone. *Just go*, something inside whispered. *This matters.*

We weren't spiritual then. We weren't "awake." We weren't sitting in moon circles calling down guidance or dissecting our childhood wounds with the language of therapists and teachers. We were just two souls on different continents, trying to find our way to each other in a world that made it nearly impossible.

Sometimes I think about those nights—long-distance calls that cut out mid-laughter, letters that took weeks to arrive, the ache of wanting someone so close but living oceans apart. There was nothing glamorous about it. No sacred rituals, no high-minded teachings, no idea of what this love would demand. Just a stubborn faith in each other we didn't yet have words for.

I didn't know then how much that yes would ask of me.
I didn't know about the fires ahead.
I didn't know about the breaking and mending and breaking again.
But if I'm honest, I think that was the gift—that innocent, unstudied beginning. Because we didn't fall in love from our wounds or our wisdom; we fell from somewhere purer, somewhere untouched by all the noise that would come later.

And later... the noise came.

Years later, when I began to step into my own spiritual path, I found myself spiraling into doubt.

It happened slowly, almost imperceptibly at first—like a shadow moving across a field at sunset. I started reading the books, attending the retreats, following the teachers who promised answers. I was learning the language of healing, mapping childhood wounds, and unearthing ancestral patterns I hadn't even known were there.

And as I awakened to the weight of those stories, as I began unearthing all the places within me where old griefs and buried fears still lived, I couldn't help but wonder if this love, this marriage, had been born from a version of me that didn't yet "know better." And somewhere along the way, a quiet question began to hum beneath the surface:
Had I chosen too soon?
Was I really in the right love... or had I built my life on a foundation I wasn't conscious enough to choose?

The spiritual spaces I wandered into didn't make it easier. Everywhere I turned, there was this quiet suggestion—spoken or implied—that a truly conscious relationship required years of self-work first. That we were meant to heal our wounds before choosing another. That until we were whole, love would always be distorted.

And I believed it for a while. I thought maybe I had done it all backwards. Maybe I should have waited until I had unraveled every thread of my past, until I had perfected the language of boundaries and shadow work and soul alignment. Maybe, I thought, the reason love felt heavy sometimes—the reason we clashed and triggered and broke open in ways I didn't yet have tools to name—was because I had entered it without being fully healed.

I started looking back at us like maybe I had made a mistake—like I should have waited until I had language for my shadows, until I had untangled the wounds I didn't yet know were mine, until I was "fully whole" before letting someone else hold my heart. I thought maybe I had gotten it wrong simply because I'd chosen young.

I questioned everything. Him. Us. Me.

I imagined alternate timelines where I waited, where I became some wiser, healed version of myself before letting love in. I wondered if the right thing would've been to walk away until I "knew who I was."

And while I know it's often offered with good intentions, underneath it lives something heavier—a belief that love is something you must earn through perfection. That wounds make you unworthy. That triggers disqualify you. That love is a reward for the healed and the prepared, and the rest of us must wait until we're flawless enough to deserve it.

I watched so many women believe this.

Priestesses. Healers. Seekers.

Women who carry galaxies in their hearts and still wait.

Wait until they've shed every fear.

Until they've integrated every shadow.

Until they've "cleaned up" their energy enough to finally be received by someone "worthy."

They think that when they finally become a fully healed woman, then love will come.

But they're not just waiting on themselves.

They're waiting on him, too—the perfect man, the conscious king, the one who speaks their language, knows their soul, does his work, holds the polarity, feels like God in form.

And the thing is... he doesn't exist. Not like that. Not as some flawless, ready-made soulmate stamped with divine certification. *Hate to break it to you,* my higher self teased one night, *but he's not coming pre-assembled.*

And so, when someone shows up who isn't all of that—who still has fears, who stumbles with communication, who's figuring it out in real time—they turn away.

Not because he isn't enough.
But because they think their love will only be safe inside someone else's completeness.

But what if that belief is what's keeping so many of us alone?
What if love doesn't come after the healing... but it *initiates* it?

What if love is the container,
the temple,
the fire,
where the healing begins?

I know it was for me.

Because here's the truth no one tells you: the work comes anyway.

You don't get to skip your healing by falling in love first. You don't bypass the fire just because you said yes early. The mirror finds you either way. The shadows rise either way. The patterns surface whether you've memorized the language for them or not.

And what I see now is this: Oerti and I didn't avoid the work. We walked straight into it—without preparation, without frameworks, without rules. We didn't just face our wounds; we built a life inside them.

Because when the fires came, when the storms hit and the weight of life pressed down on us, it wasn't the theories or the teachings or the perfect self I was working toward that held me. It was him.

It was us. It was the love we had already chosen before either of us knew the language of awakening or embodiment. And the longer I walked this path, the more I began to see that maybe, just maybe, I hadn't made a mistake at all.

Maybe love had chosen me first.
Maybe this was never about waiting until I was healed enough to be worthy of love.
Maybe this was about letting love become the place where the healing would happen.

And that realization... it undid something deep in me. It softened the perfectionism, the striving, the quiet shame of not having "done it right." I began to understand that some of us don't get to prepare for love like an exam. Some of us are thrown into the deep end before we know how to swim, and somehow, in the flailing and gasping and reaching for each other, we learn.

We heal because we love.
We awaken because we stay.

Real Love Is a Mirror, Not a Finish Line

Real love didn't stand at the end of the road waiting for me to finally become whole, holding some imagined crown and clapping because I'd finally fixed all the broken places. It didn't wait for me to earn it, to cross some invisible finish line where all my wounds had been sutured shut and I could finally be deemed worthy.

It came in the middle of everything—when nothing about me felt tidy or complete—and it walked straight into the chaos of my becoming.

It didn't ask me to be ready. It didn't ask me to have answers. It showed up with its hands open, steady, patient, and willing to stand inside the storm without needing to rescue me from it.

"Oh, you mean we're not getting a warning before the soul work begins?" I remember thinking once, half laughing, half praying. My higher self just smirked: *Sweetheart, the syllabus has always been... surprise.*

Love didn't fix me. It didn't save me. It didn't try to make me smaller so I would be easier to love. It stood with me in the heat, inside the fire itself, holding up a mirror I wasn't sure I wanted to face. And in that mirror, I saw the parts of me I had buried so deep I'd almost convinced myself they didn't exist—the moments I closed my heart without realizing it, the places where I disappeared when things got hard, the old, quiet ache that still believed I wasn't lovable if I wasn't perfect.

And love didn't shame me for any of it. It didn't threaten to leave if I didn't get it right. It didn't force me into a shape I didn't belong in. It told the truth without violence, and in its steadiness, I heard something I'd never known before: *I am not going anywhere.*

My healing didn't happen because I waited until I was ready, because I perfected myself first and earned my place at the table. It happened because love met me when I wasn't ready, when I was tangled and messy and full of edges, and instead of breaking me apart, it broke me open. It cracked the sealed rooms where I had stored my unspoken fears and old grief, the silent beliefs I didn't even know were shaping my choices, and the shadows I thought I had already outgrown.

And here's the thing: we didn't get it right all the time. We still don't. Sometimes we miss each other entirely. Sometimes we circle the same argument like we're auditioning for a play no one wants to star in. But somewhere along the way, I stopped believing that love was about getting it right. The sacredness was never in the perfection. It was always in the choosing.

Choosing to pause when my ego wanted to win the fight.
Choosing to stay when everything in me wanted to run.
Choosing to unclench my throat and speak, even when silence would have kept the peace.
Choosing to forgive, not as some grand single act, but over and over again—every time truth peeled back another layer and asked us to grow beyond what we had been before.

"You're telling me we're signing up for advanced coursework with no prerequisites?" I muttered to myself more than once. And there it was again, that quiet voice: *You came here for this.*

Real love is where you're forced to meet your own face. Not the one you curate for the world, not the one that looks composed and self-knowing, but the one beneath it all—the raw one, the tender one, the furious one, the soft one, the shining one.

And somehow, in the middle of all those faces, you're still held. You're still chosen. You're still loved—not despite your edges, but because of them.

Love didn't wait for us to be perfect. It gave us a place where we could finally stop pretending. It gave us somewhere to stumble without being shamed, to soften without being punished, to be seen without having to edit ourselves into something easier to love.

So if you're still waiting for the person who has already "done the work," the one who will never trigger you or disappoint you, the one who will only speak the right words and will never get it wrong—you might be waiting forever.

But if you are willing to open to someone real, someone who carries their own shadows but chooses to walk beside you anyway, someone who doesn't have the map but still wants to take the road with you—you may just meet the kind of love that doesn't arrive to complete you, but to unmask you, revealing the you that's been waiting to be seen all along.

What Sacred Relationship Really Offers

Sacred relationship isn't where you arrive when you've finally finished healing. It isn't the prize at the end of all your work, the moment where you've mastered every trigger and earned a lifetime of ease. It isn't soft edges and safety wrapped in silk.

It's where your soul chooses, again and again, to rise.
Not because it's easy, but because something deep inside you recognizes what is real—and dares to stand in it anyway.

"We're doing this again?" I've whispered into the quiet more than once. And the softest reply always comes back: *Always. Until it opens.*

Sacred love doesn't promise harmony. Some days it feels soft and weightless, but many days it feels like friction against bone. It asks you to step into fire you didn't know you carried. It will bring you face-to-face with every part of yourself that still wants to shut down, escape, perform, prove, or disappear—every survival pattern that once protected you but now keeps you small. And somewhere in the middle of one of those moments, I actually thought *"Oh good, my inner seven-year-old and my inner lawyer have decided to co-host today's argument. Perfect."*

And even there, in the rawest places, there is someone standing at the doorway, hand steady, saying softly, *"I'm not leaving."* And of course, my ego whispered, *"Maybe I'm leaving."* But my body sighed back, *"No, we're staying."* Turns out the body always knows before the mind catches up.

Sacred relationship isn't about finding your missing half. It's about meeting someone whole enough to hold space for your becoming while letting you hold theirs too. Two souls who know they are already enough on their own—and yet choose each other because something ancient in their bodies knows they came here to create together.

It's about growth that refuses to be tidy. Healing that doesn't require you to hide your wildness or silence your voice. Love that doesn't need performance or perfection to stay committed.

It's not about always agreeing. It's about learning how to disagree without burning the bridge between you. There were times I swore I was done, and then five minutes later, I'd hear myself saying *"Fine, but also...are you hungry?"* Because apparently my higher self and my nervous system can't fight and starve at the same time.

It's about finding the words when they tremble in your throat and saying them anyway. It's about listening even when you don't want to, staying in the discomfort long enough to discover the deeper truth beneath it.

And it's not about avoiding triggers—that's one of the oldest lies. That "real" love feels effortless. That conflict means you chose wrong. But sacred love will press into the bruises you've tried to hide, not to wound you but to bring them to the surface so they can finally dissolve.

It sounds like this:
"This hurts, and I want to stay."
"This is hard, but I'm not walking away."

And when the breakdowns come—and they will—sacred relationship doesn't bury them beneath false peace. It turns them into altars.

Altars where the old stories are named and released instead of quietly carried forever.
Altars where shame loses its grip.
Altars where the unspoken finally has somewhere to breathe.

Because sacred love isn't sterile or scripted. It's holy and unruly. It will strip away everything that isn't real. It will pull up the grief you've been holding since childhood, the rage you swallowed, the longing you forgot how to name. And when you bring those parts forward, trembling and unsure, it whispers back:
"Give them to me. You are safe here."

Sacred union isn't a soft dream. It's a forge. It burns away everything false, tests you until you stand bare in your truth, and then invites you to choose each other anyway.

Two souls, unarmored, no guarantees, standing across the flame saying:
"I will hold your fire. Will you hold mine?"

And when the answer is yes, something ancient begins to move. What you create together isn't just love. It's legacy. It's repair for the ones who came before you. It's threads of alchemy weaving through your bloodlines, undoing generations of silence and exile and ache.

You become the healing your ancestors never received.
You become the prayer your future children will rise from without even knowing why.

So don't wait for the perfect one, the one with polished edges and a spotless past, the one who will never get it wrong. That love doesn't exist—and even if it did, it wouldn't transform you.

Call in the one who is willing.
The one who can sit in the fire and not turn away.
The one who will stay when the old wounds resurface.
The one who won't always know how, but will always choose to try.

That is sacred relationship.
And that is the kind of love that doesn't just change your life.
It reshapes the way you belong to yourself.

The Priestess Who Waits Forever

There is a kind of woman who doesn't settle. Not because she is difficult or demanding, but because she carries an ancient knowing in her bones— that her love was never meant for shallow waters. She waits for depth. For truth. For the frequency that hums beneath the surface and tells her she has found home.

She knows her body is a temple.

She knows her love is not casual.
She knows her heart was made for the holy.

But somewhere along the way, she swallowed a lie disguised as wisdom—the lie that she must heal it all first before she is worthy of being fully loved. That she must scrub away every shadow, soothe every ache, outgrow every trigger, and rebuild every piece of herself before she is allowed to open.
And so she waits.

She waits until the triggers are gone.
Until her nervous system is perfectly steady.
Until her grief softens and her business blooms and her calling crystallizes. She waits until the day she becomes the perfect priestess version of herself—sovereign, polished, untouchable. And only then, maybe then, she believes she'll be allowed to let love in.

And somewhere deep inside, a quieter voice whispers:
We both know you'll wait forever at this rate.
I roll my eyes at her honesty, but she isn't wrong.

Because the truth? That day never comes.

Because healing is infinite. Because becoming is endless. And love was never meant to sit on the other side of perfection, patiently holding a crown until you earned it. Love was always meant to be the fire that transforms you. The mirror that reveals you. The place where the deepest work begins, not where it ends.

The ancient ones are watching.
Mary Magdalene. Isis. Hathor. Inanna.

And the unnamed women whose bodies carried devotion, whose footsteps made the earth holy, even when no one wrote their stories down.

And they are whispering now:

Let yourself love before you are ready.
Let yourself be seen while you are still unraveling.
Let him witness the wild, unpolished, untamed parts of you.
Let him kiss the ache you thought you had to carry alone.
Let him rise beside you.
Let union be the ritual, not the reward.

"But what if I ruin it?" I ask the silence.
And Magdalene, somewhere in the marrow of my being, smiles:
"Dear one... you can't ruin what came to remake you."

Because waiting forever in the name of healing is another kind of exile. It is self-abandonment dressed up as wisdom. Sovereignty tangled with self-protection. Freedom turned into a cage.

And the deeper truth is this: some women are not single because they are broken. They are single because they've over-spiritualized their availability to love, turning their heart into a checklist, mistaking readiness for worthiness, hiding tenderness beneath performance.

If you are that woman—the priestess waiting until the day she feels perfectly whole—hear me now: you are already whole enough. Whole enough to be kissed in your contradictions. Whole enough to be held in your trembling. Whole enough to be loved inside the places you are still learning to love yourself.

Let love come into the temple now.

Let it rattle your bones.
Let it break your practiced silence.
Let it teach you what your meditations never could.
Let it move like prayer, living and untamed.

Let it be messy.
Let it be sacred.
Let it be real.

My Union Was My Initiation

I didn't walk into this relationship healed. I walked in open. Wounded. Curious. Terrified. I carried more than I even realized— grief I hadn't named, patterns I couldn't see, abandonment stories woven into my silence. And still, he loved me.

Not in the way the fantasy promises. Not in the polished dream where love is always soft and effortless and never demands more of you than you want to give. He loved me in the way truth loves us— fiercely, relentlessly, without permission, stripping away everything false until only what's real remains.

This wasn't a gentle awakening.
This was an initiation.

Our love rattled me. It cracked open pieces of me I didn't know existed. It burned away the shapes I had twisted myself into just to belong, just to feel safe. It pulled forward every shadow I thought I had healed—the ones I swore were gone, the ones I'd meditated through and affirmed away, the ones I thought I'd outgrown. But in love, those shadows didn't vanish.

They stepped closer.

They showed up in my voice when it trembled.
In the silence where I swallowed the words I needed to say.
In the way I closed my body when safety felt far away.
In the ache I still carried from my father.
In the part of me that wanted to leave before I could be left.

And there I was—heart open, ego burning—watching myself speak words I didn't mean, withhold when I longed to soften, collapse into old stories I thought I had rewritten. But in the middle of it all, I wasn't losing myself.

I was meeting myself.

I was finding the part of me that had never been given permission to exist—the one that didn't perform, didn't please, didn't pretend. The one that still longed, achingly, to be held.

This love stripped the mask from my face. Not to shame me, but to ask softly: *"Can you love her too?"*

And slowly, I said yes.

Because in that sacred seat beside my shadows, I didn't just fall apart. I came alive. There were nights I wanted to run, moments I didn't recognize myself, times when I saw exactly how afraid I was of being fully seen. But Oerti stayed steady.

He stayed when I crumbled.
He held me when I couldn't speak.
He never once asked me to hurry up and heal.

Instead, he said, *"Jump. I'm here. I've got you."*

And I remember whispering back, *"What if I don't land?"*

He just smiled. *"Then I'll fall with you."*

And that changed me.

This man became my mirror, my storm, my grounding. Not because he was perfectly healed, but because he was willing. Because he didn't need me to be perfect either.

Together, we walked through fire.
Not once. Not twice. Over and over again.
The kind of fire that doesn't ask permission before it burns. The kind that drags up wounds so old you almost forgot they were still living inside you.

We've faced distortion.
We've faced projections.
We've faced family dynamics so ancient they echoed through our bones.

We were given every reason to give up—and we didn't. Not out of habit. Not out of fear. But because something deeper than logic tethered us—something soul-woven, a thread we didn't choose but recognized the moment we touched it.

And the truth? That kind of fire would have collapsed a love built on ego, image, or fantasy. But it didn't burn us down.

It burned us clean.

We didn't just survive it.
We let it rewire us.
We let it strip away the roles we thought we had to play.

We let it remind us who we were beneath all the roles and all the pretending.
Not the perfect versions of ourselves. The real ones.

The ones who sit in the heat, trembling, and still whisper:
"I choose you. I choose this. I choose us."

Our union didn't delay my becoming. It deepened it. This was not a detour. It was the doorway.

This love became the altar.
The initiation.
The place where I finally stopped leaving myself behind.

And I wouldn't trade it. Not the storms. Not the shadows. Not the nights we weren't sure we'd make it.

Because through it all, we stayed.
We loved.

Let Love Find You in Your Becoming

You do not have to be finished to be loved.
You do not have to be healed to be held.
You do not have to be polished to be chosen.

You are becoming.
And even here—*especially* here—you are worthy of the kind of love that sees you, the kind that speaks to the parts of you you've kept hidden, the kind that says *yes* to the woman in motion, not the one pretending to have arrived.

Wild, isn't it? All those years I thought there was a secret checklist somewhere.

Let go of the story that says love will only come once you've mastered your softness, once your nervous system is perfectly steady, once your boundaries are flawless and your shadows erased. Let go of the belief that you must walk as the high priestess all the time, floating above the ache, glowing with clarity, untouchable in your grace.

You are not here to perform perfection.
You are human.
You are holy.
You are becoming.

(Although honestly, I did try performing perfection once. Exhausting. Zero stars. Do not recommend.)

And love is not waiting for your final form. It does not care how many scars still hum beneath your skin or how many old echoes still rise when someone touches your tender places. Love wants the real you. The one who still trembles sometimes. The one who forgets her own light but rises anyway. The one who carries both grief and radiance in the same chest and chooses to keep breathing them both.

Love is not something you earn at the end of healing.
It is something ancient, recognizing itself in you.
It is the mirror that appears the moment your soul whispers, *"I am ready to be seen."*

And it may not look the way you imagined. It may not follow the timeline you thought you had to live by. But when it comes, it will feel like home. It will feel like something in you remembering itself through the gaze of another, as if you have both walked this path before.

So let it come.

Let it find you before the edges are smooth, before the pieces make sense, before the story is complete. Let it arrive while your hands are still shaking and your heart is still learning the shape of openness. Let it teach you how to breathe right in the middle of the ache, not only after it passes.

The priestess in you does not need to delay. She does not need to perfect herself into worthiness. She is not meant to hide behind readiness or wait for the day when every scar fades into silence.

She is meant to be witnessed.

And there is someone—maybe already here, maybe just around the bend—who will not run from your depths. Who will not flinch at your truths. Who will not ask you to be softer, smaller, shinier, or easier to hold.
Let him witness the wild, unpolished, untamed parts of you.
(And yes, it will feel awkward at first. You might want to edit yourself. Don't. That's where the magic starts.)

They will rise with you.
Not above you.
Beside you.

Let them find you as you are. Not because you are complete, but because you are real.

Love is not waiting for the perfect you.

It is waiting for the honest you.
The willing you.

The one who says:
"I don't know what this will become.
But I am here.
I am open.
I am ready to be met, seen, and held."

Let that be enough.
Let that be holy.
Let that be the beginning.

And then, in the quiet after this soft opening, I hear them.
Not above me.
Not outside me.
But through me—
a remembering beneath the skin,
voices older than scripture braiding themselves into my breath.

Magdalene's presence moves first, steady as riverstone, and I feel her inside my ribs, whispering that I was chosen the moment I chose to remain soft in a world that begged me to close. That my longing was never too much. That my ache was never a flaw to be scrubbed away before I could be worthy of being held.

Mother Mary comes like still water—a quiet that fills the entire body. She reminds me that love is not a thing to chase, not a role to earn, not a reward for perfection. Love is the stillness we return to. It asks only this: *be open.* Let yourself be seen before you are certain. Let yourself be held before you are complete.

And then Isis rises, ancient and unyielding, her truth pressing through my bones: *You were never meant to rise alone. You were never meant to hold every weight by yourself, to stitch every wound in silence. Let yourself be met. Let your fragments breathe in the arms of another. Let someone hold the pieces you've been carrying for lifetimes.*

Hathor arrives laughing—wild, honeyed, untamed—and her voice dances inside my hips, reminding me of what I've almost forgotten: *your joy is holy. Your pleasure is prayer. Your laughter is worship. Stop postponing the feast. Stop waiting until you are ready.* I could almost hear her teasing: *Do you really think the universe is handing out gold stars for suffering? Eat the strawberries. Kiss him back. Let yourself live.*

They move as one inside me now.
Not distant guides.
Not voices from above.
But the women whose knowing has always lived in my blood.

And through them, I remember:
Love is not the crown at the end of your healing.
It is the fire that transforms you.
It is the hand that meets yours while your knees are still in the dirt.
It is the song beneath the ache,
the invitation to be known in all your unfinishedness.

I didn't heal first.
I loved first—
and the healing followed.

(Turns out, the love I thought I had to 'earn' was the thing that undid all the earning.)

I didn't wait until I was whole to be worthy of love.
I let love come into my becoming,
and that –
that is what made it holy.
Perhaps this is the quiet revolution:
to stop postponing your belonging,
to stop waiting until you are weightless and unscarred,
to stop believing you must polish yourself into something easier to
hold.

Because the love that is meant for you
is not arriving for your perfection.
It is arriving for your truth.
For the wildness that will not dim itself.
For the part of you that still quivers at the edges
and says yes anyway.

So let this be the moment you stop delaying your own heart.
Let this be where you choose to let yourself be met
inside your becoming,
inside your ache,
inside the untidy, trembling places
that are already enough to be loved.

There is no finish line here.
Only the beginning—
again and again.

CHAPTER EIGHT

The Crown Was Never in Their Hands

And still...I rose, crowned by what they could never take.

The Offering That Wasn't Received

There are offerings you give with your hands, and there are offerings you give with your soul. This chapter is about the second kind—
the kind that takes something from you that you don't always get back.
The kind no one sees, the kind no one applauds, the kind that lives in the private chambers of your heart where no cameras reach and no proof exists. It's the kind you give because something ancient inside you says:
this is yours to pour out, even if it costs you everything.
I didn't know that some offerings return as silence, not recognition.

I have given those offerings more times than I can count. And I thought if I just gave enough, maybe this time it would land.
I have stood in the quiet of my own knowing and said yes when every bone in me whispered no, yes when I was tired, yes when my hands were empty but my heart still opened itself like an altar. I gave when I had already been cut. I gave when I wasn't asked to. I gave when the return was silence, suspicion, and slander, and still—I stayed. I

stayed in rooms where I felt my own presence dissolving, where my prayers evaporated before they could reach anyone's ears, where the walls carried more weight than the people inside them. I stayed because something inside me still believed that love—real love—has the power to change even the things that pretend they cannot be moved.

I poured myself into spaces that had no intention of holding me. I sat at tables where smiles were rehearsed and words were careful but the air carried a weight my body could taste, and still, I showed up. I have carried other people's grief like it was my own, while quietly tucking mine into corners no one would ever find, promising myself I would come back for it later but knowing, deep down, I might never have the strength to pick it up again. I've stood on bridges I built with my own hands—plank after plank carved from my breath and my prayers—while watching others set fire to the far end and walk away without even turning back to watch the smoke rise.

I opened my home to those in need. I let them cross the threshold into the softest parts of my life, into the rooms where my children's laughter curls against the walls, into spaces layered with tenderness and care, and I fed them with my own hands—food I had baked with prayer woven into it, salt sprinkled with hope that what we shared would mean something. *Maybe if I love them this much, they'll see me.* And I watched them plant seeds of betrayal beneath the very table where we broke bread together, smiling as though they weren't already imagining the day they'd twist the knife.

I welcomed them into the sanctuary I built with love—
the one I built brick by brick, layered with every sacrifice, every whispered petition to God, every silent tear—

and still, some tried to dismantle it, brick by brick, with projections and fictions so carefully spun they could have been mistaken for scripture.

There were nights I sat awake questioning my own memory, my own lived reality, because their stories were so practiced, so rehearsed, so loud, and yet... my body always knew.

My bones knew where the truth lived. "Am I losing it?" I whispered into the dark.

And something inside me answered, *No love. They are loud. But you are not wrong.*

My heart never wavered, even when the world called me dangerous for saying out loud what I could feel in the marrow of me.

I've carried the weight of other people's storms while trying to soothe them with my prayers, and somehow I became the one blamed for summoning the thunder. I gave to communities I believed in—poured hours and heart and hope into visions I thought we were holding together—until I learned the hardest truth: that what shines the brightest sometimes hides the deepest rot. That what looks holy on the surface can be rotting beneath the altar. I stayed anyway, longer than my body wanted me to, longer than my spirit could hold, because I thought if I just loved harder, prayed louder, bent deeper, something would change.

But the poison crept in slowly, silently, and then all at once, and one day I saw it spilling into places I could not allow—into the bones of my children, into the innocence of the home I had sworn to protect. That was the day I knew I couldn't stay. And still, even as I walked away with blistered hands and a breaking heart, I left blessings behind me. I gave one more time. Because that's who I am.

Not because I'm foolish. Not because I can't see. But because faith has lived inside me longer than fear ever could.

And yes—I have loved people who were never going to rise with me. I have spoken truth in rooms where the ending was written long before I opened my mouth. I have told the truth when the world preferred the lie, when it was easier for them to believe the fiction, when standing with me would have meant confronting their own shadows. I have watched the people I prayed for become the people who sharpened their knives against me.

They didn't just ignore the offering. They used it against me.

They took my generosity and turned it into a weapon. They took my clarity and called it threat. They twisted my devotion into manipulation, my voice into volatility, my power into danger. They gossiped. They plotted. They whispered in corners I had once blessed with prayer. They told lies so beautiful they became evidence, so convincing they began to hold legal weight, so polished that even people who once knew my heart began to doubt it.

And I stood there. Not with vengeance. Not with fury. But with heartbreak running like saltwater through my veins, watching as pieces of my life were rewritten before my eyes.

Because the grief of the woman who gives like this is not that her offering goes unseen. It's that her devotion gets rewritten into threat. It's that the world bends her open hands into claws and calls her dangerous. It's that her love gets weaponized in someone else's story, while she's left holding the silence of the truth inside her chest.

And still—I would not take any of it back.

Not one offering.
Not one prayer.
Not one unguarded act of tenderness.
Because the crown was never in their hands.
It has always been in mine.

And it isn't the kind of crown the world can understand. It isn't gold or jeweled or meant for display. It is quieter than that. Heavier than that. It is the crown of knowing. The crown of breath. The crown of having walked through fire and refusing to come out charred. It is the crown of the woman who gave everything and still rose, standing barefoot in the ashes, untouchable, unshaken, and more alive than they ever imagined I could be.

The Woman Who Walked Away Without Needing to Win

There is a kind of woman who walks away without the apology. Without the vindication. Without the neat bow the world insists she should wait for. She walks away without being understood, without being defended, without the satisfaction of someone finally saying the words she deserved to hear—and still, somehow, she walks taller than ever before.

Not because she won. Not because the story ended in her favor. But because something inside her stopped needing to prove that she was worthy of the space she took up. Because there comes a moment when a woman finally realizes there is no courtroom in the world that can hand her back what she gave away freely.

I have been her.

I have walked out of rooms I helped build—
rooms I once believed would hold me, keep me, protect me—
while others stayed behind in the rubble, clutching the pieces and
convincing themselves the collapse was mine to carry.
I have walked away knowing that the walls I painted with prayer,
the foundations I poured with my bare hands, the air I breathed life
into would now be rewritten without my name in it.
And still, I walked.
I walked without certainty, only trust. And somehow, trust was
enough.

I have seen the way envy wears its disguise—soft, careful, deliberate.
How it dresses itself in concern, with tilted heads and lowered voices
and sentences that begin with "I'm just worried about you," when
underneath, there is venom pooling beneath the tongue. I have seen
the way someone can call you sister one day and stranger the next,
without ever admitting that what unsettles them most is not what
you've done, but the way you dared to become something they can
no longer control.

I have seen the way people cling to the version of the story that keeps
them comfortable, even when their bodies are screaming the truth
in places they refuse to listen. They will choose the clean lie over the
messy truth, not because the lie is truer but because the truth asks
something of them –asks them to see, asks them to feel, asks them
to confront where they, too, have been complicit. I've watched them
look right into my eyes, knowing they felt me in their gut, and still,
they walked away with the version of me they could survive.

And there's a grief in that no one prepares you for—

the grief of realizing that people you've held prayers for, tears for, space for, will discard you the second your light stops bending to their shadows.

That some will love the idea of your fire until it burns through the comfort of their illusions. That they will celebrate your rise right up until it threatens their own reflection, and then, they will turn.

I could have fought. I could have defended myself in every room, at every table, called out every name, presented every truth like a weapon. I could have shattered their stories with the sharp edge of my knowing. And God, there were nights I wanted to. Nights I sat awake rehearsing the words, carving my defense into the ceiling as though the stars themselves would testify for me. But something deeper than anger whispered through me:

That's not how truth works.

Truth does not perform.

It does not plead.

It does not grovel for its place at the table.

Truth doesn't chase the story; it lets the story choke on its own silence.

I wanted to clap when I realized this. "Fine," I thought, "let the silence do the talking. I've done enough of the heavy lifting."

So I walked away. I walked away without clearing my name, without dragging their lies into the light, without the apology that will never come. I walked away holding nothing in my hands but everything in my chest—my breath, my spine, my name carved into the softest place inside me where no one else can reach. I walked away knowing that even when the entire world misunderstands you, you can still be free.

Because the crown was never in their hands.

They never held my power. They never carried my worth. They never had the right to name me, so they could never unname me. They never built the ground beneath my feet, so they could never take it away.

Let them tell their stories. Let them rehearse their lines until they believe them. Let them gather around their half-truths and shrink their lives to fit inside the fiction they've built. Let them drown in the comfort of their distorted chorus if they need to.

But me? I will not shrink with them.

I will not rewrite myself to fit the pages they hand me. I will not dim to make their shadows feel softer. I will not betray myself just to be believed.

I will rise, again and again, wearing the kind of crown they'll never understand—
the one built of breath and knowing and blood and prayer—
and I will do it without their permission.

Because I have stopped waiting for anyone else to hand me back my life.
Because I have stopped needing the jury.
Because I finally know who I am, and that knowing is the one thing they can never take from me.

And that is how a woman walks away without winning—
and still leaves carrying everything that matters.

Love That Was Real—Even When It Wasn't Reflected

There is a kind of love you give that never circles back.
The kind you offer with both hands open, heart trembling, holding nothing back. You give it raw, whole, messy, true—the very best of what you have—and it slips into silence.
A silence so loud it hums against your ribs.

And sometimes, worse than silence, it meets suspicion. It meets misunderstanding. It meets sabotage in disguise. You find yourself watching something pure become twisted,
watching your devotion turned into distortion by someone who never knew how to hold the weight of it.

This is the kind of ache we're not taught to name.
The grief of love that was real, yet never received.
Not because your offering wasn't true, but because the one you gave it to had no capacity to hold it.

Because sometimes your presence asks people to face the parts of themselves they're not ready to see. Your light casts shadows they've spent a lifetime avoiding. Your devotion pulls truths they've buried too deep. Your love calls them higher—and they are terrified of heights.

And so, they turn away. Or they attack. Or they disappear into the safety of a smaller life where they don't have to stretch.

And there is a moment –
maybe many—
where you're tempted to follow them.
To shrink yourself down, to question the size of your love.

To wonder if maybe you should have spoken less, given less, loved smaller, stopped showing up altogether.

But here is what I know now:
You did not love wrong.

You loved courageously. You loved like the earth loves—without contracts, without proof, without needing applause or return. You gave from the essence of your becoming. You gave what you were born to give. And the truth is, you just loved bigger than they knew how to hold.

Even if it broke your heart, it expanded your soul.
Even if no one spoke your name, the field felt you.
Even if gratitude never crossed their lips, your offering rippled into places you will never see.

That kind of love is never wasted. It weaves itself into the unseen, folding into generations that haven't yet been born. It becomes memory and medicine, written into the fabric of time. It becomes legacy. It becomes gold.

It becomes you.

When the Pedestal Breaks the Real Woman Rises

There is a quiet kind of performance that lives inside so many sacred spaces.
It isn't announced, but it is learned.
A pressure to look like you've arrived. To soften your voice until it sounds like prayer.

To keep your tears pretty and your grief private.
To glow instead of grieve.
To float when you are breaking inside.

Somewhere along the way, you start believing your worth is tied to your image. That your value is in your ability to keep the edges smooth, the pain polished, the story easy enough to be loved. You become the one they come to for answers, for healing, for guidance— and without meaning to, you begin to believe that your job is to stay above it all.

To keep your aura clean.
To keep your emotions light.
To keep loving, forgiving, floating, transcending. Always.

But let me tell you the truth.
That isn't sovereignty. That's theater. That's survival in a costume of holiness.

And it is a cage.

I have lived inside that cage.
I have known the weight of it pressing against my ribs while I pretended to breathe freely. I silenced my rage and dressed my grief in poetry. I softened my no's until they sounded like maybes. I swallowed the words that would have freed me because I thought staying palatable would keep me safe.

But that version of me?
She was a shadow. A watered-down replica of the woman I was born to be.

And she is no longer here.

Because true sovereignty is not about floating above your humanity.
It is about grounding yourself deeper into it.
It's not about polishing your softness until it sparkles under the right light—
it's about being real enough to roar when the moment calls for it.

The real woman cries in her car.
Screams into pillows.
Lets her knees hit the kitchen floor and stays there until her breath returns.
She says "no" without wrapping it in apology.
She walks out of rooms where her presence is no longer met with truth.

And here's the paradox: she still blesses what she leaves behind.
That is power. That is grace. That is holiness stripped of performance.

You don't need to glow to be God.
You don't need to float to be free.
You don't need to earn your crown.
You were born wearing it—invisible, indestructible, alive.

So let the pedestal crack beneath the weight of pretense.
Let the curated image burn.
Let the woman you've been hiding rise from the ashes, unfiltered and untamed.

Not the one performing softness to be loved.
The one who knows she is love.

The raw.
The unapologetic.
The not-for-sale.

The no-longer-waiting-for-permission.
The woman who has stopped bowing to systems she came here to dismantle.

You Were Always the Offering

For so long, I thought my worth lived in what I gave away.
The dinners I cooked. The doors I kept open. The resources I poured out until my hands were empty. The way I carried everyone's chaos and called it love. The way I let people take and take and take because somewhere inside, I believed that being needed meant I was valuable.

I gave my time. My care. My softness. My loyalty. My trust. I gave my voice when no one else would speak. I gave my home, my table, my prayers, my energy. I gave even when my body whispered enough. I gave until I was scraped hollow—convinced that maybe, just maybe, if I kept pouring myself out, one day it would come back.

But there comes a moment when you wake up inside the exhaustion and realize something unshakable: You were never meant to trade yourself for belonging.

Because here's the truth I couldn't see back then:
The offering was never the food, the resources, the prayers, the nights spent showing up for everyone who disappeared when it was your turn to need them.
The offering was you.
Your presence. Your essence. Your way of loving. Your way of seeing what others pretend not to see.

It was never about what left your hands. It was about the light inside them.

And yes, there is heartbreak in realizing how many people never saw you. How many misused the gift of your open heart. How many took and called it theirs. It's enough to make you want to close everything down—to hide your tenderness, to armor your giving, to make your love untouchable.

But you cannot betray yourself like that.
Your generosity is not the problem.
Your open heart was never the mistake.

The mistake was thinking that the weight of someone else's hunger could be fed by abandoning your own.

What I know now—deep in my body, deeper than any words—is this:
you don't need to downsize the magnitude of your love. You don't need to dim the radiance of your care. You don't need to make yourself smaller to fit inside the places that were never built to hold you.

You were always the offering. Even before they recognized it. Even when they never could.
And you still are.

The world bends when a woman stops apologizing for the vastness she carries.

Final Invocation: For the Woman Who Gave Everything

For the woman who gave until her palms ached.
For the one who poured prayers into bowls no one ever bothered to drink from.
For the one who built bridges just to watch them burn behind her, while the smoke carried her name into mouths that never knew her.

For you, who loved anyway.

I want you to hear me when I tell you this:
You were never too much.
You were never the problem.
You are not the story they wrote about you.

There is nothing broken in you.
Not one thing.

The places where they misused you?
Those are the places where your power sharpened.
The rooms where they lied about you?
That's where your truth grew louder than their fiction.
The moments they turned your devotion into weaponry?
That's where the alchemy began.

They could take your name, but they could never take your knowing.
They could twist your story, but they could never touch your source.
And that crown they tried to break in their hands?
It was never theirs to hold.

You rise now—not because they saw you, but because you finally see yourself.

You rise because you are done auditioning for rooms unworthy of your magic.

You rise because there is something inside you too ancient to stay silent, too sovereign to stay small, too holy to keep begging for a seat at their tables when you were born to build your own.

And yes, there will still be nights where the grief leaks out of you quietly, when your chest caves under the weight of all you carried, when you wonder why love had to cost this much.

Let it.

Let the ache move through you without shame.

Because you are not here to harden.

You are here to become.

You are the beginning and the offering.

The blessing and the threshold.

And one day, you'll look back at all the places you thought you were dying and see them for what they really were:

Initiations.

Doorways.

Rites of passage dressed as endings.

So take a deep breath, woman.

Pull the crown back onto your own head, even if your hands are still shaking.

Pause here. Feel the weight of it. This is yours.

No one can take from you what was carved into your bones before you arrived.

You are untouchable.

Unshakable.

Unfolding still.

And when they tell the story of your becoming,
make sure it's your voice they hear—
steady, alive, and finally free.

CHAPTER NINE

The Chapter That Wasn't Finished

I need to be honest with you.

I've written this chapter before.
Three times.
Maybe four. Maybe more. I've stopped keeping track.

Each time, I thought this one would be the one that finally landed—
the one where the words would arrive the way they live inside me:
uncontained, breathing, messy and real. I sat with drafts that looked
beautiful on the surface. Sentences carefully sculpted. Transitions
that curved in perfect arcs, like someone had taken a soft cloth and
polished all the edges smooth.

And I wanted to believe them. God, I wanted to.
I wanted to believe I had finally crafted the version of myself worth
handing to the world.

But every time I came back and read them, I knew.

I knew because the breath wouldn't move through me.
I knew because my pulse wasn't in them.

I knew because they felt too clean, too quiet, too finished—like a staged photograph where everyone is smiling but no one remembers what was happening outside the frame.

And I promised myself, when I began writing this book, that I would never again trade the truth of the living moment for something polished enough to be acceptable.

I cannot write a chapter that looks alive but isn't breathing.
I cannot offer you language smoothed into something pretty if it means sanding down the ache.
I cannot give you closure when I don't have it.

Because the truth is this: I am still inside it.
I am still in motion.
I am still becoming.

Some nights, that becoming feels like grace.
Other nights, it feels like breaking.

There are hours when I wake at 3:12 a.m., my body restless long before my mind catches up. The house is silent except for the soft rush of the air vent above me, but my chest is loud—thoughts scatter like birds startled out of trees.

I lie there in the dark, tracing the faint cracks in the ceiling with my eyes, wondering if anyone else is awake right now, asking the same unanswerable questions: Am I doing enough? Have I given too much? How do you know when you've become the woman you were born to be, and what if the answer is never?

Sometimes I reach for him.

Oerti sleeps heavy, his arm curled against his chest, one hand open, palm warm. I rest my fingers there—just for a moment—like I'm anchoring myself back into the gravity of us. There's a safety in his breathing, slow and steady, the kind of safety I didn't know how to trust for so many years. And still, even with his warmth right here, my mind drifts.

It drifts to every version of me who thought she had to carry the weight of her becoming alone.
It drifts to the younger me who built walls so high, love couldn't climb them, and then wondered why she felt so cold.
It drifts to the woman who learned how to survive without ever learning how to receive.

Some nights, I slip out of bed and walk barefoot into the kitchen.
The tile is cold beneath my feet, grounding me back into my body. I choose the chipped mug I always reach for, fingers curling around its familiar edge. *This one's survived more drops than I have,* I think, and somehow, that steadies me. The house is quiet except for the hum of the fridge and the far-off sound of one of the girls laughing in a dream from the other room. And it's here, in these hours, that I start talking to God like an old friend I both love and question.

This is where I think about all the versions of me who have sat in this same silence before.

The girl who learned survival before she ever learned safety.
The woman who thought giving until she vanished was the same as being loved.
The mother who once locked herself in the bathroom, while the washing machine clicked endlessly in the background and I sat on

the tile floor, forehead pressed against my knees, trying to remember how to breathe.

I carry them all.

Every woman I've been still lives somewhere beneath my skin. Some are soft and quiet now, like old photographs fading at the edges. Others still stir when I write, asking to be witnessed, asking not to be erased. And maybe that's the thing about becoming—it's never a straight line.

It's a spiral.
A return to the same thresholds you thought you'd already crossed, only to find that this time, the question has a different weight.

There's an ache beneath my ribs I've never been able to name.

Some days, it's a quiet hum, like a song you half-remember. Other days, it presses against my sternum so hard I feel like my bones might split beneath the wanting. I used to believe this longing meant something was wrong with me—that craving more meant I wasn't grateful enough, healed enough, whole enough.

But I know better now.

This ache isn't absence.
It's not proof of lack.
It's not emptiness at all.

It's the hunger of expansion.
The body remembering there is more to hold, more to live, more to burn for.

Do you know that kind of hunger?
The one that comes even when you are living inside the exact life you once prayed for?

The drawings taped to the fridge, Bliss's curls tangled around her fingers, the soft sound of Zoe and Maya laughing in the other room, the smell of coffee filling the kitchen while Oerti's voice drifts in from the hallway—and still, beneath all that sweetness, something inside whispers: More. And I almost laugh at myself, whispering back, *Really? After all this?* But the ache doesn't answer. It just stays, quiet and steady, like it knows something I don't.

And then comes the shame, doesn't it?
The quiet voice that says you should be content, that longing for anything else makes you ungrateful for everything you already hold.

For years, I believed that voice.
I let it keep me small.
I tried to bury my hunger beneath gratitude, beneath prayer, beneath pretending. I convinced myself I didn't need more when the truth was that I did—not more things, but more aliveness, more depth, more wild, unpolished truth.

And here's what I know now: the wanting isn't a flaw.

The ache is holy.
It's proof I'm still alive.

....

Some mornings, before anyone wakes, I move through the quiet like it's its own kind of holy.

The walls are still dreaming, the blinds leaking pale threads of light, the floor cool against my skin. I sit cross-legged on the kitchen floor, my back pressed to the cabinets, coffee warm between my palms. I listen to the silence like it's speaking—because it is.

And sometimes, he finds me there.

He leans against the doorframe, watching without speaking at first, like he knows these are the moments I need before I can find words. There's something about the weight of his silence that steadies me, something about knowing he's seen every version of me—the broken ones, the restless ones, the ones who tried to disappear—and still, he stays.

We don't always talk about it, this hunger, this becoming, this wild need to write a book I've rewritten more times than I'll admit. But sometimes, when his hand finds the back of my neck, when his thumb presses just there, when his forehead rests against mine, it's as if he's saying what neither of us has language for: *You don't have to finish becoming before you're loved.* And something deep inside me exhales, *Finally... someone heard me.*

And maybe that's the lesson I'm carrying into this chapter.

That love doesn't wait for the perfect version of us.
It meets us right here, mid-sentence, mid-breakdown, mid-draft—
all the places we've deemed too unfinished to offer.

I think about this chapter.

How I've written it and deleted it, started and stopped, convinced myself over and over that I could shape this becoming into something neat enough to share.

How I've chased the perfect ending when what I really needed was permission to leave the ending open.
How I've been terrified that handing you this mess—the real one, the breathing one— would somehow make me less.

But I can't pretend anymore.

I can't dress this chapter in language that hides the bruises beneath the skin.
I can't pretend I'm already on the other side of this becoming, standing polished and finished with a crown in my hands.

I'm still here, standing barefoot at the edge of it, trembling and alive.

And maybe that's the whole point.

I think this chapter was never meant to close neatly.
I think it's meant to breathe.
To stretch.
To hold you wherever you are in your own unraveling.

Because you and I—we're still here.
Still becoming.
Still learning how to carry both the ache and the beauty without choosing one over the other.

And maybe the invitation isn't to write the perfect ending,
but to live the unfinished middle –
to stay open, stay hungry, stay honest enough to admit we don't know yet.

So here it is.

Not the chapter where I tell you I've arrived.
Not the chapter where I pretend I've made sense of it all.

Just the page I'm standing on right now.
Heart open. Hands open. Breath moving through the mess.

This is the chapter that isn't finished—
because neither am I.
The story is still moving through me, and for once, I'm letting it.

CHAPTER TEN

The Ancestral Fire

I used to think it was just us—just me and him, our love, our mess, our mistakes, believing we could hold it all if we just kept holding each other. Two people trying to figure it out, gripping hands through storms that came like waves against the shore, fighting and mending, breaking and rebuilding, again and again, as if love itself could be tamed by sheer devotion. I didn't know then that love doesn't just live between two people, but it carries the weight of everyone who came before. Every choice, every silence, every unspoken prayer in the lineage finds its way into the room with you.

I used to believe it was that simple: if I could just love him enough, if I could heal my wounds fast enough, if I could stay soft, patient, open—maybe we could outrun the ache. There were nights I would lie awake beside him, listening to the rhythm of his breath while moonlight threaded faint silver onto the ceiling, wondering if this was what love was supposed to feel like. Was everyone else holding their breath this much, or was I the only one terrified the ground beneath us would give way? Sometimes, in the quiet dark, I whispered into the silence, barely letting the words rise: *Please... show me how to keep us from breaking.*

The Voice Beneath the Skin: You were never meant to hold it all alone.

But I didn't know that yet. I thought strength meant carrying everything—for him, for us, for the children we hadn't yet met but already felt on the edges of my heart. I believed that if I just kept loving harder, if I didn't falter, if I held everything together tightly enough, we'd make it through untouched. But the deeper I went—into my body, into the spaces no one else could see—the more I began to understand.

It wasn't just us. It had never been just the two of us. This wasn't only the story of our love; this was old, ancient—blood and bone and breath. This was the weight of generations, his family, my family, patterns woven into us long before we ever touched this earth.

I began to see it everywhere—in the way we moved, in the words we didn't speak, in the silences that stretched too wide and stayed too long. It was in the beliefs we didn't know we were carrying, the grief that lived in our bodies before language, the fears inherited like heirlooms carefully passed hand to hand, held close but never named. It was in the way he looked at me when I was "too much"—when my voice rose, when my heart opened wide, when I overflowed with feelings he didn't know how to hold. It was in the way he disappeared into himself, carrying weight in silence, because somewhere deep in his bloodline he had learned that a man must be the strong one: the provider, the protector, the one who never bends, never asks, never lets his knees meet the ground.

And beneath all of that, there was his mother's voice, faint but unrelenting, lingering like the softest ghost of a candle burned hours ago. It was woven into our walls, into his choices, into the things he didn't even know he believed. I still remember the day she asked if I had married her son for his two cars and the house with the pool. I can feel it in my body even now—the stillness in the room, the weight of her gaze, the way the words left her lips casually but landed sharp, carrying something much older than the question itself.

I was so young then. Too young to understand the weight of it. Too young to see how deep it would burrow. And yet it pierced me instantly. I felt small, unseen, unworthy of the love I carried for him. Inside, my chest screamed: *Can't she see it? Can't she feel it? Doesn't she know?* But on the outside, I smiled—polite, steady, unbothered—because I had already learned what too many women learn too soon: how to swallow pain before it surfaces.

And I carried that question like a thorn beneath the skin for years. I didn't touch it, but I always felt it—a quiet sting whenever doubt brushed too close, an echo I couldn't silence.

Years later, when everything felt like it was burning—when the walls of our life trembled, when the weight pressed so heavy I thought I might dissolve beneath it—I felt her. Not the mother I knew in life, but her essence, speaking in the language beyond words. It wasn't a vision. It wasn't a dream. It was quieter than that—a knowing rising from somewhere deep, wrapping itself around me like a prayer I didn't realize I'd been waiting to hear.

Me: "Is this you?"
The Voice Beneath the Skin: You've always felt her. You just didn't know how to name it.

And in that moment, something loosened. I understood her more than I ever had. I could feel that she carried the weight of that day too—the sharpness of her question, the ache beneath it. And then, softly, she let me hear what she could never say while she was here: *It wasn't judgment. It was fear.*

Fear for him. Fear for what the world might take. Fear that no one would stand when the weight became unbearable. Her storms had carved her edges, and she hadn't been taught another way to ask, so she asked through sharpness, guarding love as though it might vanish if she wasn't vigilant enough. And suddenly, I saw it clearly: her love was always fierce, but it was shaped by her pain, by the wounds she carried that no one ever helped her hold.

I thought of the stories she shared with me—the humiliations, the quiet cruelty, the way her in-laws chipped away at her dignity until she swallowed her grief just to survive. I see it now, how it hardened her, taught her to guard, to question, to measure love before giving it. And I see it in me too—the times I smiled while breaking, the times I carried what wasn't mine, believing that's what devotion required.

And still, in that quiet moment, I felt her hand press softly into the center of my back, her presence settling into me like warmth. I didn't need her to say more. I only needed to know she was here, offering her blessing, her permission to love him in the way she couldn't. And for the first time, I knew we would make it. Not because we had figured it out. Not because we were unbreakable. But because this love—this fire—was bigger than us.

And then, there is his father.

The man who has always lived beneath our roof, who sits at our table and folds himself into the edges of our days, and yet somehow... has never fully stepped into the light of them. There are times I catch him in the doorway, leaning slightly to one side, his hands folded from habit rather than intention, his face turned just enough that I cannot read it. He is there, and yet not quite here, like a shadow that never leaves but never settles fully into belonging.

He carries the weight of provision like an oath carved into his spine. You can see it in the shape of his shoulders, the slow, deliberate way he moves, the quietness he wears as if he was born with it stitched into his breath. He doesn't speak much—not because he has nothing to say, but because no one ever asked how he felt. After enough years of not being asked, I think he stopped believing his words had anywhere soft to land.

His tenderness—and there is tenderness—lives buried beneath layers of survival. Beneath a belief passed down like scripture: that praise makes a man arrogant, that softness makes him weak, that silence is safer than sentiment.

Me: "Was it always like this for him?"
The Voice Beneath the Skin: Always. And before him. And before that. This isn't his silence alone—this is borrowed.

He doesn't know how to affirm his son, so he offers correction instead. Not once, but endlessly—a thousand small interruptions to Oerti's becoming, like a reflex his body learned long before his heart had a chance to choose another way. And that leaves its mark. Because when a boy reaches for his own knowing and is met with doubt, when the light in his eyes is measured before it's trusted, he begins to wonder if his wings were ever meant to open at all.

This wasn't cruelty. It was quiet erosion, the kind you don't notice until years later, when you go searching for the fire in your chest and realize you've been carrying someone else's ashes instead. Love was there, steady in its own way, but it hummed beneath an undertone: be different, be better, be less you.

Me: "Why couldn't he see him?"
The Voice Beneath the Skin: You can't name what no one ever named in you.

And I see now that Oerti's father never received praise, not because he didn't earn it, but because somewhere along his lineage, someone decided approval was dangerous—that softening boys would leave them unprepared for a hard world. And so affirmation went missing, and with it, the freedom to trust your own fire.

Even now, I sometimes catch glimpses of his wound—like the night he told me he was born premature and left to die because no one believed he would survive. He said it softly, almost apologetically, like he was sharing a fact rather than an open wound, but I could hear it in his breath, see it in his jaw, feel it in his silence. That story has shaped his life; it lives in the way he withholds, the way he stays close but never fully reaches.

And I see how it shaped Oerti too. The hesitation. The pause before speaking. The constant seeking of confirmation outside himself, even when something deeper in him already knows. This is the inheritance we don't name—the silences, the unspoken rules, the unshed tears—the subtle ways we learn to leave ourselves.

Me: "And this silence... it didn't begin with him, did it?"
The Voice Beneath the Skin: No. This silence is ancient. You're the one here to end it.

And that—right there—is what we are doing. Healing the quiet distortions, the muted absences, the things no one speaks of but everyone feels. Reweaving the threads no one thought could be touched. And as I watch Oerti father our daughters, soft where hardness once lived, steady where doubt used to be, I know: this is the medicine.

Not fixing the past. Just loving differently now.

And then there's my father.

His absence was not measured in miles or years but in something softer and harder all at once—an invisible mark pressed deep into the center of my chest, a bruise no one could see but one my body kept tracing anyway. He didn't leave with slammed doors or shouts. He left with silence—no words, no explanations, no space to ask why. And there are absences like that, the ones so complete they don't announce themselves; they just dissolve into the air, seeping through your bones until one day you realize you've been building your whole life next to a shadow you didn't choose.

That absence traveled with me into every room. It wrote itself into my breath. It whispered into the way my chest braced when joy dared to arrive, into the way my throat tightened when love came too close, into the quiet rehearsals I ran in my mind for the moment someone might leave again.

Me: "Why does it still ache?"

The Voice Beneath the Skin: Because you were never given the words... only the wound.

I carried that wound without knowing it. It threaded itself into my longing, into the part of me that feared love would always vanish no matter how soft I became, no matter how fiercely I stayed, no matter how much I gave. I twisted myself into shapes that would never scare anyone away, swallowed tears so no one would have to hold me, dimmed my light so no one would feel blinded by it—thinking if I was careful enough, small enough, good enough, I could make someone stay.

The Voice Beneath the Skin: You kept yourself small so you wouldn't be left. But in the shrinking, you left yourself first.

It has taken me years to unlearn that silence. Years of peeling back old rooms in my body, sitting in the ache I used to run from, naming the fears my tongue had swallowed whole. And somewhere along the way, I realized it was never just about him leaving. It was about all the ways I abandoned myself trying to avoid being abandoned again.

And sometimes, when I watch Oerti with our daughters—when Bliss curls against his chest, or Maya races across the yard, barefoot and laughing, Zoe doing cartwheels and handstands in every corner of the house—I feel something I can't name. The love they receive now rewrites a story he couldn't give me then, and some quiet part of me exhales.

But in the still moments—when my breath slows, when the ache loosens its grip just enough—I feel him. Not the man I knew, but the essence beneath his absence, the thread of him that lingers, untethered to time. And his whisper—oh, his whisper—rises softer than breath in the dark:

"This time, it's different. This is where you tell a new story. This is where the pattern ends. This is where you stop waiting for the leaving. This is where you stay."

Me: "Stay? Even when it's hard?"

The Voice Beneath the Skin: Especially when it's hard.

That voice—his, mine, God's, all layered into one—has been with me every time I wanted to run, every time I thought love was too heavy for my hands, every time the ache told me to protect myself before I could be left again. It's there, reminding me: I am not the little girl waiting by the door anymore. I don't have to hold my breath for love to stay. I don't have to earn tenderness by disappearing beneath it.

I am allowed to be too much, too wild, too messy, too big, too bright— and the ones meant for me will never ask me to make myself less.

And this—this unwinding, this reclamation—has become the work. The slow, steady untangling of old vows written into my blood. The rewriting of a story I thought was mine to carry forever.

And then there's my mother.

My mother—the woman who has always been the ground beneath my feet, the steady current beneath every breaking wave. She never asked for recognition. She never needed applause. She carried more than any of us ever saw, and somehow, even when the weight was unbearable, she never let it crush her.

When I think of her, I don't see a woman bowed beneath the weight of life.
I see a woman who stood inside it—who carried hope the way some people carry breath, steady and constant, never questioning whether it would run out.

Her life was not easy. There were nights when the cupboards were nearly bare, when even bread felt like a luxury, when the hum of the fridge was louder than anything inside it. But she never let us feel lack. She never looked at us with fear in her eyes. Instead, she held something deeper—a knowing I didn't yet have language for.

She would lean against the counter, brushing loose strands of hair from her face, and say softly, almost like a prayer:
"Po nuk doli, do teproj."
"If this doesn't come through, something better will overflow."

And somehow, it always did.

I remember the soft knocks at our door—late evenings, quiet afternoons, sometimes in the middle of dinner. Neighbors came, cousins came, strangers came, their voices hushed but urgent, their faces carrying the weight of fever, pain, and worry. My mother was a doctor, but more than that, she was a healer the community trusted. She never asked for anything. She never turned anyone away.

She would open the door, gather them inside, and serve. No hesitation. No calculation. No thought of repayment. She gave her hands, her knowledge, her prayers—stitching wounds, checking pulses, easing pain, offering herself in a way that left no one untouched.

And then, days later, or sometimes within the hour, they would return.
An elderly neighbor leaving a basket of warm bread on our doorstep. A cousin sliding a few folded bills into her hand, embarrassed by the smallness of it, but grateful anyway. Someone arriving with eggs, or bananas, or honeycomb wrapped in paper, whispering, "Thank you, God bless you."

To anyone else, it might have looked like luck, coincidence, provision out of thin air. But I see it now for what it was: reciprocity.
She wasn't just waiting on miracles.
She was summoning them—weaving herself into the quiet rhythm of giving and receiving that held our entire family afloat.

Voice Beneath the Skin: This was her faith, love. Not that God would send something eventually, but that God already lived in the hands of those around her.

Her faith was never loud, but it was alive.
It wasn't something she debated or tried to prove. It was woven into the way she lived—in the way she set the table even when there wasn't enough to fill it, in the way she tucked us into bed without letting us feel the ache of her worry, in the way she always trusted there would be enough.

And maybe this is what made her extraordinary: she accepted all of us exactly as we were.
Every silence. Every rebellion. Every raw, imperfect piece. In her presence, we were never required to earn belonging. She loved us as if there were no condition, no threshold, no distance too far to close.

Even now, she keeps showing up like that.
She is the grandmother who never arrives empty-handed, who remembers everyone's favorite dish, who bends her entire body into celebration when the grandchildren burst into the room. I watch her sit cross-legged on the floor with Bliss tangled in her lap, whispering soft secrets into her curls, and I see the same unspoken promise in her eyes that she once gave me: "You are safe here. Always."

And then there's Maya, running barefoot across the yard with her soccer ball, wild hair sticking to her forehead, laughter spilling out of her chest as though gravity could never catch her. My mother stands at the edge of the grass, her hands folded loosely in front of her, watching her granddaughter glide across the earth. She doesn't clap or shout or instruct. She doesn't need to. She radiates a kind of quiet knowing: "Let her fly. Let her trust her feet."

Sometimes, I swear I hear her whisper it again, this time like a prayer offered to the wind:
"Po nuk doli, do teproj."
And I realize—it was never just about bread.
It wasn't just a sentence; it was a worldview. A covenant with God. A quiet knowing that even when the walls trembled, we were held. That provision lives in places logic can't explain. That grace multiplies in the hands of those who give even when their hands are empty.

It was about faith passed through generations, about living as if the overflow was inevitable.

Her life taught me many things, but this is the deepest:
That love can hold anything.
That hope multiplies when it's embodied, not spoken.
That generosity is its own prayer.
That tenderness can be an inheritance.

I carry her in me now.
In the way I keep going when everything says stop.
In the way I mother my daughters with open hands and steady breath.
In the way I choose trust, even when the path isn't visible yet.

This—this is the fire I inherited from her.
Not the burn of destruction, but the warmth of devotion.

Not the pressure to hold it all, but the quiet reminder that love has always been enough.

I've seen her faith move mountains, though she's never called it that. I've seen her turn scarcity into sufficiency with nothing but prayer and persistence, the way she believed—fiercely, unapologetically— that God never runs out. And somehow, she was always right.
She gave without calculation, without resentment, without needing to be seen. Her love wasn't performance; it was presence. It was a river, constant and quiet, carving through stone.
And I see it now how much of her lives in me.

The way I make space at my table even when I am exhausted. The way I hold everyone before I remember to hold myself. The way I love fiercely, fully, without keeping score.

For so long, I thought this was just what women did. That carrying everyone and being carried by no one was simply part of the role. That swallowing your needs was the cost of belonging. That turning your exhaustion into generosity was proof of worth.

But now, I see the quiet cost. I see the cracks she hid beneath her steady hands, the nights she went to bed not just tired but emptied, the grief she never named because naming it would have required her to put it down—and she didn't believe she was allowed.

The Voice Beneath the Skin whispers softly:
She taught you endurance, yes... but you are here to choose softness where she could not.

And so I do.

I let myself weep the tears she never let fall. I say the words she never had permission to speak: "I can't do this alone." And I do not carry shame for it.

Because this is how I honor her.
By choosing to live the prayers she whispered but never claimed for herself.
By letting my daughters see me in my fullness: the strong and the trembling, the certain and the undone, the quiet and the burning alive.

I want them to know what she never did:
That love doesn't have to be earned through exhaustion.
That softness is not a weakness but a power.
That they do not have to make themselves small to belong.
That God does not run out.

And maybe this is what it means to turn a lineage—not to reject what came before us, but to hold it with reverence, to bless it, and to choose differently where the old stories would have us stay silent.

And when I finally let myself be still,
I feel them.

Not as words, not as visions, but as a quiet hum beneath my skin. A tide rising inside my body that I didn't realize I'd been carrying all along.

The Voice Beneath the Skin: Be quiet now... listen.

And then they're there.

The grandmothers.
The grandfathers.
The seen and unseen.
The named and the nameless.

They are not hovering above me; they are inside me—in my breath, in my pulse, in the way my ribs rise and fall like an ancient drum.

We've been here the whole time.

I imagine their hands layered over mine—weathered, calloused, soft with time—the hands that once built homes, planted seeds, tended children by candlelight, and now find me across centuries to steady my shaking palms.

The room holds its breath, and then their voices move through me like blood through bone:

"Child... we are here.
We are the ones who crossed oceans in the dark, carrying more hope than bread.
The ones who buried babies beneath willow trees and whispered their names into the earth so the wind would remember them for us.
We are the women who pressed grief into the folds of bread and kissed your mothers without telling them why we cried at night.
We are the men who bent our backs beneath suns that did not rise for us, who built homes we were never welcome in, who swallowed salt on our lips and called it sweat because naming it grief would have broken us completely."

I breathe them in, and I feel my chest tighten with an ache that isn't mine but lives in me anyway.

The Voice Beneath the Skin: This is why you feel so much, love. You were never just holding your own.

"Every time you pause where we rushed, you rewrite us.
Every time you choose softness where we hardened, you free us.
Every time you let your heart break open where we stitched ours closed,
you become the prayer we didn't know how to pray."

I close my eyes and let their presence settle into me until I can no longer tell where they end and I begin. In this silence, I feel myself belonging not just to my own life, but to all of theirs, carried forward through me.
And I whisper without sound:
"I'm trying... I hope I'm doing this right."

The Voice Beneath the Skin: You are. This was always the work.

And I understand it now.
It was never just me.
Never just us.
Never just this love.

This fire.
This vow.
This tenderness we hold between us...
it carries all of them.

And when I choose differently,
when I breathe where they held their breath,
when I stay where fear told them to run—

I free all of us.

CHAPTER ELEVEN

Where Most Leave, We Stay

There were nights I thought we wouldn't make it. Not because the love had faded (that was never the question) but because love was asking more of us than I thought two people could possibly hold. No one tells you, before the fire, that real love isn't the kind you find in neat Instagram captions or wedding vows recited under fairy lights. They don't prepare you for the truth that the kind of love our souls ache for—the old kind, the vow-before-time kind, the one seeded into your bones before you even met—will split you open before it settles you. It does not ask politely for your edges. It tears them.

I thought staying in love would feel like soft skin, easy mornings, safety without effort. Sometimes it does. But more often, it has felt like facing a mirror you didn't ask for, one that insists on showing you the part of yourself you thought you'd outgrown. There were nights I cried quietly into my pillow, wondering if we had reached the edge, if we had cracked beyond repair. There were mornings I walked into the kitchen, made coffee, and stared at him across the counter thinking, *I love you, but God, I don't know how to love you here.*

And the thing about real love is that it doesn't give you time to hide. It pushes everything to the surface: your grief, your rage, your mother's unspoken ache, your father's silence, the patterns you thought you buried, the little girl inside you still waiting by the door, hoping someone will choose her. It asks the question no one prepares you for:

Can you stay?
Not just in the relationship, but in yourself.
Can you stay in your body when it trembles with old memories?
Can you stay in the room when silence stretches and every instinct wants to run?
Can you stay in the mirror when you recognize the pieces of you that you swore you'd never become?

This isn't the love they taught us.
This isn't movie love, poem love, soft-filtered-reel love.
This is the kind of love that rearranges your cells and rewrites your lineage.
The kind of love that pulls all the ghosts into the room and says, *We are doing this now.*

And here's the secret no one tells you: most people leave. Not because they don't feel it—the depth, the pull, the holy ache of it—but because no one showed them how to stay. No one told us how to stand barefoot in the fire when the mirror of love reflects the things we've avoided for decades. No one gave us instructions for what to do when the story we told ourselves about who we are begins to dissolve in the presence of another human being holding our heart in their hands.

We live in a world obsessed with escape. With "fresh starts." With clean slates. With erasing rather than rewriting. We know how to leave; we are fluent in walking away.

But no one taught us the sacred art of returning.

Returning when the wound opens again.
Returning when the silence gets loud.
Returning when your hands are shaking and your body whispers, *Protect yourself*, but your soul whispers, *Stay*.

Staying isn't about abandoning yourself. Staying is bringing all of you—the messy, raw, unpolished, breaking parts—to the table and saying, *I'm here. I won't run from myself anymore.*

I used to think staying meant never questioning. Never doubting. Never collapsing on the kitchen floor at 3 a.m., whispering to God, *Why does this feel so hard if we're meant for each other?* But I know better now. Staying isn't tidy. Staying is unglamorous work. Staying is laying your chest open and saying yes even when your ego is screaming no. Staying is burning through the illusion of love until you find the actual thing beneath it.

And God, there have been times I wanted to bolt.
Times I wanted to climb into my car barefoot, drive until the highway disappeared beneath me, and start over somewhere far away where nobody knew my name or the shape of my ache. I didn't leave—but in my head, I packed the suitcase a hundred times.

Somewhere, deep beneath the storm, I think my soul was waiting for me to discover something I didn't want to know: that leaving would have been easier, but staying was the initiation.

There was one night—I'll never forget it—when I found myself holding Oerti's phone in my hand. Not because I wanted to find something, but because my body wouldn't stop bracing for an impact that wasn't even coming. Trauma installs smoke alarms in empty rooms. It whispers warnings your mind can't quiet.

I didn't want to believe the story my nervous system was screaming at me. I hated that part of me—the suspicious, anxious, double-checking, "what if he leaves me like they did" part. But shame doesn't make a wound heal; it just drives it deeper. And that night, my wound was loud.

The girls were curled into their routines—hair damp from showers, Bliss chasing a stuffed animal around the hallway, Maya juggling her soccer ball against the wall like the house was her stadium, Zoe doing her splits and handstands—and we couldn't let them see it. So we said we were going to get gas, even though the tank was already half full. I grabbed my jacket; he grabbed the keys. Neither of us spoke on the way out.

The door closed behind us, and we carried the weight of silence with us down the driveway.

We drove until the glow of the house disappeared behind the curve of the street, until the porch lights faded into something smaller than the ache between us. The air in the car felt sharp, the kind that presses against your ribs until you remember to breathe. The dashboard lights lit his face in soft flashes, steady, unreadable, while my chest kept storming.

We parked beneath the half-lit awning of an empty parking lot and sat there for a while, both of us staring at the rows of flickering bulbs, pretending to count the minutes, pretending we weren't bracing for another break we didn't know how to name. A moth kept head-butting the bulb like it, too, had unresolved issues.

It started with my voice—small, shaky, a whisper trying to sound like reason but cracking anyway. And then his, rougher, clipped around the edges, like someone speaking through clenched teeth. One sentence became five, five became ten, and before I knew it, we were both spilling, louder now, our words colliding midair, the car too small to hold everything we had buried for months.

There was yelling, yes. And crying. And silence folded between them like sharp paper cuts. I told him what my body was holding, the ache I didn't know how to name, the ghosts of old betrayals that weren't even ours but still lived under our skin. He told me he was tired of being questioned, tired of proving what his heart had been saying all along, tired of watching me fight battles that belonged to someone else's story.
"I can't keep doing this. Either you trust me... or you don't."

And I froze.
Because it wasn't anger in his voice; it was surrender.
And something in me shattered in that moment—not because I doubted him, but because I finally realized I was the one still feeding the fire that was burning us both.

It was never about betrayal.
It was about the phantom of betrayal.
The wound that lived in my body long before Oerti ever touched my hand.
It was my father's silence, my mother's swallowed prayers, my nervous system waiting for abandonment like it was a natural season of love.

That night changed something in me.

Because the thought of him leaving—just the thought of it—was so much more unbearable than any imagined story my fear could invent.

We sat there for a long time. I don't know when I finally stopped crying that night.

At some point, the silence inside the car stretched long enough to feel almost sacred.

The heater hummed low, fogging the edges of the windows, and the only light came from a lonely streetlamp leaning just close enough to watch us. My palms were damp, my sleeves soaked, and the smudges beneath my eyes probably looked like I'd auditioned for an amateur production of Black Swan.

My knees were pulled into my chest, cheek resting against the cold glass, and my breath kept fogging and clearing the same small patch of window, over and over, like I was trying to carve my own little escape hatch into the night.

Oerti didn't move.

Didn't touch me.

Didn't try to fix it.

He just sat there, one hand on the steering wheel, the other resting on his thigh, shoulders dropped under the weight of it all. He breathed slowly, deliberately, like if he exhaled any faster, the whole car might collapse in on itself.

And in that stillness, something inside me softened.

We didn't resolve anything.

We didn't get gas.

The girls thought we had.

We were two grown adults parked in the dark, having what I like to call a "silent marital apocalypse," and honestly? If there had been a Marriage Olympics, I think we'd have medaled.

I thought staying meant fixing.
I thought we had to have answers before we were allowed to breathe again.
But sitting there, mascara streaked down my cheeks, Oerti staring into the void like it owed him money, I realized maybe staying was simpler than that.
Sometimes, staying just means breathing in the same car while the silence does its slow, holy work.
Sometimes, it's letting the storm pass without trying to wrestle the clouds into shape.

At some point, my tears slowed, though my body still trembled in tiny, leftover aftershocks—like my nervous system hadn't gotten the message that the worst part was over.

I looked at him.
Not the way you look when you're searching for proof, but the way you look when you realize proof was never the thing you needed in the first place. He was tired. So was I. Our love was tired too—not fragile, not breaking, but weary from holding so much without knowing how to set any of it down.

And yet, we were still here. In the same car. Breathing the same heavy night air.
That had to mean something.

I leaned my head back against the seat, staring at the faint condensation dripping down the passenger window. And out of nowhere—maybe because silence was starting to feel like its own language—I laughed. Not the bright, easy kind of laugh, but the cracked, exhausted one that sneaks out when your body can't hold any more tears.

He turned to me, brow raised, lips pressed into the softest almost-smile.
"What?"

I shook my head, wiping at my face with the sleeve of my sweatshirt. "I just realized we told the girls we were going to get gas. We've been sitting here for... what? Forty-five minutes? They're probably inside imagining we're lost somewhere between Gate and Mars."

For the first time all night, his shoulders dropped. The smallest sound—something between a sigh and a laugh—slipped out of him, and I felt the tension between us shift, just slightly.

And maybe that was the beginning of forgiveness.
Not the big, cinematic kind with sweeping gestures and carefully timed apologies. But the small, ordinary kind, the one that lives in the way you let someone laugh again without punishing them for the hurt.

We drove home slowly, the streetlights blurring past us, neither of us ready to fill the quiet yet. And when we walked through the door, the girls were sprawled on the couch, watching something on the TV, oblivious to the hurricane we had just survived outside the walls of their world. Bliss looked up first, cheeks sticky with ice cream, and yelled, "Did you get me a surprise?"

I remember thinking: this is what we're doing it for.
This messy, chaotic, imperfect little life we're building.

This house that holds laughter and slammed doors, banana peels on the counter, mismatched socks under the couch cushions, whispers in the dark when no one else is awake.

This is the actual sacred.
The soft magic that hides beneath the exhaustion, the sighs, the folded laundry that somehow still never ends. It's the same kitchen we've fought in, made up in, danced barefoot in at midnight because "our song" came on and we both pretended we didn't know the steps—until Zoe walked in, rolled her eyes, and muttered, "God, you guys are so weird," before stealing a grape and disappearing back to her room.

It's that love.
The love that lives beneath the noise of everything else, the one that remembers why we keep choosing each other, even when the ache is loud.

And we didn't. We didn't have a surprise for Bliss. We didn't have gas.
But we had stayed.

And that was everything.

That night became a quiet turning point. Not because everything healed in an instant—it didn't. But because I understood something I hadn't before:

Staying isn't a single decision; it's a thousand tiny ones.

It's saying, I choose you when the stories in your head are screaming run.

It's choosing silence instead of the sharpest words, not because you want to swallow yourself, but because some things are truer than anger can hold.

It's remembering, over and over, that the person in front of you is not the sum of every wound you've ever carried.

Staying is holy work.

Not because it's painless, but because it asks everything of you—your pride, your patience, your rehearsed exits—and hands you something larger in return.

And it's messy. God, it's messy.

It doesn't look like the soft-lit montages, or the movie couples who never get mascara-streaked faces and heater-fogged windows at midnight.

It looks like driving circles in silence.

It looks like choosing presence while your hands are shaking.

It looks like making cheese and bresaola sandwiches at 2 a.m. with swollen eyes and puffy cheeks, because small bodies are sleeping peacefully in the next room and somehow life, in all its tenderness, goes on.

I used to think staying meant holding on tight enough that nothing could fall apart.

But it isn't that at all.

Staying isn't gripping harder; it's softening deeper.

It's letting go of the illusion that you can control the storm and instead learning how to breathe in the middle of it—together.

And maybe that's why it feels so sacred.

Because every time we choose to stay, it's not just us we're healing. It's every version of us that thought leaving was the only way to survive. It's every woman who swallowed her truth just to keep the peace, every man who braced his heart against being misunderstood, every ancestor who loved without knowing how to be held.

Sometimes, when I think back to that night, I don't remember the words at all.
I remember the fog on the windows.
The tremble in my hands.
The weight of his silence beside me.
And the truth that still sits like a quiet ember in my chest:

We could have left.
But we didn't.
We stayed.

And that changed everything.

I lay in bed later that night, staring at the faint cracks in the ceiling, listening to the sound of his breathing beside me—steady, grounding, the kind of quiet that means we've survived something without naming it yet.

And somewhere beneath the silence, I felt it.
That other pulse.
The one I've come to know so well—the current that moves beneath words, the voice that isn't a voice but somehow speaks louder than anything I can hear.

It rose slowly, like something remembering its way back into my body, and for a moment, I forgot to resist it.
I just let it come.

You think staying is about the other person, it murmured, soft as breath beneath my skin.
But staying begins in you. It always begins in you.

I felt it before I understood it.
All the times I had abandoned myself—leaving my body when the ache got loud, swallowing my truth when I thought it would cost too much, quieting my longings before anyone else had the chance to reject them.
And how every time, without meaning to, I had trained my nervous system to believe love meant disappearing first.

The knowing kept unfurling, slow, deliberate, like it didn't want me to miss a single word:

The mirror is not here to hurt you.
It is here to free you.

I thought about Oerti's silence in the car, the way he had sat there without filling the space, without trying to fix me, without offering the thousand reassurances I thought I wanted. How, somehow, his quiet became an anchor—not because it gave me answers, but because it invited me back to my own breath.

I thought about the fight we didn't finish.
The things we didn't resolve.
The gas we never got.
And yet, there we were—inside the same night, beneath the same roof, choosing the same home again.

And maybe that's what I'd been missing all along:
That staying is not a grand vow carved in stone.

It's a small, trembling yes whispered into the mess, over and over and over.

I let the weight of it settle into my body, let it dissolve against the exhaustion finally pooling in my muscles.
And somewhere between that quiet knowing and the soft hum of the heater, I heard it again—closer this time, like an ancient promise pressed into my bones:

The ones who stay are not the ones who never break.
They are the ones who keep returning—to themselves, to each other, to love.

I exhaled into the dark, slow and unsteady, and reached for him beneath the blanket.
He found my hand instantly, like his body had been waiting for the signal.

And we didn't speak.
We didn't need to.
The staying was its own language.

And then—as though the air thickened around me—another layer arrived.
Not louder, but deeper.
A warmth pressing into my bones like memory uncoiling itself:

Child... we have been here the whole time.

It wasn't one voice.
It was hundreds.

The grandmothers. The grandfathers. The ones whose hands built the ground beneath my feet. They didn't hover above me; they crowded inside me, humming like low-lit bees in the marrow of my bones.

We are the ones who stayed, they said.
When hunger thinned our bodies but not our hope.
When silence stole our language but not our songs.
When the weight of leaving pressed against our throats but we planted our feet anyway.

Their words weren't words exactly; they were memory.
I saw flashes of them—bent backs planting seeds they'd never live to harvest, quiet rebellions sewn into bread, lullabies hummed to children who would carry their stories without knowing their names.

You are not just staying for you, they breathed.
You are staying for us.
I felt my mother then.
Her hands stacking bowls of beans when there was barely enough for the table.
Her voice carrying that soft Albanian promise—po nuk doli, do teproj—like a secret covenant with the unseen: "If this doesn't come through, something better will overflow."

And suddenly, I thought of the knocks on our door, back when I was little.
Neighbors, cousins, sometimes strangers, arriving late at night with fevers or headaches or prayers stitched into their voices. My mother—our constant healer, our quiet priestess—would gather

them inside, hands steady, heart wide open, serving without calculation, without hesitation, without keeping score.

And days later, they'd return—someone leaving eggs on the doorstep, a cousin slipping folded bills into her hand, a basket of warm bread left with no name attached.

She didn't call it magic.
She called it Tuesday.

And I swear I heard her laugh somewhere in my chest right then, that knowing little laugh she gives when life proves her right—the one that says, "See? God never runs out."

It was her voice, but it was all their voices, braided together now.
The Magdalene frequency.
The ancestral drumbeat.
The quiet rebellion of love that chooses to stay, even when the world says run.

Staying has nothing to do with certainty.
It has everything to do with devotion.

And devotion—real devotion—isn't pretty.
It's makeup-stained.
It's sitting in a parked car in an empty parking lot at 8pm, wondering how your life became this.
It's passing him a crumpled napkin and both of you laughing through snot because your nose sounds like a dying accordion and somehow that ridiculous sound saves you both from drowning.

This isn't movie-love.
It's floor-love.
Parking lot love.

The kind of love that lets you scream until your throat burns, sit in silence until your breath steadies, and then, somehow, reach for each other anyway.

Not because it's easy. Not because the fight isn't exhausting. Not because love feels soft and perfect and holy every single moment. But because something deeper than exhaustion pulls you back into the gravity of each other. Something ancient in the body remembers: we came here to do this together.

And this isn't curated love.

This isn't the kind of love you see on perfect Instagram squares with matching sweaters and laughing eyes. This isn't candlelit silence and uninterrupted tenderness, where the music swells and the answers are obvious and the arguments are solved in thirty seconds flat. This is the kind of love where your eyeliner is smeared halfway down your cheek and the radio's stuck on static and you're too stubborn to turn it off because the silence feels louder than the sound. It's the two of us choosing to be ridiculous and holy at the same time.

This is the kind of love where someone eventually says the wrong thing, and someone else breathes too loudly, and one of you mutters "wow" under your breath in a way that could start an entirely new war if the other one hears it. It's absurd, and messy, and human in a way that would almost be funny if it weren't so holy.

And maybe that's the thing I wish someone had told us sooner:
the sacred lives inside the mess.

It lives in the hand you reach for after the screaming.
It lives in the breath you take together when neither of you knows what comes next.

It lives in the quiet choice to stay seated in the same car, in the same dark, holding the same silence, even when every part of you is begging for escape.

And God, the ache can be so loud sometimes.

There were nights it woke me at 3 a.m., pulling me out of sleep like an undertow I couldn't fight. I would lie there staring at the ceiling, the shadows stretching long and thin across the walls, my chest carrying all the stories my body hadn't yet untangled. Stories that weren't even mine but lived inside me anyway—my father's leaving, his mother's fears, the silence Oerti learned from his father, the echoes of every woman before me who swallowed her voice to keep the peace.

This is the part no one writes on Instagram. This is where ancestral weight shows up disguised as an argument about tone, or dishes, or who forgot to pick up Zoe from practice last Tuesday. You think you're fighting about this moment, but you're really sitting in a car under bad gas station lights, holding your grandmother's ache, your mother's silence, and your own longing all at once—trying to decide if you will choose differently this time.

Sometimes, that's what staying really is:
not forgiving him, but forgiving the generations.
Not choosing "us" as we are today, but choosing the lineage we're here to rewrite.

And that's the thing about Oerti—he stayed, too. Even when my edges were sharp and my shadows louder than my voice, he stayed. Not because it was easy for him, but because something deeper than either of us kept pulling us back into the gravity of each other.

There were nights we sat across the couch, knees pulled up, both of us drained from another round of unearthing the same old wound—the one that shapeshifted but never quite disappeared. Sometimes, we'd sit there for hours, not touching, just breathing in the same room, until one of us would sigh and say softly, "Okay. I'm still here." And somehow, that was enough to loosen the tightness between us.

That's the thing I want to tell anyone holding this book with a tired heart:
staying isn't always beautiful, but it is holy. It's made of both the tears and the ridiculous laughter in between them. It's the devotion of sitting in the fire together—even when one of you wants to bolt—and remembering that the fire is refining, not destroying.

It's learning to hear the deeper question beneath the argument.
It's learning to reach for each other even when your bodies are screaming "protect yourself." It's letting the quiet weight of his hand on yours at a gas station become the gospel of staying.

And no, this isn't a fairytale.
It's messier than that.
Holier than that.
More human than anything I was ever taught about love.

The truth is, I didn't know what we were doing half the time. There were nights I stared at him and thought, *We are never going to make it.* And then, five minutes later, I'd be convinced we were unbreakable, destined, tethered by something older than vows.

That's the thing no one warns you about sacred love—it will make you feel like both things are true in the same breath.

It's not the kind of love where the soundtrack swells and everything resolves in three minutes and thirty-eight seconds.

This is the kind of love that leaves you sitting in a car outside a gas station at 10:43 p.m., mascara smudged, forehead against the window, saying things like:
"I don't even know who I am anymore,"
and him whispering back,
"I know. But I do. I know who you are."

It's the kind of love where one minute you're yelling, and the next, you're laughing—because somehow, mid-argument, he mispronounces "detoxification" like "detoxifishion," and I choke on a sob and say, "You're actually impossible," and he says, without missing a beat, "Statistically speaking, impossible people live longer." And I hate him for making me laugh.
And I love him for knowing I needed to.

That's the kind of alchemy no book prepares you for.

Because staying isn't always soft.
Sometimes it looks like sitting in your car, holding your knees to your chest, while the man you love stares straight ahead and says nothing—not because he doesn't care, but because he's learning how not to defend himself, how not to armor up, how to just be there, even when the silence between you feels louder than sirens.

And sometimes staying means waking up the next morning, making coffee in the same kitchen where your heart cracked open last night, and remembering you still have to make breakfast, pack lunches, find Maya's left shin guard because apparently it vanished into another dimension overnight, braid Zoe's hair before school, get Bliss to stop brushing her doll's teeth with actual toothpaste, and

271

somehow, somehow, not let your tender chest spill all over everyone before 8:07 a.m.

This is staying.
Not perfection.
Not harmony every second.
Not bypassing the ache, but folding it into the life you're building anyway.

Because beneath all the arguments, beneath the projections, beneath the echoes of everyone who came before us—there's this quiet thread that keeps pulling us back to each other.

And sometimes I feel it strongest in the smallest moments.
The ordinary, unphotographable ones.

Like when I'm in the laundry room, buried under piles of mismatched socks and still-damp towels, muttering about how we literally have too many clothes and not enough drawers, and he comes up behind me, wraps his arms around my waist, and says, "You're my one and only," into my hair. And I melt, not because the fight is resolved, but because I remember:
This is what choosing each other feels like.

Or when Maya bursts through the door barefoot, holding her soccer ball above her head like a trophy, yelling, "I made the team!" and before I can even stand up, he's already scooped her into his arms, spinning her around the living room while Bliss shouts, "My turn! My turn!" from the couch. And I stand there, watching my girls pile on top of him, and I think:
This.
This is why we stayed.

Because staying isn't just for us.
It's for them.
For the laughter we haven't had yet.
For the dinners we'll eat on the floor when the table's too full of laundry.
For the small, holy, quiet moments when I catch him watching me like it's the first time, even when it isn't.

This isn't curated love.
This isn't pretending our wounds didn't travel here with us.
This isn't us arriving "healed" and "whole" and "ready," like some cosmic prize for perfect self-work.

This is ancient work wrapped in human skin.
This is rewriting the patterns no one before us had the space or safety to rewrite.
This is choosing the slow miracle of repair over the fast relief of escape.

And I think about the ones who came before us—
the women who swallowed their pain so the family would stay together,
the men who left rooms quietly because they didn't know how to say, I need you,
the ancestors who endured in silence so we could stand here, holding this particular fire.

Sometimes, when it's really hard, I close my eyes and feel them around me.
Not as ghosts, not as words—but as breath.
Like they're leaning in, whispering without sound:
This is the work we couldn't do. You are doing it now.

And then I look at him.

At the man who has walked through every storm with me, even when I dragged us into some of them kicking and screaming.

At the father who tucks our daughters in at night and whispers prayers into their hair when he thinks I'm not listening.

At the partner who has stayed, not because he is unscathed, but because he is willing to be transformed.

And I think:
This is love.
Not the kind that saves you.
The kind that remakes you.
The kind that burns you clean.

The world lied to us about love.
Or maybe not lied—maybe it just... forgot.

It told us that when we found "the one," we'd know. That it would feel effortless, like puzzle pieces sliding into place under soft candlelight. That we'd wake up every morning to golden light slanting across the sheets, smiling, hair perfectly tousled, coffee steaming, two perfectly matched hearts syncing without friction, without questions, without needing anything more than the movie-worthy moment.

It didn't prepare us for car rides where silence stretches so long you wonder if you'll ever find your way back to each other.

It didn't prepare us for the nights when we turned away from each other in the same bed, holding our own grief in separate bodies, pretending to be asleep.

It didn't prepare us for how trauma remembers even when we forget, how it wakes you at 3 a.m., heart pounding, whispering, don't trust this, don't trust him, don't trust yourself.

It didn't teach us how to love when the nervous system is still bracing for abandonment.
It didn't give us language for holding someone else's wounds without confusing them for our own.
It didn't warn us that deep love would surface everything we thought we'd already healed.

And so we learned the hard way.

We learned that sacred union is not the absence of rupture.
It's the devotion of repair.

It's knowing that some nights we'll both get it wrong—the timing, the tone, the words— and yet we still come back to the table, and talk until the edges soften. Sometimes, we don't even talk. Sometimes, we just pass a mug of cold tea back and forth in silence, letting our breathing be the truce.

It's realizing that "perfect matches" don't exist. We don't find them. We become them by choosing presence over performance.
By asking better questions when the easy ones fail us.
By letting our wounds sit side by side on the same couch instead of pretending they don't exist.

And, God, sometimes it's funny.
Sometimes, right in the middle of the ache, one of us says something absurd and it dissolves the heaviness without fixing a single thing.

Like the night we were halfway through the fight about whether he "never listens" or I "never let things go," and Bliss came tiptoeing into the living room in her unicorn pajamas, holding her toothbrush in one hand and saying, dead serious:
"You guys are too loud. The baby doll is sleeping." We apologized to a doll at 9:17pm, and I'm not kidding.

And just like that, the entire storm inside the room shifted.
Not gone. Just softened.

Because sometimes staying isn't about resolution.
It's about remembering you're still on the same team, even when your shadows are wrestling in the hallway.

And the truth?
Oerti isn't my perfect match; he's my evolving one.

Not because he isn't extraordinary.
But because he's human. Because I'm human. Because love this deep requires us to grow into each other, over and over again—through seasons of rupture and repair, contraction and expansion, forgetting and remembering.

This is the part no one talks about.
How love forces you to meet yourself.
How it places mirrors everywhere—in arguments, in intimacy, in silence—and asks:

Can you stay?

Can you stay with yourself when your voice trembles?
Can you stay in his presence when your chest is screaming to run?

Can you stay soft enough to receive his love even when every part of you wants to fold your arms and say, "No, I'm fine"?

Because that's what staying really is.
Not denial. Not bypassing.
It's choosing the repair over the escape.

It's looking at the person across from you, seeing the jagged edges and the tenderness and the places they don't know how to love themselves yet—and saying:
"I'm here. I choose you anyway."

And here's the thing I've learned:
The staying doesn't happen in the grand gestures.

It happens in the gas station parking lot at 11 p.m., where we're both crying into the dark, whispering things we don't even know how to say out loud.
It happens in the kitchen, where his hand brushes mine as we pass plates in silence after a fight, and I remember we are still here, still breathing, still trying.
It happens in the tiny, unglamorous moments—like folding the socks together, picking up spilled Legos at midnight, answering texts about missing permission slips while trying not to burn the rice.

And sometimes, staying is knowing when to laugh in the middle of it.
Because if you don't let yourself laugh, you forget that joy is medicine too.
Because the truth is, staying was never just about us.

Not really.

It was never only about a woman and a man learning how to love each other better, though God knows we have had to do that, over and over again, in a thousand different ways.

It was about breaking contracts we never signed but inherited anyway.

It was about rewriting the story for every woman in my bloodline who swallowed her no because the world told her to.

It was about giving my daughters a living example of what devotion looks like when it's no longer tethered to self-abandonment.

Some nights, when the house is finally quiet, I sit in the stillness and I swear I can feel them—the women, the mothers, the unnamed ones who came before me. Not hovering above like saints, but inside the ache in my chest, in the warmth at the base of my spine, in the steadying pulse beneath my skin.

They don't arrive with trumpets. They don't need to.

Their knowing moves differently—subtle, tidal, inevitable—like something inside me remembers before I do.

And when I listen closely, I hear them.

Not in words, but in breath.

Not outside of me, but through me:

"Child... we know this fire.
We know what it is to stay when everything inside you wants to leave.
We know the temptation of silence, the hunger for ease, the exhaustion of carrying what feels unfixable."

I close my eyes, and I feel their weight layered into mine—women who crossed oceans carrying babies and salt, women who tucked their grief into the hem of the day so their children would never taste it, women who said I'm fine when they were breaking, because no one ever taught them they were allowed to fall apart and still be loved.

They stayed, but many of them stayed inside themselves only halfway.
Bodies present, hearts buried.
And they whisper through me now:

"Do it differently, love.
Stay, but don't vanish inside your staying.
Stay, but keep your voice in the room.
Stay, but keep your softness intact.
Stay, but stay with you, too."

And it undoes me—this reminder that staying isn't about folding into someone else's shape.
It isn't about being chosen.
It isn't about holding everything together so tightly that nothing breaks.
It's about allowing yourself to be fully here, with the mess, with the ache, with the laughter that still finds its way through.

I think about my girls.
About the day they will love someone the way I love him—wide and wild and scared and holy all at once.
I think about the nights they'll sit cross-legged on their own kitchen floors, mascara smudged, hair tangled, whispering into the dark: "Is this worth it? Can I keep going?"
And I want them to have a different answer than I did.

I want them to know that love isn't about pretending the cracks aren't there.

I want them to know that rupture doesn't mean failure, and repair doesn't mean weakness.

I want them to see me choosing softness even when it feels impossible, because maybe if they see me forgive in real time, they'll forgive themselves more gently, too.

Because this is the quiet inheritance we're shaping.
Not castles or crowns.
Not the illusion of perfection.
But a new memory in the body:

That love can stay.
That tenderness can stay.
That you can stay, fully, without leaving yourself behind.

And in this way, we are healing something ancient.
In the staying, we're mending the places where love used to collapse. In the choosing, we're stitching together the fractures we didn't cause but were born carrying anyway. In the breath, in the laughter, in the reaching for each other even after the storm, we're giving our children a map—one written in something older than language, carved into marrow, passed hand to hand like a prayer.

This love rearranges timelines. This is the kind that changes what's possible for the ones who come after us. The kind where the decision to remain becomes medicine not just for you, but for the lineage that dreamed you into being.

And so we stay.

We stay when it's inconvenient. We stay when it's humbling.

We stay when the staying asks everything of us and offers no guarantees in return.
We stay because something in our bones knows this is the work.

And one day, when my daughters ask me how we did it –
how we made it through the storm, how we held on when the winds wanted to tear us apart—I won't give them a formula.
I'll hand them this:

I'll tell them there were nights where I screamed into the steering wheel,
mornings where I prayed on the kitchen floor, afternoons where we forgot to speak and had to learn each other's language again from scratch.

I'll tell them we laughed until we cried,
and cried until we laughed.
That we failed beautifully,
and failed often.
That we burned pieces of the old us to the ground so that something truer could rise in its place.

And I'll tell them the truth that changed everything:

We didn't stay because it was easy. We stayed because it was holy—because love, the real breathing kind, was worth the becoming it asked of us. And when they're standing in their own storm one day, may their bodies remember that.

CHAPTER TWELVE

The Beauty After Remaining

What love becomes when it has nothing left to prove

There is a quiet that comes after the fire and it does not arrive the way you think it will, not as silence heavy with defeat or some neat, curated ending tied with a ribbon, but as something older and stranger. A current the body doesn't trust at first, because the body remembers the heat, remembers the fracture, remembers the sound of its own undoing, and so when the quiet enters it feels almost dangerous, like stepping barefoot into a room you thought was lost. Like touching a door you were certain had been sealed and finding it give beneath your palm, soft as breath, soft as something waiting.

I stand there anyway, bare soles pressed against the tile of my life, realizing I survived, realizing survival has its own frequency, its own texture. The air shifted somehow, denser and cleaner, sharp in a way that makes me want to cough and laugh at once. And then I notice the weight in my hands loosening, the knives I didn't even know I was gripping sliding back into drawers, my fingers unclenching as if the body has finally agreed to release its watch.

About time, something inside me mutters, half exasperated, half amused, and I almost laugh aloud at myself because of course I was gripping invisible weapons in broad daylight, of course I was sleeping with my shoulders drawn up to my ears like a soldier in a foxhole, of course my bones forgot they were meant to be scaffolding for breath and dance, not just armor.

And there, beneath the ribs, beneath the memory of every wound and tremor, a single unlit room opens, a room I've always lived in, but could not return until now, and the stillness waiting there carries its own heartbeat, steady, indifferent to my doubt. It doesn't ask me to trust it, doesn't demand I promise to stay; it simply keeps pulsing until my body, stubborn as it is, begins to believe.

See? You don't have to prove anything, the current whispers, sly and tender at once. *You just have to stand here and not run.*

And so I do.

When we look at each other now it is not the same looking as before, it is slower, quieter, stripped of the fog and stripped of the thousand small defenses we carried like second skin. Stripped of the old habit of scanning for safety, of measuring the weather inside each other's eyes before daring to open the door. Instead there is this soft astonishment, this sudden recognition that the war beneath our skin has ended even if the scars still hum.

For the first time in longer than memory I am not searching his face for the boy I once met, not measuring him against the man I secretly insisted he should become, and he is not scanning me for the girl who lit every room with borrowed fire just to outrun the ache of being dimmed.

 Without realizing it we have stopped negotiating with the ghosts, stopped dragging their shadows into this moment, stopped letting their breath script the silence between us. Here we are instead, standing in the aftermath, soul-bared, raw, unarmored, the same and yet truer somehow.

And when his gaze lands inside mine I can feel the old names dissolving, the ancient contracts unbinding, the old mirrors breaking into soft light, and something inside me whispers that we are meeting for the first time again. Not as the shapes we rehearsed for each other, not as the roles we clung to when we were both still afraid of being seen, but as two currents that have finally remembered how to flow beside each other without colliding, without damming, without drowning.

I swear the air between us has changed its texture, heavier with something unspoken, tender with something holy, and my body knows it before the mind dares to name it: we are here, still, and we are new.

Don't look away, the current teases gently, almost laughing. *This is what you came for.*

And I don't.

It happened in the kitchen, not in some polished moment I could frame. The kettle clicked off, loud enough to remind me of the ten other things I hadn't finished, and his hand brushed mine as he passed me a mug already warmed the way I like. Something in my chest startled awake, like a door I didn't know was still locked had just come undone.

"Really?" I muttered under my breath, rolling my eyes at myself. "A mug of tea is the miracle?"

Yes, the current inside me answered, half amused. *Don't argue with it.*

And I laughed—actually laughed at myself—standing there, hair tangled, strands sticking up in every direction, surrounded by dishes and clothes no one had put away. The absurdity of it nearly undid me.

Later, in the doorway, our eyes caught and held too long. Immediately the old reflex lit up inside me—that bracing, that inner voice rehearsing disaster like a script it had memorized.

"Okay, here we go," I muttered in my head. "This is the part where he pulls away and I pretend I don't care."

Stop rehearsing endings that aren't happening, the other current shot back, a little sharper than usual.

"Well excuse me for trying to be prepared," I whispered under my breath, shifting the laundry basket on my hip.

Prepared for what? Love? Presence? God forbid something actually works out for once.

I almost snorted—right there in the silence of the doorway, hadn't even washed my face or brushed my teeth, hair that had lost the battle hours ago, laundry spilling down my arm like I was auditioning for the role of "overwhelmed mother of three." Hardly a cathedral moment.

"This is absurd," I muttered, rolling my eyes. "Chipped paint on the wall, basket of socks about to topple, and suddenly I'm supposed to believe this is holy?"

Exactly, the current whispered back, sly now. *If it only counted when the floor was clean and your eyeliner was intact, you'd never recognize it. This is where holiness hides—in chipped paint and socks you keep stepping over.*

I exhaled in surrender, right there in the doorway, because it was true—my body wasn't flinching. His nearness didn't feel like danger. And that ordinary ridiculousness, mascara streaks and all, felt like the most honest miracle I'd ever been handed.

The ache was still there, of course—I wasn't healed, not by a long shot—but it had changed texture. Less like glass shattering inside me, more like a bruise the light already knew how to touch.

There was no big speech, no moment that would make sense on film, no orchestral swell. What came instead was this steadying, this downward rooting that felt almost anticlimactic at first.

"Really? This is it?" I thought, folding towels at the kitchen counter. "This is what the poets meant?"

Yes, the current inside me replied dryly. *The poets forgot to mention laundry day. Don't hold it against them.*

Love stopped showing off. That's what happened. It quit climbing for fireworks and started sliding under everything, under the arguments, under the ledgers of who hurt whom and when, under the long silences that didn't fix themselves overnight. It pressed itself flat to the soil like a palm, steady, unmoving.

And of course, I resisted it at first. "So we're just… staying? No grand performance? No dramatic reunion speech?"

You wanted Broadway? the current teased. *You got a life instead. Congratulations.*

And it was right, because the miracle wasn't in the spectacle. It was in the small decision to keep showing up anyway. Not because everything was resolved, not because either of us had suddenly become saints, but because leaving would have been easier and we didn't.

Presence slipped in where punishment used to live. Growth took the place of perfection. The real thing stood in for the performance.

It wasn't pretty. It was better.

I can still feel the quiet of those evenings—him passing me a dish towel, me rolling my eyes but taking it anyway, the hum of the dishwasher in the background, the way my body softened even when my mouth stayed stubborn. No lightning, no thunder, just the steady hum of devotion rooting itself into soil I hadn't trusted in years.

And the current whispered, softer now: *This is it. This is holy. Don't wait for it to sparkle—it's already here.*

Staying itself became a vow older than understanding, a vow to the breath, to the ache, to the body that remembers what the mind resists, and it whispers without sound: *I choose you. Not as the polished thing you're trying to become, but as the wild unfinished pulse you already are.*

And in that choosing something tender and almost unbearable unfolds. A stillness that does not erase the storm, a steadiness that does not require certainty, a presence that carries its own weight without demand.

And I realize that this, more than the fire, more than the ruin, more than the endless nights spent on opposite ends of the couch wondering if love could survive its own hunger, this is the miracle. This kneeling into what remains without asking it to perform, this knowing without proof, this quiet covenant that does not need to be spoken because it breathes itself into the space between our hands, between our bodies, between the hours where nothing happens and everything is happening at once, and the river beneath the river hums its low, unbroken hymn: *stay, stay, stay.*

Presence comes quietly, almost shy, as if it has been waiting at the edge of the room for years. And when it steps forward it does not demand recognition, it does not rearrange the furniture of our lives. It simply begins to replace what could no longer hold us, dissolving punishment into softness, undoing the fantasy of perfection we kept mistaking for love, all the courtroom moments of right and wrong... feel unnecessary, almost tender in their smallness, as if it belonged to a life we have already shed.

The miracle wasn't the big reconciliations, the "aha" moments people imagine. It was the quiet ones. My forehead finding his shoulder, not as apology, not as plea, just because it was late and the day had been too much. A knee brushing mine under a blanket. Ordinary gestures that didn't need translation.

That's altar work, the current interrupted, sharper now. *Stop waiting for incense. It's this.*

And I knew it was right. Because love had stopped performing. It was rooting instead. It was folding clothes, carrying groceries, listening badly but trying again, breathing side by side.

There was nothing grand about it. And maybe that's the point.

It's not smaller, the current said, softer now. *It's truer. Stop confusing spectacle with holy.*

And I let that line land—right in the middle of the mess, right in the hum of the dishwasher, right where the miracle was hiding in plain sight.

Right here, right now, I realize it isn't the grand gestures that build a life, it isn't the fireworks or the declarations. It's this slow stitching of ordinary moments into a tapestry so wide the mind cannot name it, only the body can trust it, because somewhere beneath the noise of the world the river has been humming its low hymn all along, teaching us presence in fragments we did not know were prayers and none of it shouts but all of it speaks, saying only this: you are seen, you are safe, you are still chosen.

Touch didn't change because it had been wrong before. I had always loved the way his hand found me, the way his presence carried steadiness even when the rest of life was unraveling. What changed was the air around it—the ghosts fell away, the courtroom dissolved, the ache stopped hijacking the moment.

So when his fingers brushed mine one evening, nothing new happened—and yet everything was different. It wasn't a plea. It wasn't an apology. It wasn't carrying the weight of everything unsaid. It was just touch. Simple. Present. Free. A gesture stripped clean of history, the way a pilgrim kneels before water knowing she doesn't need to drink the whole river in one day, knowing that the river exists whether she arrives with thirst or not.

Do you feel that? the current hummed inside me. *No bargaining. No translation. Just skin remembering skin.*

I almost smiled to myself, realizing how rare that kind of simplicity had become. Not because his touch was ever unwelcome, but because my body had been busy running interference, always negotiating with the ghosts. And now, finally, it didn't have to.

When my palm rested at his jaw I felt the history flicker. All the years of us trying to fix with closeness what words hadn't carried, but it passed through me like weather instead of lodging like glass. The body could finally trust what it had always known: his nearness was safe, steady, wanted.

"Of course this is where God hides," I muttered under my breath, half laughing at myself. "In messy kitchens, in warm palms, in flushed cheeks."

Exactly, the current teased back, amused.

And I laughed, low and quiet, because it was both absurd and tender—the way his breath caught under my hand, the way my body leaned without second-guessing, the way touch became less about mending and more about meeting.

It wasn't new. It was just honest.

See? the current whispered, gentler now. *This is what love feels like when you stop dragging the ghosts into the room.*

Something silent passed between us that doesn't belong to thought or speech or even this lifetime, the vow without words. Not hurried, not grasping, simply there. There is no hunger laced with fear here anymore, no desperate choreography to prove we are whole. We have retired from that ritual entirely, and instead there is only arrival— skin arriving into skin, breath softening into breath. And I realize we are no longer touching to erase absence but to create presence. No longer seeking fusion to hide our fractures but meeting as two rivers that have stopped fighting gravity, letting current find current without resistance. In that quiet, where pulse speaks to pulse, the room dissolves, the years dissolve, even the names dissolve, and what remains is this single, unbroken knowing beneath the ribs: we are here, still, and we are infinite.

There comes a moment when the person you've loved for so long suddenly feels unfamiliar, not because they disappeared, not because they betrayed the story you thought you were writing together, but because they have finally arrived inside who they are.
There it is, the unveiling, the breathtaking strangeness of seeing the soul in front of you as if for the first time, as if all the years have been rehearsal for this exact arrival. And I looked at him the way I imagine the earth first looked at rain, like recognition layered beneath surprise, like devotion braided with awe. In that instant I do not want to fix, or frame, or predict the shapes he will take next, I only want to witness, to sit inside this opening and let it swallow every name we ever gave each other. I realize I have been saving a chair for this exact version of him, this exact becoming, without knowing it.

I remember looking at him across the room, really looking, and I wasn't searching for the boy I met or measuring him against the man I insisted he should become.

He was just... here. Himself.

Don't ruin it by overanalyzing, the current warned, half smirking.

"I'm not," I whispered back, already grinning at myself. "I'm just—surprised."

Of course you are. You've been squinting through fog for years. Clear air always feels strange at first.

He wasn't scanning me either—not for the girl who lit rooms too bright, terrified of being dimmed. That girl had retired, thank God. What stood between us now wasn't performance or strategy. It was presence. It was the quiet astonishment of two people seeing each other without mirrors in the way.

The ghosts we used to negotiate with weren't at the table anymore. The courtroom was gone. There was no contract left to uphold except the one written in the marrow: stay, see, breathe.

It felt raw, unarmored, the same but truer. And in that moment I knew we were meeting for the first time again, not as the versions we rehearsed, not as the roles we thought we owed each other, but as ourselves.

And yes, I was standing there with pajamas, hair uncooperative, picking up toys and clothes—hardly the setting for revelation.

Perfect, the current whispered. *It has to happen exactly where you think it shouldn't. Otherwise you'd never believe it.*

This is the quiet after remaining: the place where the armor that once saved you begins to loosen without being asked. Where vigilance falls from the body like old bark peeling from a tree in spring. Where survival, once sharp-edged and necessary, begins dissolving into something softer, rounder, deeper, and the timeline that used to keep score—every rupture, every storm, every unfinished conversation—blurs at its edges, washed in a light I do not have to earn.

And suddenly gratitude is everywhere, thick in the throat, dense in the bones, not because everything was resolved or tied in a clean ribbon but because we are still here, because the fire came and we did not vanish. Because we stayed, and in staying, something holy bloomed in the ash. I wake beside you now not searching, not bracing, not rehearsing who I should be in order to keep your nearness, but arriving, soft and whole, into the moment that meets us.

The mornings are quieter now, full of small permissions like the shape his breath takes before his eyes open. The low ache behind my sternum when I remember the nights we almost didn't make it here, when goodbye hovered like an unspoken ghost between us. The gratitude is so wide some mornings it spills out of my chest without warning, like rain sliding from a roof into open earth, soaking everything it touches.

Love stopped performing, the current reminded me one night as I tucked in a shin guard back into the shoe rack instead of cursing it under my breath. *It's rooting now. Downward. Quiet. That's the miracle.*

And this, I think, is what it means to begin again—not returning to the place where we first met, but meeting the river where it carries us now, deeper and slower and wilder, knowing the water has changed us both. Knowing we are not the people who stepped into the fire, and still, somehow, miraculously, we find each other here, again, and again, and again. The devotion rises quiet and unsummoned, not as promise, not as proof, but as presence whispering without words: you stayed, and so did I, and the earth beneath us has learned our names.

There is a sweetness here now, one that did not exist before the burning. A sweetness so delicate the body almost doesn't trust it, like waking to birdsong after too many nights of sirens, or like stepping into a room where every lamp has been turned low and realizing your eyes can finally rest.
It is not the sweetness of nostalgia, not the kind that pretends the ache never carved itself through us. But the sweetness of a body unclenching, the nervous system unfurling petal by petal after seasons of curling tight in defense. The sweetness of realizing we are no longer rehearsing the catastrophe before it comes.

Tenderness announcing itself in the most unphotographable ways with gazes across the table that linger half a heartbeat too long and tell me without words that I am seen, that I am safe, that I am still chosen. And this—this ordinariness—has become the scripture we live by, folded laundry still warm from the dryer, the dishwasher humming its own low hymn, the forgotten shin guard rescued from under the couch as if retrieving a relic, the quiet sacrament of you knowing exactly what espresso setting I like before pouring the coffee. Small gestures no camera would ever notice but my body records them like gospel, because in the aftermath of storms, this is the treasure.

Even the children joined in with their own sermons. Zoe minted sarcasm into a love language, Bliss enforced role playing with her and her toys with full legal authority, demanding apologies for violations, Maya sprinted barefoot all over the house, joy radiating because she megged one of us with her soccer ball.

The ordinary, luminous because I was finally present enough to notice.

This is what survived, the current murmured, softer now. *Not the fireworks. The sweetness.*

And I believed it.

We stopped trying to repair each other into versions we thought would save us. Stopped sculpting one another into softer shapes that might hold our ache without spilling it. Stopped performing fluency in languages we never truly spoke but kept rehearsing out of fear of being misunderstood. And somewhere along the way the silence between us shifted, not into absence but into space.
Inside that space something tender and almost unbearable began to bloom—the desire to be known without translation. We began to meet each other differently, not as problems to solve but as landscapes to walk slowly. The way we talk now is less about victory and more about understanding, less about being right and more about being real, less about defense and more about belonging.

And the question I used to carry like a stone beneath my ribs— will you stay if I fall apart?— has dissolved into something quieter, softer, certain, because we have already held each other through the private collapses no one witnessed: the nights we sat on opposite ends of the same couch, our silence sharp enough to cut, our grief spilling across the floor like an untended river. We found our way back to the middle, through apologies offered not in speeches but in folded laundry and warm mugs of coffee left waiting. The body remembered how to lean even when the mind had no words.

Even Bliss putting diaper rash cream all over her toys, became kind of a preacher, reminding us that devotion lives in absurdity, that holiness doesn't mind the mess.

Love was never meant to be clean, the current reminded me one night as I watched him clean the kitchen with sleeves rolled passed his elbows.

Maybe this is the truest thing I know now: staying isn't a theory or a ceremony or a vow written down. It is the thousand small choices to return, again and again, to the same room, to the same gaze, to the same body, and let the air settle around you until the river beneath the river reminds you that there was never anything to prove here, there was only this: the slow miracle of being known and the even slower miracle of letting yourself be loved anyway.

And yes, there is laughter here now, the kind that surprises you, arriving like a stray dog padding soft and unannounced back into the yard, tail low, eyes bright, testing the edges of belonging before curling itself at our feet as though it never left. And we let it, we make space for it without forcing it to explain where it's been, because somewhere along the way we stopped believing that joy has to be earned.

So we laugh deeper now, not the brittle laughter we used to weaponize, not the sharp kind meant to cover rupture, but the full-bodied kind that folds us into ourselves, where shoulders drop, ribs loosen, and for a moment we are just two people with open mouths, letting sound carry the weight we used to hold in silence.

There are nights when we sit in bed, exhaustion draped across us like a blanket, and one of us says something small, unplanned, not even funny enough to repeat, and yet we dissolve into laughter

anyway. The kind of laughter that pulls tears from your eyes and leaves your
chest aching in the best way.

Some nights, when the house finally exhales and even the walls seem to rest, I can hear the transmissions again. Not words, not sermons, more like frequencies moving through entire being.

Don't overreach, the current teases. *You don't have to decode it all. Just listen.*

So I do. I sit there with the dishwasher cooling, the children asleep in their tangled blankets, his hand warm against mine, and I let the under-voices braid through my ribs.

One voice remembers staying at a cross, not out of naivety, but because love had carved itself deeper than fear. Another remembers gathering what was shattered, not to save a man, but to call the world back into wholeness. A third reminds me that joy is not decoration but priestess, that laughter is not shallowness but doorway.

And always, beneath them all, a mother's pulse. The kind that holds the field steady even when the field is grief. The kind that refuses to abandon her post, even when the cost is everything.

I don't argue with them anymore. I don't line them up like soldiers and demand their names. I just let them braid through my breath, like tide rolling in and out, like a hum that remembers itself.

We remained, the current whispers finally, steady as heartbeat. *Awake. And now so do you.*

And there's nothing to do but nod because I know it's true.

I lie there in the dark, eyes open, heart slow, body warm against his, knowing without thought that we are not just living our own story anymore, we are standing inside a continuum of devotion larger than either of us. That our staying has never been ours alone, that the fire did not burn us out of belonging but into it, and the river under the river hums its one, unbroken hymn: keep breathing, keep loving, keep becoming.

It turns out staying has nothing to do with certainty and everything to do with devotion. And devotion is not pretty.

It leaks mascara down your cheeks and leaves tissue shreds stuck to your face. It passes a crumpled napkin across the center console at a stoplight. It laughs through snot because your nose, mid-sob, decided to sound like a dying accordion and that sound, absurd and merciful, stopped both of you from drowning.

See? the current chuckled. *Even grief has a sense of humor when you let it.*

I wanted to roll my eyes, but I couldn't. Because it was true. Devotion never asked us to be glamorous. It asked us to stay in the car with the windows fogged, to stay on opposite sides of the couch until the silence softened enough for our knees to touch again, to stay in the dark without abandoning ourselves or each other.

That's all it ever was: the oldest ritual I know. Two people sitting in the same night, refusing to leave.

No center stage and glowing lights. Just makeup stains on pillowcases and a laugh so sudden it felt like grace in disguise.

This is the altar, the current murmured, gentler now. *Not the vows you rehearsed. The mess you kept living through together.*

And I knew it was right. Because devotion never came with a spotlight. It came with an unremarkable Tuesday, with folded laundry, with arguments that turned into apologies whispered against tired skin, with joy arriving like stray dogs you were foolish enough to think had left for good.

That is the miracle: that the same breath can hold rupture and relief, ache and belonging, despair and delight. That love can make room for all of it without trying to name it beautiful.

Maybe that's the secret none of the stories told us—that devotion isn't a crown, it's an offering poured out, breath by trembling breath.

As I lean into him, I find ourselves becoming something vaster than the two of us, something unnamed and infinite, something that has always belonged to the field, and I close my eyes and let the current take me, knowing at last that we are the fire, we are the water, we are the vow.

On the other side of devastation there is no parade, no announcement, no grand reconciliation, there is only this wide and unspectacular and miraculous presence.

We see each other differently—not as the sum of what burned or the wounds we carried through the fire, but as something unstoried, unguarded and infinite.
And I realize, with the same awe as the earth receiving rain for the first time, that we are no longer trying to complete each other, no longer dragging the courtroom of yesterday into today, no longer

bending ourselves into shapes that might make the other stay, because the staying has already happened.

What's left now is the holy ordinariness of our mornings, the quiet of our bodies finding each other beneath blankets without needing to fuse, the unscripted laughter that slips out like breath, the knowing glance across the table that carries entire volumes without a word, the divine hidden in the way you pour my coffee without asking and the reverence stitched into the smallest gestures. Reverence for the breaking, reverence for the returning, reverence for the living miracle that nothing dissolved us even when we thought it might.

I understand at last that there is no finish line, no final arrival, no complete healing waiting in some other room. There is only this breath, this gaze, this table, this life, and the knowing that we are still inside it, still inside each other, still being remade by the quiet miracle of staying.

The river carries us forward—infinite, unbroken, alive.

And I don't need to know where it's taking us.
This life, unspectacular and unfinished, is enough.

CHAPTER THIRTEEN

The Book Within the Book

Once, the veils parted and I only listened, trembling as the priestesses spoke. I thought their words were the codex itself. But mystery does not stay still. It circles back, asking more, until one day I found myself inside their voices, not apart from them but among them, as though the book had turned itself inside out—and that is where this chapter begins, in the field that opened beneath my feet.

It began in the place I cannot name. Half sleep, half prayer, half some realm that refuses explanation. One moment I am lying in my bed, trying to hush the noise of thought, and the next I am elsewhere. No thunderbolt, no announcement. Just a slip, a tilt, the way twilight sometimes convinces you the veil is thinner than it should be.

I stand barefoot in a field so wide the horizon feels alive. Grass rises and bows in a rhythm older than memory, and a tree spreads above me, its trunk thick with centuries, its leaves whispering words I almost understand. Here, nothing threatens. The unknown is vast, but it feels more like invitation than danger.

And then I see her. A girl, hair wild with wind, her toes pressed into the earth as though she belongs more than I do. She looks at me as if

I am the latecomer. Her hand slides into mine, warm and steady, and she says, "We made it."

"Made it where?" I ask, startled by how sure she sounds.

"Here," she shrugs. "Where else?"

I want to laugh, but something in me bristles instead. "I don't know if 'here' is enough. Shouldn't we know where we are going?"

She tips her head at me, her eyes narrowing in that way children do when they are certain the adults are missing the point. "You always want to know first. That's why you miss things. Don't you feel it? This place is safe. This place is right."

I bite my lip, realizing how much I don't trust safety when it comes unannounced. "But what if we're wrong?"

Little Light frowns, tugging harder at my hand. "You're the one who brought me here. Don't blame me now."

The words sting. I don't remember bringing her anywhere. I want to argue, but before I can, the air shifts. The field folds into itself, becoming a doorway, and suddenly we are inside a library.

It is immense. Rows of books rise like cliffs, not in flat aisles but in a vast curve, as if the whole library were shaped inside a sphere, the shelves bending upward and around until they disappear into shadow, stacked upon stacked, the sky itself built of bindings and spines. The dust does not settle; it hangs suspended, shimmering as though time itself has been holding its breath, waiting for someone to arrive who would dare touch what has been sleeping. The air is thick with the scent of parchment and something older—stone, cedar, salt—and every breath tastes like history.

The shelves glow faintly from within, as if the books are not lit by lamps but by their own remembering. Each one hums at a pitch too low for the ear but not for the body. My ribs vibrate. My palms tingle. It feels less like walking into a room and more like stepping into a living organ, a womb of knowledge, spherical and infinite, every surface lined with stories that seem to lean toward me, eager to be opened.

Little Light spins in the center of the chamber, laughing at how her echo circles back in perfect rings. She spreads her arms wide as though to gather it all and whispers, "It's round so nothing gets lost."

And she is right—no corner, no ending, only curve after curve, a horizon folding into itself, carrying more memory than one lifetime could ever read.

I whisper, "How could there be so many stories?"

"Because no one ever stops telling them," Little Light answers, skipping ahead. "Not even when you're tired. Not even when you think it's over."

I walk slowly, almost afraid that if I move too fast the whole thing will vanish. Every step stirs the air, and the dust turns to constellations for a moment before settling back into its invisible hum. The shelves lean closer as I pass, not menacing but curious, as though the books are aware of me, watching, waiting. Some are so massive they look carved from stone, their spines cracked like old riverbeds. Others are slim and delicate, stitched with threads that catch the light like veins of gold.

I trail my fingers across the spines of the books, each one humming. The sound is soft, like bees in a distant hive.

And then I see it.

Amid the fullness of volumes pressed tight shoulder to shoulder, there is one space left bare, exactly the size of the book I carry. The shelf curves inward, carved perfectly to cradle what has not yet been placed there, an absence that feels louder than all the presence around it. Little Light runs ahead, crouches down, and peers at the empty spot with wide eyes. She looks back at me, grinning as though she's just found the answer to a riddle: "See? They left it for you. Only you."

My throat tightens. The weight of travel, of centuries and lifetimes, presses through me in an instant, and still I cannot lift my hand. The knowing is too much. The absence is too exact. The empty space glows faintly now, as if it recognizes me before I have the courage to recognize myself. My hands tremble as I slide it into place. The gap hums, low and insistent, as though it has always known my hands would bring the thing it longs to hold.
The shelf exhales, and the air brightens. Something in me loosens too, as though a knot untied.

Little Light claps her hands. "See? You did bring me here. I told you."

I shake my head. "I don't even know what's happening."

She looks up at me, suddenly serious. "You don't have to know. You just have to keep walking."

Before I can argue again, the book dissolves into pulse, and the shelves vanish like smoke. We are standing on a dark plain.

The silence is heavier here, but not empty. Beside me, a guide appears—tall, cloaked, carved from the same night that surrounds us. He does not speak, yet his presence steadies me.

The ground beneath my feet begins to glow. With every step, constellations burst open, stars unfurling like lanterns along the path. They do not burn as the stars I know; they bloom, tender and bright, as if each one has been waiting for the press of my foot to awaken. The darkness is no longer empty but alive, trembling galaxies that recognize me. I am walking on the night sky itself, and the sky is answering back.

At the edges of the path, trees rise as if summoned by breath. Their trunks are spun of light, silver-threaded, transparent and yet solid enough to hold the world. Branches arch overhead, heavy with leaves that shimmer like fragments of moon. Some leaves drift loose and fall around me, glowing softly as they descend, dissolving before they touch the ground. The air smells of earth after rain, of cedar and something older, like incense that has never been lit but has always been burning.

The guide walks at my side, steady and slow, his stride longer than mine yet perfectly in rhythm. He doesn't need to speak; his silence is instruction. With every step, the path lengthens, stretching forward as though created just in time for us to arrive. Behind us, the stars dim back into darkness, so that there is only forward, only now.

Little Light skips ahead, her bare feet leaving their own bursts of starlight in the soil. She twirls once, laughing and the trees lean toward her like they, too, remember her. She doesn't question it. She doesn't hesitate. She belongs here without effort. Laughing and skipping she says, "Look! Look what we're planting!"

I shake my head. "This isn't planting, it's… I don't know what it is."

"Yes, it is," she insists. "Every step is a seed. You just don't believe it yet."

I sigh. "How can you be so sure?"

"Because I'm you," she says simply, with a grin, before sprinting forward again.

Her words hang in the air, sharp as starlight, and for a moment I want to call her back, to demand proof, to insist that things make sense before I trust them. But the guide lays a hand on my shoulder—not pushing, not pulling, just steady. And I realize sense may not come first. Only steps.

We walk like this—her wild, me uncertain, the guide silent—until the path bends toward a doorway of gathered light. I stop, trembling.

"I don't think I can," I whisper.

"You already are," the girl replies. She tugs my sleeve. "Don't you see? You're always afraid right before it opens."

And before I can argue, before I can name the fear, I find myself stepping through.
The chamber hums as though the walls themselves are breathing. Golden dust floats in spirals, catching the glow of unseen suns. At the far end, Isis waits, her robe trailing like tidewater, her gaze fixed and steady.

Little Light grips my hand so tightly it almost hurts. "She's here," she whispers, trembling with delight.

I want to bow. I want to surrender. But instead the words tumble out sharp, defensive:
"Why me? Why now?"

Isis tilts her head, neither offended nor surprised. "Why not?"

"Because I don't feel ready," I say, crossing my arms as though they could shield me. "I don't even know what's happening. You stand there like it's obvious, but it isn't. Not to me."

Little Light tugs at me. "It's obvious enough. You just don't want to see it."

I pull my hand free. "And how would you know? You're only a child."

She stamps her foot. "I'm the part of you that still believes before you smother it with doubt. I know more than you remember."

Her certainty needles me. "Belief without proof is dangerous."

"Not as dangerous as never believing," she snaps back.

I turn toward Isis, frustrated. "And you—you speak in riddles. Seeds, galaxies, fragments –but what if I just want something clear? What if I need answers, not poetry?"

For the first time, Isis moves closer. Her voice fills me like water poured into clay. "Clarity without mystery is a cage. You ask for answers, but answers alone cannot hold you. Only wonder can."

I shake my head, angry. "But wonder doesn't help me when I'm afraid. Wonder doesn't steady me when I'm falling apart."

Little Light's eyes flash. "That's not true. Wonder is the rope you keep refusing to grab."

"Enough!" I shout, my voice echoing against the glowing stone. "You make it sound simple, both of you, but you're not the one living in this body, in this time, with this fear."

The chamber stills. Even the dust seems to pause in mid-air.

Then Isis speaks, calm but firm. "You think fear makes you separate. It does not. Fear is the thread that ties you to every woman who has stood here before you. They too trembled. They too wanted proof. And still, they stepped."

My throat tightens. "And if they failed?"

"Then they rose again," Isis replies. "As stars do when they collapse. As mothers do when they are forgotten. As love does, endlessly."

Her words hang heavy. I want to believe them, but something in me resists. "It's not that easy."

"Of course not," she says gently. "If it were easy, you wouldn't be here."

Little Light squeezes my hand again, softer this time. "She's not against you. She's with you. So am I. Why can't you see that?"

Tears rise, unbidden. I whisper, "Because I don't know how."

Isis's eyes soften, blazing with something I cannot name. "Then let that be your first truth. Not knowing is not failure. It is opening. Live inside it. Let it shape you. The book you carry is not finished. It never will be. That is its holiness."

The golden dust brightens, galaxies spinning above us, their light reflected in Little Light's wild eyes. The guide, silent and patient, inclines his head.

And in that moment, torn between fear and longing, I feel the smallest shift inside—not a full surrender, but the faintest crack where light can enter.
The galaxies shimmer overhead, slow spirals of light turning like prayer wheels. I press my palms together, desperate for steadiness.

"I don't know how to carry all of this," I admit, voice cracking. "The wounds, the weight of the past, the voices that still echo. It feels too heavy. It feels like I'll drown in it."

Isis steps closer, her eyes never leaving mine. "You mistake inheritance for burden."

I frown, stung. "How can you say that? I've lived inside their silence. Their distortions. Their unspoken grief. I carry what they couldn't."

Little Light tugs impatiently at my sleeve. "But you also carry what they could. Their love. Their survival. Their songs, even the ones no one else heard."

I shake my head. "That doesn't feel true. The pain is louder."

Isis raises her hand. The golden dust stirs and begins to move, not like smoke, not like ash, but like something alive. It thickens, then loosens, then gathers again, swirling into shapes that shimmer just at the edge of recognition. Faces emerge first, half-formed, then dissolve back into light before reappearing sharper. Voices thread through the chamber—soft at first, then rising—an old woman's lullaby carrying notes I almost remember, a man's laughter cut short yet echoing as if it never ended, children chasing each other through tall grass, hands planting seeds into soil cracked with thirst.

The fragments weave together until it feels like the chamber itself is breathing, each inhale filling with the scent of bread baking, earth turned under, incense burning at altars long forgotten. Their memories ripple through me: the weight of a child pressed to a chest, the cry of mourning, the sigh of a first kiss, the prayers whispered in languages I do not know but somehow understand.

The walls seem to fall away as generations spill outward like stars, not bound by time or silence. They do not look at me with accusation. They do not hand me their sorrow to carry. They arrive whole—joy and ache braided, pain and persistence inseparable, their voices a chorus not of demands but of presence.

"Do you see?" Isis asks. "They are not only their pain. They are also their persistence. You are not the graveyard of their wounds. You are the ground where their unfinished prayers take root."

Her words press into me, but I resist. "If that's true, then why does it hurt so much to love? Why does love tear me open again and again?"

For the first time, Isis smiles. Not a soft smile, but one edged with fire. "Because love is meant to. It is not a cushion. It is a blade that carves you into more than you were before. You ache because you are expanding. You weep because your vessel grows wider. This is how galaxies are born."

I turn away, covering my face. "But what if I don't want to be carved anymore? What if I want it to stop?"

Little Light darts in front of me, her small hands gripping my arms. Her eyes blaze. "If you stop, then so do I. And I don't want to stop. I want to keep planting, keep running, keep becoming. Please don't quit on me."

Her plea rips through me. My knees weaken. I fall, not in worship but in exhaustion.

Isis kneels too, her robe pooling around her like water. She places her hand over mine -warm, steady, impossibly alive. "You are not asked to be without pain," she says. "You are asked to let love be larger than pain. That is the only way through."

The galaxies pulse above us, brighter now, as if the stars themselves lean in to listen.

The guide, silent all this time, finally speaks—his voice deep as earth, rare as thunder: "The doorway is near. But it will not open until you believe you can walk with all of this—the wound, the love, the doubt, the light. Not instead of each other. With each other."

The words settle like stone. Little Light presses her forehead to mine. Isis withdraws her hand but her gaze lingers, fierce and unyielding.

And in the quiet that follows, I realize: the doorway is not ahead. It is already opening inside me.

The chamber quiets. The golden dust begins to settle, as though the stars themselves are bowing in acknowledgment. Isis does not move again. She simply holds her gaze on me—a gaze that is neither indulgent nor demanding, but eternal.

"You have enough to walk with," she says at last. "Not everything. Never everything. But enough."

Little Light squeezes my hand so hard it almost hurts. "See? She's not sending us away. She's sending us forward."

I look around. "Forward to what?"

The guide gestures toward the far wall. At first, I see only stone, but then a faint shimmer appears, as though the dust itself is rearranging into shape. A second doorway begins to form, not carved or built but breathed into being. It glows faintly, pulsing like a heartbeat.

My chest tightens. "I'm not sure I can."

Isis's voice fills the chamber one last time, low and steady. "You are not asked to be sure. You are asked to step. Certainty is the last veil. Love is what tears it."

Little Light pulls on my arm. "Come on. We're not supposed to camp here forever."

I linger, afraid to release the steadiness of Isis's presence. "Will I see you again?"

Her eyes blaze, softer now but no less fierce. "You will not stop seeing me. Once I have entered you, I do not leave. I live in your marrow, in your breath, in the space between questions. Look there, and you will find me."

The words fill me like wine, warm and dizzying. I bow my head, not in submission but in gratitude.

The guide steps ahead, and the doorway of light widens, spilling radiance into the chamber. I hesitate, palms damp, heart loud.

Little Light tugs, impatient as ever. "We're wasting time!" she declares, laughing as she darts toward the threshold.

I take a trembling breath and follow.

The light folds around me, and the chamber dissolves. I step into a space softer, gentler. The air smells of roses, though none are in sight. The walls glow pale, as though lit from within by candlelight. It feels less like stone and more like embrace.

And there, waiting, is another figure—not as vast as Isis, not as fierce, but radiant with tenderness. Her robe is white, simple, woven as though of morning itself. She turns toward me with eyes that carry oceans of sorrow and oceans of joy, and I know without being told:

It is Mary.

The light softens as I cross the threshold. The air feels different here—less fire, more breath. It smells faintly of roses, though none are in sight. The walls glow pale, as if woven from candlelight, and the silence is not heavy but tender, like a lullaby waiting to be sung.

She is already here. Not crowned, not distant, but simple and radiant, her robe white as dawn. When she turns to me, her eyes are oceans—sorrow and joy bound together, inseparable.

Little Light lets out a delighted sigh. "I knew it would be her."

I freeze, afraid to speak. Afraid to disturb the gentleness. But the words tumble out anyway: "I don't know if I can bear your gaze."

Mary smiles, a smile that feels like forgiveness for every moment I have thought myself unworthy. "Then do not bear it. Let it bear you."

The words land like balm and blade at once. I shake my head. "You make it sound so easy. But love has torn me open too many times. I don't know if I have anything left to give."

Little Light squeezes my hand hard. "She's not asking you to give. She's asking you to receive."

Mary nods. "Children know. You forget that receiving is also holy."

I swallow, ashamed. "But if I keep receiving, won't I become selfish? Isn't the point to pour myself out?"

Her eyes deepen, sorrow shimmering through joy. "Did I not pour myself out? And still—was I not asked to receive first? Life itself entered me not through striving, but through surrender. Do you think surrender is selfish?"

Her words pierce me. I whisper, "I don't know how to surrender without feeling weak."

Mary steps closer, her voice low and steady. "Weakness is not the opposite of love. Pride is. Pride tells you that you must earn worth. Love tells you that you already are worth."

Little Light nods vigorously, tugging at me. "She's right. You keep trying to prove, when you could just be."

I bristle. "Being doesn't protect me. Being doesn't stop the wounds, the gossip, the distortions. Sometimes I feel like if I don't fight, I'll disappear."

Mary's hand rises slowly, resting over her own heart. "Did I not disappear, in the eyes of many? A girl from nowhere, a woman whose story was questioned, whispered about, doubted? And yet—here I stand. Do you see? Disappearance is not the end. It is a doorway. What vanishes in the world becomes eternal in God."

Tears blur my vision. My chest aches with both relief and resistance. "But it hurts so much to trust that."

Mary's gaze does not waver. "Of course it hurts. Love always hurts. But the hurt is not proof of its failure. It is proof of its depth."

Little Light leans against me, resting her head on my arm. "Can we stay here a little longer? It feels safe."

Mary smiles again, softer now, and spreads her arms as though to gather us both. "You may stay as long as you need. But know this: safety is not the gift I came to give. The gift is courage. The courage to let love live in you, even when the world misunderstands it."

The chamber glows brighter, the candlelight walls seeming to pulse with her words. The guide remains silent, watchful, steady.

And I, trembling in both ache and relief, whisper, "Then teach me how to live love even when it wounds."

Mary's eyes fill with tears, not of weakness but of solidarity. "I already am."

The candlelight dims as we leave Mary's chamber. The air cools, heavy with earth and stone. I feel my stomach knot, my breath shallow.

Little Light frowns, tugging at my arm. "This one's different."

The guide nods, silent but steady, as we step forward. The walls shift into cavern—rough stone, dripping water, shadows pressing close. A hush hangs heavy, not gentle like Mary's, but expectant, as though the air itself is waiting for what must be lost.

At the far end, she stands. Inanna. Barefoot, robed in midnight, eyes like obsidian wells. There is no crown on her head, only a gaze that strips me bare.

I shiver. "I don't think I belong here."

Her voice rises, low and resonant, echoing off the stone. "No one belongs here. Yet everyone arrives."

I step back, afraid. "I don't want to descend. I've been through enough."

Little Light squeezes my hand, whispering, "We already are."

My chest tightens. "But I don't want to lose more. I've lost too much already."

Inanna takes a step closer, her shadow spilling across the chamber. "You think loss ends you. But loss is the gate. Without it, you cannot enter what is real."

I shake my head, hot tears rising. "I don't want to pay the price. I want love without losing, truth without tearing. Why can't it be enough to have survived what I already have?"

Inanna's eyes blaze. "Because survival is not the same as transformation. You are not asked to endure. You are asked to descend."

Little Light clings to me, her voice sharp. "She's telling the truth. But I don't like it either."

Inanna kneels then, her robe pooling like darkness itself. Her voice softens, though it does not lose its weight. "Child, you cannot keep carrying armor and call it wholeness. Lay something down here. Let something die. Only then will your next doorway open."

I tremble, whispering, "But what if what I lay down is all I have left of me?"

Inanna's gaze does not waver. "Then what rises will be truer than you have ever known."

The chamber falls silent. The dripping of unseen water echoes like a clock.

The guide steps forward, laying his hand on my shoulder. Little Light presses her forehead into my side. My palms sweat, my breath comes hard.

I whisper, barely audible, "Then take it. Take what no longer belongs."

Inanna's eyes blaze brighter, and the cavern itself seems to inhale. The chamber waits. The silence is heavy, pressing on my chest. I feel as if the stones themselves are holding their breath.

Inanna's eyes never leave mine. "You cannot step forward carrying everything. What will you lay down?"

I shake my head, panic rising. "I don't know. I don't know what to give."

Little Light looks up at me, eyes wide and wet. "You do know. You just don't want to."

The words sting. I turn away, ashamed. My fists clench at my sides. "If I lay it down, what if I vanish too? What if it was the only thing keeping me together?"

Inanna steps closer, her presence cool and steady as stone. "Then let yourself vanish. The false must fall before the true can breathe. What you cling to is not your life. It is your mask."

My breath catches. I know what she means. The armor. The endless proving. The voice that insists I must explain myself to survive. The weight of it feels carved into my bones.

I whisper, "If I put it down, I'll be defenseless."

Inanna kneels before me, her gaze sharp and tender all at once. "Defenselessness is not weakness. It is the gate through which power enters."

The guide places his hand on my shoulder, firm, silent. Little Light presses closer, whispering, "Do it. Please. We can't carry it forever."

My knees give out. I fall to the stone floor, trembling. The armor I've worn—invisible but heavy—begins to rise from me. It does not fall easily. It clings, fights, digs its edges into my skin. I weep as I tear it free.

When it finally leaves me, it clatters onto the ground with a sound that echoes through the cavern like thunder. The stones themselves seem to exhale.

I collapse forward, breath ragged, body shaking. "What's left of me now?" I whisper.

Inanna places her hand gently against my cheek. "What was always there. The self that does not need defending."

The chamber brightens, the dripping water catching light as if stars are hidden in each drop. Little Light kneels beside me, stroking my hair, whispering, "You did it. We did it."

The guide steps forward. The stone wall before us shimmers faintly, a new doorway forming, pulsing like a heartbeat.

Inanna rises to her full height, her robe swirling like the night sky. "Go now," she says. "There is more to face. But do not forget—you left the false here. Do not pick it up again."

She steps back into shadow, and the chamber hums one last time before falling still.

I rise on unsteady legs, lighter than I have ever felt, and take Little Light's hand. Together we step toward the doorway, where another presence waits.
The doorway of stone and shadow folds away, and I step into warmth. Not fierce like Isis, not gentle like Mary, not dark like Inanna—but something startlingly familiar.

The chamber is smaller here, almost ordinary. Its walls are rough clay, lit by lanterns that flicker like heartbeats. The air smells faintly of myrrh and salt. There is no grandeur, no radiance meant to overwhelm. Only presence.

And she is there. Magdalene. Not veiled in mystery, not adorned like a queen—but robed in crimson, her hair loose, her face marked with the softness of tears.

She looks at me as if she knows every wound I have ever carried. Not from vision, but from living.

Little Light runs forward first, unafraid. "I like her," she says simply.

Magdalene smiles at the child, then at me. "You are trembling."

I cross my arms, defensive. "I've laid everything down already. I don't know what else you want from me."

Her eyes hold mine without flinching. "Not what I want. What you refuse."

The words sting. "And what is that?"

"Your own tenderness."

I laugh bitterly. "Tenderness doesn't protect me. Tenderness is what got me hurt."

Magdalene steps closer, her robe brushing the clay floor. "No. Betrayal hurt you. Lies hurt you. Tenderness did not. Tenderness is what allowed you to survive it."

Little Light tugs at my sleeve. "She's right. You wouldn't still be here without your softness. You only think it's weakness because they didn't honor it."

I shake my head, tears rising. "But every time I open, I get cut. How many times am I supposed to bleed?"

Magdalene lifts her hand, slowly, and places it over her heart. "As many times as love calls you. Not because pain is holy, but because closing would be worse."

Her voice trembles now, not from weakness but from truth lived. "Do you think I did not ache when I watched him bleed? Do you think I did not rage when the world mocked what was sacred? And still I loved. Still I stayed. Not because it was easy, but because love is stronger than humiliation. Stronger than distortion. Stronger than death itself."

The chamber flickers, lanterns flaring. Her words press against me like waves.

I whisper, "But what if I can't stay open? What if I close without meaning to?"

She leans close, her forehead almost touching mine. "Then open again. And again. And again. Tenderness is not something you keep perfectly. It is something you return to."

The guide inclines his head. Little Light clasps my hand, whispering, "See? We don't have to be perfect. We just have to come back."

The clay walls seem to pulse with breath, as if alive with her words.

Magdalene takes my hands into hers. They are warm, calloused, real. "Do not let them trick you into believing your softness is your downfall. It is your resurrection."

Tears spill freely now, falling onto the clay floor. I nod, unable to speak.

And the lanterns flare brighter, as though the chamber itself is sighing in relief.

The lanterns flicker as Magdalene keeps my hands in hers. Her palms are warm, roughened, not the hands of an untouchable saint but of a woman who has worked, washed, carried, wept.

"You think tenderness failed you," she says, voice steady, "but it was tenderness that made you survive the distortion. Tenderness is why your heart still beats with longing instead of stone."

I shake my head, hot tears spilling. "But they twisted everything. They told lies until people believed them. They made me a stranger in my own story. How do I live with that?"

Her eyes deepen, full of grief and fire. "Do you think I was not twisted into lies? Do you think I was not called names, dismissed as less than holy, erased from the very pages of the story I bled for? They tried to turn me into shadow so their version could shine brighter. And yet –" she squeezes my hands, her grip fierce now—"here I am. Their lies did not erase me. Love preserved me."

Little Light presses close, whispering, "See? They didn't win."

I want to believe it, but bitterness rises. "But what if the distortion is louder than the truth? What if no one ever knows?"

Magdalene's face trembles, not with weakness but with memory. "Then you live as though you are known anyway. Because you are. Truth does not need a crowd to be real. It only needs one heart strong enough to carry it."

The chamber swells with silence. Her words strike something deep in me, something I have been avoiding.

Still, I resist. "But it hurts. To stay soft. To keep opening. Every time I do, it feels like I bleed again."

She nods, tears glinting in her eyes now. "Yes. I bled too. Not with nails in my hands, but with whispers in my name. Every distortion cut me. Every silence wounded me. But do you see? The bleeding did not end me. It made room for more love than I knew I could carry."

Her tears fall freely now, yet her voice does not waver. "Love does not spare us the wound. It transfigures it. The scar becomes the mark of belonging. The tear becomes the doorway."

Little Light looks up at her, then at me. "So we don't have to stop hurting to be whole?"

Magdalene kneels to meet the child's eyes. "No, little one. You only have to let the hurt be loved."

The chamber trembles, the lanterns flaring bright as dawn. The clay walls seem to sigh, as though the earth itself has heard and agreed.

I fall to my knees, unable to hold the weight of her words. Magdalene lays her hand over my heart, steady and sure. "Your tenderness is not what broke you. It is what will raise you. Do not abandon it now. Let it be the stone they could never roll away."

The silence that follows is not empty. It hums with presence, with memory, with promise.
The clay walls of Magdalene's chamber soften, the lanterns dimming until only their glow remains in my chest. I rise slowly, unsteady, tender. The guide gestures, and once more a doorway opens—this

time wide, golden, pulsing with warmth like sunlight breaking over water.

Little Light bounces on her toes, tugging my arm. "This one feels different. Lighter."

We step through.

The chamber explodes with brightness. Columns carved from alabaster gleam like rivers of milk. Music hums in the air, though no instruments are seen. The scent of honey and wildflowers drifts on the breeze. It is not solemn here. It is alive.

And there she is—Hathor. Crowned with the horns of the cow, circlet of sun blazing between them, yet her smile is wide, playful. She looks less like a distant goddess and more like a friend who has been waiting for me to finally join the dance.

Little Light runs ahead, clapping. "I knew there'd be music!"

I hesitate at the threshold, still raw with tears. "I don't know if I belong here. I'm not... joyful enough."

Hathor laughs, a sound like bells and river water. "Joy does not ask if you deserve it. Joy invites you anyway."

Her words feel almost irreverent after so much solemnity. I cross my arms, defensive. "But isn't joy... shallow? Compared to what I've just faced?"

She steps closer, eyes gleaming with mischief. "Do you think the stars are shallow when they shine? Do you think the child's laugh is less holy than the prophet's prayer? No, daughter. Joy is not escape.

It is endurance. It is what keeps the soul from collapsing under its own weight."

Little Light twirls, hair flying. "See? Even she says it—joy is what keeps us alive!"

I shake my head, still heavy. "But what about the wounds? The losses? Doesn't joy dishonor them?"

Hathor cups my face in her hands, her touch warm and grounding. "No. Joy is what proves the wounds did not win. Grief shows you what you love. Joy shows you that love is still possible."

Her laughter spills again, this time softer. "They will try to convince you that seriousness is holy. That only sorrow can sanctify. But I tell you—laughter heals the bones. Dance restores the breath. Pleasure is prayer when it is received with love."

My chest tightens, the ache and longing rising together. "But I don't know if I remember how to rejoice. Not fully. Not without fear it will be taken away."

Hathor presses her forehead to mine, her voice low and tender now. "Then begin small. One note hummed. One bite savored. One kiss given without defense. Joy is not a possession to be kept. It is a river to be entered again and again. Do not fear its ending. Fear never stepping in."

Little Light grabs my hand, spinning me clumsily in a circle. "Dance with me! Just once!"

I stumble, laughing through tears. The sound surprises me, as though it belongs to someone braver than I have been. Hathor claps her hands, and the whole chamber seems to echo with delight.

The guide smiles for the first time.

And for the first time in this long journey, I feel not only broken open—but alive.

The temple of chambers dissolves, and I find myself drifting into whiteness. Not empty, not void, but full—as if every breath is spun from light. The ground beneath me is soft as down, a vast cloud stretching in every direction.

I sink onto it, my body loosening for the first time. I no longer feel pressed to rise, to question, to defend. I simply lie down, my cheek against the softness. Beside me coils a great white dragon, scales gleaming like pearl, breath rising and falling in steady rhythm. Its presence is not fierce but protective, not fire but peace. With each exhale, the air smells faintly of rain before dawn.

Little Light dances ahead, barefoot on the cloud, her laughter ringing clear as bells. Around her gather the priestesses—Isis with her flowing robe, Mary with her eyes of ocean, Inanna barefoot and unflinching, Magdalene robed in crimson, Hathor crowned with light. But here they are not solemn or commanding. They are laughing with her, spinning, skirts flaring, hair loosed in the wind of the high sky.

I watch, chest easing, heart wide. For once, I do not ache. I do not argue. I simply let the scene be what it is: divine, human, radiant, alive.

The dragon shifts closer, laying its great head beside me. I rest my hand against its warm scales, and it hums low in its throat, a sound like the deep earth remembering the sky. I feel it vibrate through me, a lullaby older than memory.

Little Light calls out, spinning, "Look! We're all here now. Nothing missing. Nothing broken."

The priestesses nod, each smiling, each radiant in her own way. For a moment, time feels unnecessary. For a moment, I believe her.

And I lie back on the cloud, dragon steady at my side, Little Light dancing in circles of laughter and song—and I know that this, too, is holy: not only the descent, not only the wound, but this. The light. The rest. The joy that needs no proof.

The cloud cradles me, wide and endless, the dragon's breath steady at my side. Little Light spins across the white expanse, skirts of radiance swirling, laughter rising like bells. Around her the priestesses dance—Isis flowing with starlight, Mary luminous as dawn, Inanna fierce even in joy, Magdalene tender as flame, Hathor radiant with delight. They do not teach now. They simply move. Their steps weave rhythm into the sky, and the air itself sings.

I watch, resting in the warmth, my heart unclenched. Nothing to argue, nothing to prove. Only this: the softness of the cloud beneath me, the dragon's hum, the laughter that keeps time with my breath. For the first time, I know the journey is not only descent and wound—it is also this light, this play, this holy rest. And so Chapter Thirteen closes not with fear, but with wonder. Not with fracture, but with joy.

CHAPTER FOURTEEN

The Storm Remembers Her Name

On another night altogether, far from the clouds and dragons and fields of my earlier dreaming, the waters came. Not as symbol, not as metaphor, but as tempest—vast and alive, carrying centuries in its roar. It did not stop at the horizon. It climbed into the heavens, swallowing stars, tearing open the fabric of night until galaxies spilled like embers into the flood. I was ankle-deep in water, but also standing on a shoreline made of constellations, as though time itself had liquefied. Lightning split not just the sky but the seams of creation, and thunder rolled through me as if my bones were cathedral walls built to hold its echo.

I did not come to this through study. No one handed me a text or placed their palms on my head. There was no smoke, no ceremony, no lineage I could point to and say, this is where I received it. What came was not inheritance dressed in ritual. It was wilder than that—an initiation without warning, a knowing that broke through like lightning. It did not fade with waking. It pressed itself deep into bone, carved itself into marrow. The kind of knowing that shatters you open and insists you answer to your own name.

The world was breaking. Streets swelled into rivers, dragging sandals, doors, and voices into the current. People ran barefoot through water that clutched at their legs, arms outstretched for those already lost to the dark. Mothers pressed children into their ribs, names ripped from their mouths before they could reach another ear. Toys spun, papers scattered, breath came sharp and fast as if the air itself were rationed. Above, lightning tore through the sky not as weather but as rupture—splitting time, cracking open the fabric of what was known. The cries of people below rose and tangled with the thunder until it was impossible to tell if the sound belonged to the storm or to the breaking of human hearts.

Yet beneath the roar, another sound threaded through—low, steady, ancient. A hum vibrating in the salt, a pulse pressing against my skin. I knew that cadence.
I had been here in other lives. I had felt waves swallow all I loved, winds steal the voices of those I would never hear again. I had stood on shores that collapsed, carrying names that vanished into silence. The memory tasted of salt and ash and starfire.

But this time I did not run. I did not beg the sky to stop. I did not shrink or break.

I stood.

Rooted as earth before lightning. Still as a womb before the crowning. Still—not from weakness, but because stillness is command.

From that stillness, a truth older than language surged through me: *I am not the victim of the waters. I am the one they answer to.*

I looked down at Bliss first. She was pressed against me, arms locked around my neck, her breath quick and hot on my skin. Her eyes were wide, but they weren't darting, they weren't searching for escape. They were listening. It was as if she was taking the storm in, the way a child takes in a lullaby, without trying to understand it. The roar didn't frighten her as much as it seemed to meet her. I could feel it in my chest—her presence softened something in the waves, like the storm recognized her glow. She has always carried that quiet radiance, that way of turning heaviness into light without even knowing she is doing it. Even trembling, even so small in my arms, there was no dimming in her. I pressed my lips to her damp hair and whispered, "We are not in danger, my love. The water listens to us." And I swear it did. For a heartbeat, the fury curved, and we were cradled instead of struck.

Maya stood to my right, her body shaking but her feet planted, her chin lifted against the wind. Her eyes locked forward, unblinking, even as water whipped against her face. She did not waver. There is something ancient in her gaze—sharp, cutting, unwilling to turn away. Even when fear lives in her body, clarity lives in her spirit. In that moment, she wasn't a child fighting to survive; she was a flame daring the storm to look her in the eye. And I could feel it: the storm faltered before her, not out of mercy but out of recognition. Her seeing pierced it, held it accountable, named it without words. She has always had this. That steadiness in the face of chaos, that refusal to be tricked by shadows. Even in the roar, I could feel her essence pressing back. It was not defiance. It was truth.

And then Zoe. My eyes found her in the spray, her hair slick to her cheeks, her lips trembling but her gaze steady in another way. While Maya stood like fire, Zoe leaned into the space between us, into the invisible thread that bound us together. She wasn't only looking at the storm, she was holding us. I could feel her pulling us into a circle, weaving us closer even as the waters tried to tear us apart.

Her spirit knows how to mend what frays. She doesn't call attention to it—she just does it. She holds, she binds, she brings together. And in that moment, it was more powerful than the waves themselves. She was the bridge. The tether. The reason our bodies, our breath, our hearts did not scatter.

I spoke then, but my words were not commands. They came from the knowing I had always carried: "You were made for this. Swim forward. Don't look back. The water will carry you, not take you."

They nodded. Not because fear was gone—fear was there, alive and pulsing in their small bodies—but because something deeper had risen. Something that belonged to their souls, older than the storm, older than even my own breath.

And when they moved, the water shifted. I saw it curve around their strokes, easing where it had been violent, bending where it had been sharp. It wasn't my voice that parted it. It wasn't my prayer that softened it. It was them. Their essence. Their recognition. Their presence in the storm.

I raised no wand. I chanted no spell. I simply knew.

The storm had not come to destroy me. It had come to ask: *Do you know who you are?*

And from the marrow of my being, I answered *yes*.

—

Chaos pressed on all sides—mothers frantic, fathers forcing strangers into rafts, bodies colliding in the crush to survive. None of it touched me. Not because I was apart, but because I was inside something older.

"They don't know," I told the wind. "But I do."

And the wind leaned in close, slipping through the cracks of my ribs, curling against the edges of my jaw, hissing between marrow and skin: *Then remember this—one woman rooted is heavier than a thousand waves.*

It was not comfort. It was command. A truth older than speech, older than the storm itself, pressing itself into me until I could no longer doubt.

And then a thought cracked through me, sharp and commanding, as if spoken by every woman who had ever lived through what tried to end her: If I can find even ten percent of these women— the priestess hiding in plain sight, the power-holder disguised as an ordinary mother—if I can reach them, we don't just survive. We command the storm.

One woman knowing is powerful.
Ten make the sea itself kneel.

Far off, she stood barefoot on broken pavement, a child tied to her chest like a second heartbeat. Her hair clung wet against her face, her body shook with the force of it. And yet her eyes found me through the storm. Not through sound, not through words, but through the marrow's knowing. The thunder could have split the sky in two and still her gaze would have reached. Her shoulders dropped. Her grip loosened. The child's shriek broke into a whimper. Something invisible threaded between us, tight, unbreakable.

Another woman saw her. Not me—her. She caught it, the way a body braced for death suddenly softened, the way a single breath remembered itself. She stumbled mid-stride, clutching her son's hand, eyes flicking between chaos and calm. She faltered, caught between running and stopping. Then, as if the choice was made for her, she turned—not toward the false shelter of the crowd, not toward the panic, but toward us.

A third slowed. Her baby bound to her chest, cheeks streaked with salt and terror, she staggered. She saw the second woman's turn, the first woman's loosening, and for a moment she froze as though her own body was a gate too heavy to push open. Then their gazes met. First one, then the other. Something passed between them— wordless, weighty, undeniable. Her jaw unclenched. A gasp tore free of her lungs, half sob, half release. The net thickened.

The air itself shivered, carrying their recognition like fire through dry grass. The storm bent closer, curious, as if even the waters wanted to witness what was unfolding. Three women, each carrying a child, each one trembling yet standing, began to move not with panic but with power. And the ground, the wind, the sea—all of it seemed to hush, waiting to see what women bound together might command.

The storm leaned in. You could feel it—the pause between thunderclaps, the breath the sea itself took as if it had never seen such a thing. Three women, trembling, soaked, salt-streaked, yet holding ground. It was not their strength the storm recognized, but their surrender into something older than fear.

The first woman adjusted the child tied to her chest, her body still shaking but no longer clenching. Her steps, though small, sent ripples into the water that did not crash back but curved aside. The second woman gripped her son's hand tighter, not in desperation now but in steadiness, and together their movement cut a path where chaos had been. The third pressed her baby close and exhaled a cry that was not terror but release—a sound so raw it split the storm's rhythm in two.

The wind faltered, catching on that cry. The waves, once clawing and wild, bent around them as though guided by unseen hands. Even the lightning seemed to pull higher into the sky, reluctant to strike near. It was as if the elements themselves had remembered something: that three women carrying life on their bodies could summon a force greater than destruction.

And in that moment, the storm was no longer the hunter. It was the witness. Watching them. Testing, yes, but also bowing.

The net was thick now—not rope, not thread, but a current running between us all. One woman had loosened, the second had turned, the third had cried out, and together they had changed the air. The storm pressed against us, but it no longer had teeth. It was being commanded.

The sky bent lower, curious. Patterns loosened themselves from the constellations we thought we knew. Shapes unfastened, reassembling into a luminous geometry that mirrored the circle of women below. Lightning ripped seams in the night, and galaxies spilled through like lanterns shaken from hidden shelves. The heavens did not look down on us—they leaned in. They answered.

And then came the chorus. Not words, but a pressure inside the skull, a current threading bone to bone. A knowing pressed through marrow: *You don't need to reach them all. You don't need to convince. Just stand. Just hold. That will be enough.*

Replies pulsed back, carried on the same current. *I'm here.*
Another: *Steady.*
Another still: *Yes.*

The voices multiplied—not just the three women before me, not just the ones within reach. A mother half a mile away gripped her child and thought, *I can do this.* Another, from centuries past, whispered through the crack in time, *I already am.* A daughter not yet conceived sent her agreement from the edges of the future. All of them pulsing yes into the storm.

The current thickened, traveling like wire lit from within. One woman's yes sparked another's, then another's, lanterns igniting across the dark. The storm, once a predator, now carried their agreement, amplifying it, flinging it wide. Waves bent. Winds curved. Even the thunder seemed to hold its breath, listening.

The storm did not end. It obeyed.

The dream ended before resolution. But unlike other dreams, it did not dissolve when I opened my eyes. I woke with water still in my ears, salt drying on my lips, the storm alive in my chest as if I had swallowed its heart. I didn't need to see the waters part or the city saved. That was never the point. The point was not resolution. It was transmission. It was what the storm left lodged in me—a pulse that did not fade when morning came.

I carried it into waking: the heaviness of the air, the press of thunder still reverberating through bone. Even as I moved through the day— brushing hair, tying shoes, filling bowls –the storm moved with me.

Not as dread. Not as threat. But as memory: This is what it feels like to be met by something vast, and not break.

The feminine does not flee the storm.
She stands inside it.
She finds her voice there.

That voice did not arrive polished or ceremonial. It was not granted by elders, not wrapped in smoke or song. It came raw, from the heat of ordinary fires. It came with Bliss balanced on my hip while I stirred soup with my other hand. It came in the bathroom where I wept into towels so the girls would not hear. It came in mornings when my body felt emptied out and still I rose, because rising was the only way.

And when it came, it said:
You were never just a mother. Never just a partner. Never just a body enduring waves. You are the keeper of rhythm. The carrier of pulse. A womb that holds the ancient signal.

I did not ask for this. I did not reach for it. But it was given. And once given, I could not un-hear it.

When I told Maya and Zoe they would be safe, I wasn't hoping. I wasn't bargaining with chance. I was speaking from that marrow-deep place that had already answered. It was not domination that steadied the storm. It was reunion. The storm had never been against us. It had been waiting for us. Waiting for one woman to remember, and then another, and then another, until the net was thick enough to bend the tide.

That is how it spreads. When one woman's eyes meet another's and soften, something ancient stirs. When one unclenches her fist, another remembers how to breathe. When one whispers yes, lanterns of yes ignite across time, flickering in women not yet born and women long gone, all carried on the same current.

The dream ended before resolution, but its knowing stayed. It followed me into the kitchen, into the carpool lane, into the late-night stillness when everyone else was asleep. It pulsed through laundry, dishes, errands, through every moment I once thought was too small to hold anything holy. And now, when I stir the soup, when I hold a child close, when I rise on mornings I thought I couldn't—I hear the question again: *Do you know who you are?*

And my answer rises like a drumbeat, steady, unrelenting.
Yes.
Yes.
Yes.

And somewhere, I know, the others still carry it too. The woman who first loosened her grip. The one who turned mid-run. The one who gasped and let her chest unclench. They are out there now, holding their children, folding their clothes, standing in their own kitchens—and the storm still lives in them as it lives in me.

When one woman's eyes met mine and softened, something ancient passed between us. She could not hear me through the roar, but her body understood. I thought: This is how we save each other. Not by shouting louder. Not by fixing anyone. By standing so steady in our truth that others feel theirs again.

I woke before the ending. Perhaps the ending is not mine to write. Perhaps the task is only to place this knowing in your hands and say:

We were never meant merely to survive the storm.
We were born to still it—with breath, with presence, with the body's own signal.

The Storms Beneath Our Skin

The storms of this age are not always sky-born. They do not always split the heavens with lightning or batter the roof with rain. They are subtler, stranger, and perhaps more ruthless, for they hide themselves in the ordinary until we no longer see them as storms at all. They slip into our days dressed as normalcy, until disconnection itself becomes the air we breathe.

Disconnection—it is the great flood of now. You feel it when you reach for someone you love and find them buried in the glow of a screen. You feel it when words are spoken at a dinner table but no one is listening, when whole families sit shoulder to shoulder yet feel a thousand miles apart. You feel it when you stand in a room full of people and cannot find a single gaze that meets your own. The current of disconnection runs through our houses, our schools, our governments, our very bodies. It is the storm that makes us lonely in crowds, starved in plenty, thirsty though surrounded by rivers. It is the storm that leaves us strangers to ourselves.

And from this one storm, others rise like offspring. Noise, fear, anger, forgetting—each one fed by the root of separation.

Noise is a tempest that never sleeps. It fills our ears with commentary, outrage, distraction. It multiplies until silence feels impossible, until you doubt the sound of your own heartbeat because it has been muffled under the static. Noise is a storm that looks like entertainment, but it erodes the inner ground where wisdom once grew.

Fear is a flood seeded with intent. It is sown into headlines, written into contracts, woven into economies until entire nations bow beneath its weight. Fear whispers that you are powerless, that you cannot survive without permission, that your freedom is fragile glass easily shattered. And so fear builds its dams, controlling the flow of life, making us forget that the river was ours all along.

Anger too has become a storm. Once it was a sacred flame meant to cleanse, but unanchored it becomes wildfire. It burns the wrong houses, scorches the wrong people. It leaps from neighbor to neighbor until the architects of harm stand untouched, watching as we devour each other while they remain cloaked in safety.

And then there is forgetting. Forgetting is a drought. Forgetting is a famine. Forgetting is when reverence is dismissed as naïve, when gratitude is treated as weakness, when awe is left behind like an abandoned toy. Forgetting dries up the wells of the soul, and people starve in the midst of abundance because they no longer remember how to taste, how to bless, how to bow.

But storms are not only out there, circling through governments, communities, headlines. They are intimate too. They live inside our ribcage. They curl in the shadows of the body.

There is the storm of shame, a quiet hurricane that shrinks the throat and silences the voice before a word can escape. There is the storm of betrayal, splitting the heart wide open, scattering trust like shattered glass across the floor. There is the storm of grief, creeping in without invitation, stealing the color from the air until everything feels gray and heavy as ash. And there is the storm of exhaustion—

bone-deep, relentless—the storm a woman knows when she rises again and again with nothing left to give, when she continues to show up though the world has already emptied her.

All of these are storms. No less fierce than winds. No less devastating than floods. They batter the soul as surely as waters batter stone. They strip away illusions, reveal what is fragile, leave us raw and trembling.

And yet, like the waters of my dream, they do not come only to destroy. They come with a question. They come with an invitation. They come to ask: *Do you know who you are?*

Because if you can stand in the storm of disconnection and reach for another—truly reach, palm to palm, gaze to gaze, presence to presence—you stitch together what the world has torn. If you can remain still within the storm of noise, silence begins to sing again, and that song becomes medicine. If you can walk through the storm of fear remembering the compass of sovereignty, the chains lose their weight. If you can sit beside the fire of anger without letting it consume your tenderness, flame becomes hearth, flame becomes warmth. If you can dare to pour reverence into the drought, even one drop, the desert remembers it was always meant to bloom.

The storm is not only an ending. It is a clearing. It is not only collapse. It is invitation. It comes to break what was never true, to wash away what could never last, to carve channels for what has always been waiting underneath.

And so when you face the storms of this age, whether in your home or your heart, whether across oceans or inside your own breath, remember this: they are not only weather. They are thresholds. They are the sea standing before you, waiting for the sound of your voice.

They are the winds circling your body, asking if you will remember that stillness itself is command.

The storm is never the end of the story. The storm is the question that makes the next chapter possible.

—

Now I know why I am here. Not to prove. To remind.

You are the stormkeeper.
The one whose body can quiet hurricanes and re-weave legacies.
The one whose hands recall what scripture forgot, what doctrine buried.
You were born knowing how to part seas—not to escape, but to cross into more.

You are not here to be rescued.
You are here to rise.
To reclaim what is written in your blood.
To walk barefoot into the chaos and declare: Enough.

When one woman rises in her knowing, the waves shift.
When two rise, the tides turn.
When ten rise, the storm itself kneels.

Do you feel it? The blood answering? The chest opening? The skin alive as if it remembers? That is not adrenaline. That is the soul catching fire.

So come.

Come with tired bones and wild dreams.
Come with unfinished healing and sacred rage.

Come barefoot, even if only in spirit.
Come luminous, even if you have forgotten your light.
Come ready, even if your hands shake.

We are gathering now. Not as leaders or followers, not perfect or prepared, but as those carrying embers in our bellies and oceans in our eyes. We have prayed in kitchens and cried in cars and still shown up. This is how the world changes. Not with louder voices, but with deeper listening. With bodies that speak the language of the earth. With hearts unafraid of breaking.

Lanterns of Yes

I have not yet called them into circle, but I have already gathered them in my heart—in the womb of my knowing, in the still place between heartbeats where what the world resists still waits. I have stood on storm shorelines not as savior, but as woman who knows: stillness is not weakness. Tenderness is not surrender. A single breath can move mountains. I did not come to prove. I came to remind.

And it was never just about me. It has always been about them— the daughters in corners, the girls who will one day be women, the mothers who came before and the ones not yet conceived, all carrying these codes in their skin.

We felt you, they say. Even in the moments you thought you had disappeared. We saw you choose love in silence. We felt you tremble and still stay. We heard the prayers you whispered into pillows. We saw the tears behind bathroom doors, and still you rose to hold us as if nothing had split you in two.

We noticed how you stayed soft when it would have been easier to harden. We didn't always understand it, but our bodies remembered. You gave us truth instead of performance, presence instead of perfection.

And because of that, we will love differently. We will mother differently. We will walk into fire not to burn, but to illuminate.

You showed us that being a woman is not to suffer silently, but to sing pain into power. You showed us the waters are not enemy but kin—something we can speak to, and they will answer.

And the mothers behind us nod. We, too, endured. We, too, carried the silence and the song. And the daughters ahead of us pulse their yes from the edges of time: We will not forget. We are already with you.

Together we say: this is not ending. This is covenant.

To every woman reading these words, to every girl who thought she must dim, to every womb carrying memory older than her body—we say: Come.

Come with your grief, your joy, your thunder, your softness. Step into the waters not to drown, but to emerge.

Because the world shifts not when we stand in rebellion, but when we rise in knowing.

And we will rise—together.

Final Blessing

May every word here be seed in your womb.
Not rushed, but warmed in your own timing, your tenderness, your truth.

May you know you were never too much. That your emotions are compass, not chaos. That your voice is not too loud—it is liberation.

May the currents within you rise without flooding, swirl without destruction, cleanse without apology. May you speak with eyes, with hands, with prayers, with your very presence.

May the daughters hear you not because you are flawless, but because you are real. May the future mothers—even those not yet born—feel this message pressed to their hearts like a lullaby.

You are the storm-keeper. The memory-bearer. The one who chose not to vanish.

And for that, we bless you.

Now go. Wrap the world in your knowing. Shape the waters with your breath. Let the Earth reclaim herself through you.

CHAPTER FIFTEEN

The Ones Who Came Back Singing

I do not remember when the song first found me—only that it had always been waiting, like water pooled in a hollow waiting for a foot to press and send it running. It comes through me the way river comes through rock: patient, insistent, carving as it goes. When it arrives it is not polite. It is not tidy. It lifts the roof of my small certainties and lets the rain come down, and in that rising I remember that song is not a thing you hold; it is a thing that holds you.

We are the ones who came back singing. Not with lullabies thought to hush children, but with thunder braided into our throats and long rivers braided into our lungs. We returned with notes that did not ask permission, with tones that carried the grit of the road and the salt of old seas. The music that lived in our grandmothers' hands and the soft hum in the ribs of the unremembered ones unspooled itself through us; we were not students so much as instruments, struck and then learning to resonate.

This song does not flatter. It strips. It peels away lacquer until whatever remains is raw and true and incandescent. In a world that paces around polish, we chose the ragged edge—the note that breaks rather than bends. We learned long ago that perfection does not resurrect; only truth has that patience and that wildness. Truth will pry open tombs. Truth will set a throat free. So we struck the bell inside the sleeping places of ourselves and kept striking until our own marrow answered.

We sang in kitchens, where the hot oil crackled and the baby on the hip inhaled and exhaled like the tide. We sang in aisles between stacked cans, where strangers caught our eye and in that catching a private ache became a public string of sound. We sang in hospital corridors, in courtrooms where the air was thick with other people's lives, in the thin hours while a child slept and time seemed to drip like candlewax, in the car at red lights, in the dry, stubborn spaces where grief accumulates and the world expects us to tidy it and move on. Every place that thought itself ordinary became altar when we let a note slip. Ancestors heard those notes. They came—not as ghosts but as weather: skirts full of wind, palms untying the maps of memory. They handed us back the music that had been folded and hidden, and said with eyes made of old light, *Sing it forward.*

At first the voice that came through me sounded like fracture. It sounded like the sound a bowl makes when it has been dropped and rests in scattered pieces on the floor. It felt like surrender—like everything I thought could hold me had collapsed. In ruin, something soft and persistent rose. A single tone, almost a whisper, that said: *Begin here.* So I did. I began with less than I thought necessary: one trembling breath, one cracked syllable, a willingness to be raw in public and private. I let the song pass even when it stumbled. I let it be unpretty and it taught me the architecture of truth.

The voice beneath the skin speaks in the smallness as much as in the blaze. It is not only thunder; it is the sound of a spoon against the side of a pan at dawn, the quiet vowel of a child's new name, the hum in the bones when the world shifts and you have not yet learned to stand. That voice moves through the ordinary because ordinary is the place where change is actually made. The cosmos conspires not to dazzle but to steady; that quiet first learns the shape of our palms. When I let it through, my voice becomes conduit, not possession. I am not singing to an outside power; I am letting the power that lives under my ribs sing through me.

This singing is not a performance to be polished. It is a weather system that arrives and has its way. Some days it is a hush, a note so small you might mistake it for breath. Other days it thunders and the windows rattle and you realize the whole house was waiting for that particular sound. The point is not to be remarkable; it is to be faithful. We stay at our posts—the school pickup, the crowded bus, the stifling staff meeting—and in those places we loosen the glue that holds forgetting together.

You will not be told when your first true note will sound. Sometimes it arrives in the bathroom with steam on the mirror, while you scrub the face you have to present to the world. Sometimes it comes at a funeral, a small, brave syllable escaping you like a flag. Sometimes it is a grown-up thing around a kitchen table, an apology in a voice that has been quiet too long, and out of that apology a filament of tuning is born that holds generations.

Listen: this song is not a thing to be deserved. It is an inheritance, and like any inheritance it comes with unkempt corners. You were taught to earn safety and silence, and you learned to bow and become small. But now the lineages answer back. The hands that beat drums at the edges of memory push us forward. The ones who walked barefoot over coals, who swaddled grief in their skirts and refused to let it harden into stone—they are here. Their lungs fill our lungs. Their yes presses against the inside of our ribs.

When we gather, something else rises: a chorus that is not merely many voices stacked but a single large instrument made by joining hollowings. We do not harmonize because we are identical; we harmonize because we are true. The discordant parts are entryways to truth. A woman who can only whisper pulls the rest of us gently toward the place where our tones will meet; a woman who thundered and burned bridges shows the rest how to leave heat and not scar. In this choir each crack is a seam. Each fracture holds secret light.

Do not expect tidy maps. The song is braided from grief and from joy, from lullaby and from labor, from the small, unrecorded faithful things no one applauds. It is carried in the hands that wipe tears at two in the morning and in the hands that hold a newborn and in the hands that sign legal papers because someone has to. Devotion here looks like dishes at midnight and like the refusal to leave at the first sign of trouble. Devotion looks like stubbornness worn as a virtue and tenderness worn as armor.

And then there is the song of Little Light. It does not thunder. It does not surge like rivers through stone. It flickers. It skips. It arrives like a child darting barefoot through twilight, laughter spilling from her ribs faster than her feet can follow. Hers is the song of fireflies— not steady, not solemn, but insistent. It hums without words, bright as a spark leaping from kindling. Where the elder voices split sky and command oceans, hers opens windows in houses that had grown stale with forgetting. A single note from her ribs carries more oxygen than whole cathedrals of silence. She does not sing to be heard. She sings because the song cannot be contained. Every rise in her tone scatters shadows. Every fall of her breath lays a petal on the wound.

Her song teaches us that wonder is not a luxury. It is a necessity, as urgent as air.

Little Light reminds us that the chorus of the returned cannot be only thunder and grief and fire. It must also be play. Mischief. Tenderness. The small lanterns that gather by the hundreds until no night is absolute. Her melody is proof that joy is not naïve. Joy is armor. Joy is rebellion. To sing with her is to remember that it was never only about survival. It was always about radiance. And so, in the middle of storms and testimonies, in the middle of aching ribs and trembling spines, she begins to hum. A golden sound, unafraid of being small. And suddenly, all the voices lean toward her. Because without Little Light, the song would be unfinished. Without her, the night would be endless.

There will be forgetting. There will be nights when you do not know which side is up, nights when you fold into forgetfulness because the ache is too heavy and the world keeps asking for your functioning. That's human. We forget. We fall. But we also hold routes back. A single note—a hum you remember from your mother, a phrase an old woman used to say before the work of the day—can unstick an entire life. The chord begins again when you let one breath in, long and honest.

This is not mine alone to offer. It is communal. The song is the thing we hand to daughters not as instruction but as water: take it, follow where it flows, do not attempt to catalog every eddy. When I whisper to the next woman, I know. Me too, I am not offering counsel so much as a place at a riverbank. Come here. Sit. Listen. The river will move you.

There are times when the music is fury because fury must be sung. There are times when it is so soft the world will miss it if it looks away for a second. Each register is holy. Each register is necessary. We have had enough teachers who told us the scream was profane; we have had enough clergy who taught us that softness was sin. That inner voice overturns this table. It says the scream is part of the psalm and softness is the shape of prayer. We hold both without shame.

I have watched the song do what it does: it stitches. In a room where two people would otherwise be strangers, a single lifted note loosens the scab of old offense. In a hospital corridor the hum moves like a hand laid flat, and the tense jaw unfurls. In the court where words have been sharpened like knives, the song arrives and the sentence breaks into mercy. It is not a magic trick; it is persistent becoming. It insists on presence until new forms are possible.

And when someone says, I cannot, the song replies: *Then I will be your capacity.* When someone says, I am too small, the song answers: *Remember you are river.* It does not shame. It does not command. It invites. It takes what we offer—even if it is only a half-breathed yes—and with that slender thing builds a bridge.

This is the work of our era: to let the sound move through the ordinary, to make sanctuaries of the small places. Kitchens, not cathedrals, become where the world is remade. Car rides become processions. The late-night text—the one that says, I am scared— becomes an altar call. We have been taught to wait for grand stages; instead, we find stages of breath.

Do not confuse gentleness with weakness. To stay soft when everything says harden is audaciousness of the highest order. To let tenderness be your weapon is to recalibrate power. We who have come back singing are apprenticed to that paradox. We are the ones who have learned that the most radical thing is to be tender in the face of apocalypse. We have seen empires crumble and learned that tenderness outlives all of them.

And there are the long arcs, the scales beyond the individual: climate, migration, war, hunger, the slow grinding of systems that forget human faces. The song does not pretend to be all the work that must be done, but it is the thing that turns labor into liturgy. It is the thread that can make protest become prayer without losing its teeth. The courage to sing in the streets can become the courage to sit in the hallways and feed the tired and to write letters that hold both fire and precision. Where structures crack, the song presses in like root and begins to hold the soil.

The ancestors are listening. They are not waiting for spectacle; they are listening for the return of ordinary faithfulness. The maps they hand us are not routes to triumph but reminders: stay, love, repair. We carry their breath in our breath; when we sing, their lungs swell with us. This is not a performance of the past, but a continuity of service. We do not resurrect what was; we reweave it into something that breathes in this climate and in this hour.

Come close. If you hear nothing now, wait. The first note may be a tremor under the tongue. It may be the way your hand lingers on the counter. It may be a sudden, inexplicable lifting of your gaze toward someone across a crowded room. The song arrives in tiny mercies, in brief acts of refusal to numb, in the small saying of truth to the one who needs it. Say yes to that smallness. Let it widen.

When you answer, you will find the circle already there. No registry, no application. Just a nod, a seat, a palm opened. We will not ask for credentials. We will not demand a history of success. We will only want to know if you have come to stay. If you have the breath to try again. In that honest, trembling yes we will sing together.

And listen—even in the places of greatest ruin there is a thread. If you can find the thread, follow it. It will take you through grief, through the grinding disbelief that tells you you must not hope, to a place where sound and repair are possible. The song is both path and scaffold. It will not save the world alone. But it is the thing that makes saving possible because it will not let us forget to be human while we do the work.

We are the ones who came back singing, not because we were spared but because we were made to return. We are the chorus that will not let the world forget its music. We are the hands that fold the tattered maps and hand them to the next, saying simply: Here. Sing this. Walk this. Live this. We are not outside of the ordinary; we are woven into it. We do not perform beyond the kitchen. We consecrate the kitchen.

If you feel a stirring—a hum in the belly, a weight in the throat, a trembling in the hands—it is not a mistake. It is invitation. Breathe toward it. Let the note find the arc of your mouth. Give it voice. Do not wait to be perfect. The river starts with a small trickle. Let it grow by your will to keep giving breath.

We will meet you there. We have been singing in the dark, and when your voice finds its place in the chord, the dark is altered. The bell rings differently. The air holds its shape in a new way. We do not promise that sorrow will vanish; we promise that sorrow will be held, that the weight will be witness, and that from this witness something, however small, will shift.

Return. Not as a perfected thing, but as the human you are: cracked, luminous, persistent. Let the voice beneath your skin speak through you. Let the song be large enough to hold your breaking and your making. Let it be the thing that moves behind your hands as you wash dishes, the thing that steadies your speech when fury rises, the thing that quiets you back into presence when the noise threatens to drown your sound.

Welcome back to the song. Walk into it like a river—with feet that know the feeling of current against ankle, with lungs that remember how to breathe slow and true. We will sing with you. We have never truly been apart.

You do not have to catch every thread. You do not have to sing every harmony. It is enough to feel the stir—the hum in your ribs, the prickle at the back of your throat, the small ache that rises when something true brushes past. That is the song finding you.

Do not trouble yourself with understanding all at once. Songs are not meant to be dissected, but lived. Return to it as you would to a river—sometimes with thirst, sometimes only to listen. Let it wash through you in pieces. The current knows the way.

If you leave here carrying only one note, one breath, one flicker of yes—it is enough. That note will call the next, and the next. You do not need to master the song. You only need to let it move you.

CHAPTER SIXTEEN

The Fire That Does Not Burn but Belongs

I used to think fire was only the ordeal. I thought it lived only in the crucible, the fierce baptism that left my throat coated in ash and my bones rattled with thunder, the purging that tore through illusions until there was nothing left but bare truth, sharp and unyielding. I thought fire meant devastation—that to be touched by flame was always to be reduced to cinders, to lose something that could not be found again. For so long, I believed fire was only trial. But slowly, tenderly, I have begun to see its other faces. Faces that do not scorch but warm, that do not devour but illuminate, faces no less holy for their gentleness. Fire is not only purification; it is presence. Not only destruction; it is revelation.

There is a flame in Zoe, though it does not blaze like a bonfire. It flickers in her laughter when she begins to tell me her dreams, those half-sensible, half-magical visions she spins out of the fragments of the day. She speaks as though the world itself is still unfinished and she has been given the privilege of weaving it together, and in her eyes there is a spark so bright it could trick the stars into leaning closer just to listen. When she looks at me, mischief crackling, I see the way galaxies must have first been born—not in silence, but in joy, in some great burst of laughter that spilled into constellations.

She teaches me that imagination is not a lesser flame but one of the original ones, that creation itself was seeded not only in gravity and force but in delight. The universe, she reminds me, is playful. It still dares us to believe in worlds we cannot yet see.

And that flame does not live only in her words but in her body as well, for Zoe carries the fire of movement—the spark of flight—in her gymnastics. When she flips, when she stretches herself across the beam with balance taut as starlight, when she bends backward into bridges that seem to defy what bones were made for, I see a fire that remembers the cosmos did not only laugh itself into being but also leapt, tumbled, arched itself across the void in joy. Her body in motion is not separate from her dreaming but the continuation of it, the way imagination proves itself true in muscle and sinew. And I realize that this, too, is fire: the courage to trust the body to remember what the soul already knows—that flight belongs to us, that balance is not a trick but a birthright, that gravity is not a chain but a partner. Zoe's gymnastics are her liturgy, her flame made visible, her body whispering the same truth her laughter sings: creation is still happening, and we are part of it.

Bliss carries a fire of another kind. It is smaller, subtler, and yet when I catch it in her, it feels as eternal as anything I have known. She claps her little hands to rhythms no one else can hear, her body wriggling like a current of hidden music has entered her bones. She does not ask permission to be carried by it—she lets herself go, eyes alight, laughter bubbling up from some well deeper than words. And in watching her, I remember something I had almost forgotten: joy is not an afterthought, not an ornament added after labor is complete. It is an element, essential as oxygen, threaded through the fabric of being itself. Without joy, no atom would dance, no star would sing, no heartbeat would sustain itself. Bliss's rhythm is the rhythm of galaxies, her pulse the secret cadence of creation.

Sometimes I look at her and I swear she is Hathor embodied, joy and music and holy delight wrapped in the small form of a child, reminding me that the divine has always chosen the simplest vessels to reveal itself. She is a reminder that joy is not peripheral but central, that the divine once sang the world into being, and still sings through the smallest hands.

Maya's flame is different again. Hers is not laughter's spark nor rhythm's pulse but devotion's burn. I see it when she runs. The soccer field transforms under her into something like a cathedral; each sprint becomes an offering, each strike of her foot upon the earth a liturgy. Her body and her spirit are no longer separate things but one fierce stream of motion, wholly given, wholly alive. There is prayer in her sweat, sacrament in her breath, hymn in her legs as they carry her forward. Watching her, I see that fire does not only destroy or delight; it consecrates. It turns the ordinary into the holy, the fleeting into the eternal. It whispers the oldest truth: that love longs to be embodied, that devotion seeks to take form, that spirit is not satisfied to remain invisible but wants to pour itself into matter. Maya runs, and in her running I glimpse what the cosmos has always been doing—burning with desire to become visible, to incarnate beauty in motion.

But her flame does not live only on the field. It burns, too, in her discipline, in the way she refuses to give less than her best, in the way she sets her sights on a goal and will not let go until she has reached it. Her drive is not only ambition but devotion in another form—the fire that commits, that perseveres, that endures. And alongside that fierce strength lives a tenderness just as powerful. She can walk into a room and read it as though it were a book open to her; she knows when to hold back, when to soften, when to offer gentleness instead of force. And somehow, without my needing to say a word, she knows when I am running on empty. She steps in quietly, without announcement, without asking for recognition, and she gives in the small ways that matter most—a helping hand, a softened voice, a simple presence that steadies me. In those moments, I realize her flame is not only devotion but discernment, not only strength but compassion. Hers is the fire that holds both—the burn that pushes forward and the glow that knows how to comfort. And I see in her what it means for fire to become wisdom: a strength fierce enough to move mountains, yet tender enough to lay a blanket over the one who is weary.

And then, there is Oerti. His fire is the quietest of them all, and yet it may be the one that keeps us alive. It is not the dazzling star, not the sudden blaze, not the spark that startles the night. His is the steady flame, the core flame. It glows with patience, it waits, it holds its ground even when the winds rise. It is the fire you can gather around when the hours stretch long and shadows press close. His presence is the warmth that does not call attention to itself but without which everything else would falter. And sitting beside him, I see that even the universe must have such a fire at its heart—not the scattered stars, not the fleeting comets, but the deep center around which all things revolve. The burn that says, stay. *You are not alone. Here is home.*

His fire does not stop at our threshold. He looks outward, always watching over friends, always ready to carry someone else's burden for a while. He gives freely, without calculation or need for recognition, sometimes even to people he barely knows. There is in him a current of generosity that moves almost unnoticed, but it warms whoever it touches—an extra kindness, a hand extended, a gift offered for no reason but that he can. His flame is not only for his own family but for the wider circle, a light that reaches further than anyone realizes.

And yet it is also deeply personal. His fire is the quiet way he makes me laugh, not because he tries, but because something in him leans toward joy even when the air is heavy. It is the way he sits with me in the mud and does not flinch, never rushing me to climb out before I'm ready, but waiting as long as it takes until I can stand again. His fire is not the blaze that dazzles or the wildfire that consumes—it is the ember that endures through the night, the glow still warm in the morning, the presence that steadies every other flame in this home so it can burn more brightly.

And there is, too, a fire in me, though I resisted naming it for so long, thinking it could not be holy to claim a flame for myself. I thought I was only the one who tended, the one who watched, the one who kept the logs from tumbling apart. But I am beginning to see that the same fire I glimpse in them also runs through my own bones, quiet but unrelenting, sometimes wild, sometimes steady, sometimes hidden under ash but never gone. Mine is the fire of holding and of remembering—the flame that keeps watch through the night, that refuses to go out even when storms rage, that knows how to bend low without breaking. It is the fire of the woman who rises again and again, who has walked through trial and come out carrying not only scars but embers still glowing.

This fire is not only for survival. It is not only the fire that kept me alive when distortion closed in or when shadows pressed their false stories against my skin. It is also the fire that creates, that nourishes, that shapes. It is the fire that writes in the dark, that dreams when the house has gone quiet, that prays not only with words but with breath, with tears, with every step forward into the unknown. It is the fire that says yes when fear whispers no, that keeps opening even when it would be easier to close.

But this fire did not begin with me, nor will it end with me. I see now that it belongs also to the ones who came before, the women whose hands bore children while the world pressed hard against them, the grandmothers who cooked by small stoves or whispered prayers into rooms no one else entered, the mothers who endured storms that no one recorded and yet still managed to pass a flame into our keeping. Their fire was not always celebrated, but it endured, and in their endurance a line of light stretched forward until it reached me, until it reached my daughters. The flame in our home carries the breath of theirs; it is never only ours alone.

And so I have learned that fire is not only trial, not only the searing ordeal that strips and scours. Fire is the laughter of a child inventing new worlds. Fire is the rhythm hidden in small hands that clap to songs we have forgotten how to hear. Fire is the devotion of a body offering itself wholly to the moment, unashamed and unreserved. Fire is the steady glow of presence that steadies us when the night grows long. It is all of these at once, and more besides. The cosmos itself is fire, not only burning but belonging, not only consuming but creating. And in each flame I meet—in Zoe, in Bliss, in Maya, in Oerti—I see the mystery reflected back, and I know that fire, like love, was never meant to leave us empty but to remind us that we are already home inside its light.

And when I look at my daughters, I cannot help but glimpse the flames that will stretch ahead of me, fires that will carry themselves into futures I will not see. Their sparks will leap into new rooms, new worlds, perhaps children of their own or visions that belong only to them. And I realize that fire is not only inheritance but promise—it is the way eternity moves itself forward, the way the cosmos ensures that what is holy is never lost but always reborn in new forms.

When I lift my gaze outward, beyond our walls, beyond our names, I see that these small fires echo larger ones. Stars kindling in darkness, volcanoes forcing land into being, lightning striking oceans with the first spark of life—each a face of the same fire that flickers in my daughters, in my husband, in me. The universe, too, keeps a hearth. The galaxies, too, are born in laughter and rhythm, devotion and presence. To speak of our fire is to speak of fire itself, alive everywhere, forever becoming.

And lets not forget the fire of love—the flame that belongs not only to me or to him, not only to each child, but to the space between us all. The fire of union, of alchemy, the bonfire that holds our separate sparks and makes them one. Without it, none of the others would exist, and because of it, all of them do. This fire is not just passion but covenant, not just warmth but creation itself. It is the flame that makes family possible, the one that sustains us when we falter, the one that refuses to be extinguished even after trial, even after storms.

So when I speak of fire now, I do not mean only ordeal. I do not mean only trial. I mean the spark of creation that flickers in a child's laughter, the rhythm of joy that claps itself into being with small hands, the devotion that runs fierce across a field and just as tenderly steps in when I am weary, the quiet sanctuary that steadies the night and gives without asking, the ember I myself carry—hidden sometimes, glowing always. I mean the inheritance of those who came before and the promise already alive in those who will come after. I mean the fire of love itself—not metaphor but reality, the very substance by which all things endure.

And I see now that my flame is not apart from the others but woven among them, as thread through cloth. None of us orbit alone. Together we turn like a constellation, each light distinct and yet inseparable, each revealing a different face of the holy, each feeding the glow of the rest. In their weaving I glimpse the deeper mystery: that the universe itself burns this way—not as one solitary blaze but as countless flames, bound and belonging, each a facet of the same eternal fire.

Perhaps this is the truest lesson: that fire is not the thing that leaves us bare and empty, not only the element of trial, but the element of belonging. To gather near the flame is to remember ourselves in its light, to recognize that love is not fragile, not fleeting, but eternal as the fire that first sang the stars into being. And that fire, whether it blazes or whispers, whether it startles or steadies, is already here, alive in us.

And if you lean close to your own life, if you pause long enough to notice, you will find it, too. The spark that hides in the eyes of those you love. The ember that glows in your own chest when you refuse to give up. The flame that flickers in your laughter when you least expect it, when joy startles you awake. The fire that waits in silence, unannounced, steadying you when night grows long.

It may live in the rhythm of your breath, rising and falling like a tide that has carried you since the day you arrived here. It may live in the work of your hands, the way they mend, or cook, or build, or hold. It may live in the sound of your voice, in the words you dare to speak aloud, or in the songs you hum when no one is listening. It may even live in the people around you—in the child who reads a room and knows when to bring gentleness instead of force, in the daughter who somehow senses when you are running on empty and steps in without needing to be asked. That, too, is fire: the kind that does not dazzle but steadies, the flame that sees what is needed and offers itself in quiet love.

It might be carried in the memory of your parents, or in the faces of ancestors you never met but who kept the fire alive long enough for it to reach you. Perhaps it lives in a friend who never left, or in a stranger who smiled at you when you needed it most. It might even live in your body itself—in the pulse of your blood, in the warmth of your skin, in the courage of your heart that keeps beating, even through ache, even through silence.

And sometimes you will find it in the places you thought were barren. In the grief that nearly consumed you but did not succeed. In the questions that still ache without answers but refuse to let you grow numb. In the breaking that stripped you bare, only to show you the ember that nothing could extinguish. That, too, is fire—the fire that endures when all else falls away.

Look for it in your joy, but also in your sorrow. In your strength, but also in your weakness. In your prayers, but also in your doubts. Fire does not leave you. Fire waits, patient, even when you forget it is there.

And still, there is a fire beyond all the ones I can name. The flame that moves unseen, the ember that guides even when the path is unclear. It is the fire of mystery itself—quiet, hidden, sometimes hard to trust, yet steady beneath everything else. We may not always understand it, but even the unseen flame has carried us this far. That, too, is fire—the holy ember that belongs to no one and to all.

And so I say this to you: protect it. Nurture it. Let it grow. Do not mistake fire only for trial or only for destruction, because fire is also tenderness, also creation, also the reminder that we are never as alone as we fear. You are carried by the flame that holds galaxies together. You are made of the fire that does not burn but belongs.

CHAPTER SEVENTEEN

The Remembering: When She Rose, He returned

Thank you for staying when it would have been easier to leave. For holding your ground inside fires that seemed endless, for choosing presence when absence would have been simpler. I know what it costs to remain in a place where nothing is guaranteed, to walk through seasons of doubt without turning away. That choice is not small. It is the foundation upon which everything else now rests.

Thank you for carrying weight that was invisible to most. The kind that does not announce itself in words, but in the way your shoulders sometimes sag when no one is looking. The burdens inherited from fathers, from history, from a world that told you to endure without complaint. You carried them, even when no one thought to ask what it was costing you.

Thank you for giving without calculation. For offering yourself freely to friends, to strangers, to people who may never know your name. You have always moved in that quiet current of generosity that does not seek recognition, that does not keep score. The warmth you spread has reached farther than you will ever realize.

Thank you for making me laugh when laughter seemed impossible. For the way humor slips out of you unannounced, catching me by surprise and lifting heaviness off my chest. Those small sparks of joy have carried me through nights darker than I could name. Sometimes it was your unintentional smile, your quiet joke, that reminded me the world was not only fire, but also light.

Thank you for sitting with me in the mud. For not rushing me out of it, not insisting I stand before I was ready, but simply being there—steady, patient, present. You let me unravel without fear you would abandon me. And because you stayed, I could gather myself again. That is what devotion looks like: not rescuing, not fixing, but remaining.

Thank you for fathering with your whole heart. For holding our daughters with tenderness that defies the stories men were once told. For letting them see you cry. For letting them hear you say sorry. For showing them strength that is not in armor but in softness. That is how they will grow knowing love is not something to fear.

Thank you for protecting without confining. For guarding what is precious without making it smaller. For letting me bring both storm and silence, and never once asking me to shrink. Your protection has never been a cage. It has been a shelter, a place where I can rest without apology.

Thank you for your discipline and your devotion. For rising again and again, for showing up even when tired, for refusing to abandon the work of love. Thank you for the loyalty that hums beneath your skin, for the way your commitments hold steady even when no one is watching. There is a holiness in that kind of faithfulness.

Thank you for your dreams. For the visions you whisper late at night, yes, but also for the ones you carry silently in your chest when the world gives you no reason to believe. Thank you for daring to imagine futures even when history has broken faith with men like you. Thank you for not letting cynicism harden your heart, for guarding the ember that refuses to be extinguished. The world does not always honor a man who dreams—it mocks him, calls him naïve, asks him to trade wonder for survival. But you did not trade it. You kept dreaming anyway.

And in your dreaming, I see not only us, but the greater arc of what is possible: families restored, wars ended, children safe, the Earth healed. I see how your visions are not just yours, but offerings for the collective. They are seeds pressed into soil others have long abandoned. They are maps rolled up and waiting for the day we are brave enough to unfold them.

Your dreaming is not small. It is what keeps us alive. It is the ember glowing in strong winds, and the horizon that keeps calling us forward.

Thank you for your imperfection. For the clumsy silences, the half-finished sentences, the moments when you did not know how to meet me but still tried. Thank you for admitting, *I don't know*, and staying anyway. For the nights when your voice shook, but you spoke anyway. For the times you failed, not because you didn't care, but because you were human—and then came closer instead of turning away.

Because it is both your visions and your flaws that make you whole. The dreams you carry into the night and the stumbles you make in the day—both are part of the offering. Your strength is not that you are perfect, but that you keep imagining more while allowing yourself to be real. You show me that a man can dream of worlds not yet built and still admit when he is weary, that he can hold hope for the future and still whisper, I don't know, but I will stay. And in that paradox—in your daring to dream and daring to be imperfect—I see the truest devotion of all: a love that refuses to leave, a presence that refuses to die.

And thank you to the masculine beyond you.

To the fathers who rose each morning under the weight of expectations too heavy to name. The ones who built homes with their hands, who worked fields and carried tools, who shouldered the silence of generations. They were asked to bear everything and reveal nothing, and though it bent them, they still carried us here.

Thank you to the grandfathers whose names I may not remember, but whose sacrifices live in the bones of my family. Thank you for the calloused hands, the sweat on your brow, the long nights of labor no one ever praised. You, too, kept the fire alive.

Thank you to the brothers who are now learning to weep. For every man who dares to cry in front of his child, who lets his son see him tremble, who teaches by example that tears are not weakness but release. Each tear is a seed of change, softening a lineage that once forgot how to feel.

Thank you to the men who are relearning tenderness. Who choose to listen instead of argue, to stay instead of flee, to place their bodies not as walls but as shelters. Every time you choose gentleness over force, the balance of the world shifts.

Thank you to the masculine that lives in the earth itself—the mountains that hold their ground, the rivers that carve a path forward, the stones that endure across centuries, the sky that covers us without fail. Thank you to the structure of time that steadies our days, the rhythm that carries us forward when we would otherwise drift.

Thank you to the men who once distorted their power, for through them we saw clearly what power without presence becomes. Their shadows taught us what we refuse to repeat. And thank you to the men who are now returning, who are laying down armor and remembering their original strength—the kind that builds instead of destroys, that protects instead of conquers.

Thank you to the masculine as presence, as witness, as home. You are not here to dominate but to hold. Not to take but to guard. Not to flee but to stay. You are needed. You always were. And in your return, we all begin to breathe again.

I did not know, when I began remembering myself, that it would help him remember too. I thought this path was a solitary one, a pilgrimage I would walk alone through the ruins of my forgetting. I thought the work was mine: to gather the scattered pieces of my body, to listen again to the pulse of my womb, to lift my voice from silence, to stop abandoning the very places that had always carried me.

I thought I was doing it for me—for my daughters, for my ancestors, for the women who came before. I thought the rising was mine alone, an act of reclamation after years of shrinking and over-giving. But as I stood taller in my own skin, I began to notice the way his shoulders lowered, the way his eyes softened, the way his breath met mine differently. It was as if the ground between us was shifting too, as if my return to myself was a signal his soul had been waiting for.

Every time I softened, something in him relaxed. Every time I chose presence instead of defense, I saw another wall crumble in his chest. When I unclenched my fists from needing to be right, he unclenched his jaw from needing to resist. It was not instant, not dramatic—it was gradual, subtle, almost imperceptible at first. But it was real. My healing was not sealed inside me. It spilled out. It called him into places he had long abandoned.

I began to see that this work was never mine alone. I had imagined my healing as a private inheritance, something I would pass only to my daughters, a story of women restored. But he was part of the inheritance too. My rising became a lighthouse for him, showing him what it looked like to feel and still stand, to break open and still love. And once he saw it was possible in me, he began to believe it might be possible in himself.

I thought he needed me to rescue him. I thought he needed me to fight for him, to insist he join me in the waters of feeling. But what he needed was something quieter: a witness. A mirror. Someone to show him that collapse is not the end, that tears are not weakness, that tenderness is not shameful. He needed to see me sit with my own grief and survive it. He needed to see me fall apart and still rise.

That was the medicine I didn't know I was carrying, and it changed everything, not all at once but slowly, almost secretly, like water carving stone. Because when I stopped waiting to be rescued, something in him stopped hiding; when I stopped fighting to be seen, he began to see himself through my eyes, not as broken or failing but as whole, as clear, as already enough; when I stopped demanding that he feel for me, he began to feel with me, and it was as if all the roles, the defenses, we'd rehearsed for years, simply began to dissolve, and in their place was something simpler, quieter, but truer than anything we had known before.

It was never just about me. And it was never just about him. It was about us—the space between us becoming wide enough for honesty, for presence, for vulnerability. It was about creating a field where we could both fall down and both rise, not as enemies, not as strangers, but as companions.

We stopped performing. We started remembering. And the remembering did not come in one blinding moment of revelation but in the slow weaving back together of what had always been waiting for us—in the way our silences softened, in the way our bodies loosened, in the way the ground beneath us seemed steadier, as if it too had been longing for this return. And now when I watch him, when I watch how he holds our daughters, how he listens without bracing, how he allows tears to fall without shame, I know: this is the return of the masculine, not as conqueror but as co-creator, not as the one who stands above but as the one who stands beside, not as the one who must prove himself but as the one who has already remembered who he is.

—

And as all of this was unfolding in our home, I could not ignore what was happening in the world beyond our walls. As I write these words, the earth is burning. Gaza. Iran. Israel. Ukraine. Villages turned to ash in Sudan. Families scattered across Afghanistan. Fathers burying daughters in Yemen. Mothers carrying babies across the Rio Grande. Men executed in Myanmar. Women disappearing without a trace in Mexico. Earthquakes in Turkey. Floods in Pakistan. Fires devouring forests in Canada, Greece, California. Cyclones tearing through the

Pacific. Children starving in Somalia. Children shot in American schools. Children waking in the night to the sound of drones instead of dreams.

The soil is thick with blood. The air heavy with grief. Whole generations collapsing under the weight of forgetting.

These are not isolated events. They are reflections of the same wound I saw in him, the same wound I was learning to touch in myself. The wound of separation. Of power severed from presence. Of force divorced from feeling.

Every war, every famine, every border crisis, every headline is a mirror of the same fracture—the severed masculine and the forgotten feminine.

The scale is different, but the grief is the same. The forgetting is the same.

And the forgetting lives everywhere. In the boardroom where profit trumps people. In the parliament where treaties are broken. In the classroom where a child hides her tears so she won't be mocked. In the home where silence feels safer than truth. Different scales. Different faces. But the forgetting is the same.

The man who clenches his jaw so no one sees him shake is not so different from the leader who clenches his nation into submission. One hides tears; the other hides his fear behind borders and armies. Both are born of the same wound—the terror of being seen as fragile.

The girl who learns to quiet her voice in the classroom is not so different from the woman silenced in a courtroom, her testimony dismissed. One forgets herself to survive the day; the other is forgotten by the very systems meant to protect her. Different scales, but the forgetting is the same.

The couple who stop speaking to one another across the dinner table is not so different from the silence between two countries refusing to sit in dialogue. In both, love collapses into suspicion. In both, presence collapses into defense.

The boy who is told to "man up" when he cries is not so different from the soldier who pulls the trigger while his own hands tremble. Both are taught that feeling is weakness, and so both learn to turn feeling into force.

The woman who numbs her body to endure the night is not so different from the earth split open for oil, forests clear-cut for profit, oceans poisoned for gain. Both are treated as resources instead of living sanctuaries. The violation is the same. The forgetting is the same.

The addict who pours another drink to silence his pain is not so different from the government that pours money into weapons to silence dissent. One anesthetizes the body, the other anesthetizes the world—but both are attempts to bury grief that refuses to stay buried.

The refugee searching for home in a strange land is not so different from the child searching for safety in her own home where no one notices her tears. Both carry the ache of dislocation, both wander in landscapes that should have been safe but were not.

The executive who believes his worth is measured only by numbers is not so different from the empire that believes its worth is measured only by land. Both confuse expansion with life. Both mistake possession for love.

The mother who carries invisible labor while her exhaustion is ignored is not so different from the nurse in a war zone carrying bodies no one will name. Both bear what the world refuses to hold. Both break silently under the weight.

The grief is the same. The forgetting is the same. The refusal to feel, to stay, to soften—whether in a living room, a parliament, a battlefield, or a body—is always the same fracture repeating itself on different scales.

—

And so I began to understand that if the grief is the same, then the gratitude must be the same too. Not only for the tenderness that saved me, but for the sharp edges that carved me. Not only for the ones who stayed, but for the ones who did not. For even they were part of the remembering.

Thank you to the ones who doubted me, for they pushed me deeper into my own knowing. Every time my voice was dismissed, I learned to hear myself more clearly.

Thank you to the ones who betrayed me, for they revealed what could never be stolen. In their distortion, I found the truth that cannot be altered.

Thank you to the ones who tried to wound me, for they became the fire that forged me. Their attempts to break me only burned away what was never mine to carry.

Thank you to the ones who misunderstood me, who spoke lies in my name, who scattered stories that were not true. They taught me that clarity is not owed to the crowd, that integrity does not depend on being believed.

Thank you to those who left when I needed them most, for they showed me that abandonment can become initiation. Their absence taught me how to hold myself, how to find the home within when no one else remained.

Thank you to the ones who silenced me, for in their silence I discovered the sound of my own voice rising louder than I ever imagined it could.

Even distortion became part of the path. Even cruelty became teacher. Even betrayal became altar. Without them, I might never have known how strong the roots of love already were beneath me. Without them, I might never have recognized the miracle of a man who stayed.

And it is here, in this paradox of gratitude, that the remembering deepens. Because when I turn toward him—not with blame but with truth—I see not just the man before me, but the masculine as a whole.

I remember when you were whole. Before the wars, before the hunger for power, before you forgot the sound of your own heart. I remember when you sang to the fire with me, when your hands built temples instead of weapons, when you knelt beside rivers and prayed not for conquest but for rain.

I remember you before the forgetting.

And I am still here—not because I am weak, not because I do not know how to walk alone, but because something in me always carried the memory of your return. Because I could not un-know who you were before the breaking. Because I am the one who never stopped holding the thread of your wholeness, even when you laid it down.

This is how the remembering begins—not in a loud public ceremony, not in history books or sacred texts, but in the quiet moment between two souls, when a man finally collapses into her arms and she does not ask him to explain his shame, only to feel it. When he is no longer asked to perform strength, and she is no longer asked to perform forgiveness, but together they let themselves be human again.

And this is how war ends—not only with treaties, but with truth. Not only in parliaments, but in bedrooms. Not only on battlefields, but in kitchens, in bathtubs, in the places where we dare to stay when everything in us wants to run.

I carry the memory of your return. I hold within me a dwelling you can come back to, not as conqueror, not as hero, but as yourself.
And what is happening between the two of us—the softening, the unlearning, the honoring—is what the world is starving for. It is the revolution no one sees, the uprising that never makes headlines, the transformation that cannot be tallied or legislated but that remakes the very ground of a life.

This is the real revolution.

Not only protests in the streets, though they matter. Not only treaties in parliaments, though they matter. But tenderness in the home. Presence at the dinner table. Remembrance in the bedroom. Truth in the silences that once held only distance but now hold the quiet pulse of staying.

Because it is here, in the smallest spaces, that the great healing takes root. It is here, where no crowd is watching, that we decide whether war continues or whether peace is born again.

—

There is a moment—not recorded in history books, not etched into sacred texts—when the feminine turns toward the masculine, not with blame but with truth, not to shame him but to remember him. That moment changes more than any battle or ballot because it ends the performance.

The remembering doesn't arrive with fanfare. It arrives in a room with no audience: a man finally lets his weight be held; a woman doesn't ask him to justify his shame. The armor drops, and what remains is not enemy or savior, but human. That is where the old story dissolves—not with conquest but with presence, not with defense but with devotion, not in thunder but in the soft return of breath to breath.

So I say this to the ones who are listening: do not underestimate what happens in the sacred silence between two people willing to stay. Do not overlook the revolution that begins when a woman remembers her truth and invites a man to remember his.

This is not about roles.
This is not about hierarchy.
This is not about being "more healed" or "more conscious."

This is about soul.

This is about what happens when we return to the center. When we lay down the scripts. When we stop trying to perform and begin to simply be. When love becomes less about perfection and more about presence.

Because that is where the real transformation lives—not in titles or appearances, but in the quiet meeting place where two souls dare to remain.

The Voice of Union

We are not two.
We are the echo of one breath, divided only so we could know the joy of reuniting. We are the river and the stone, the storm and the stillness, the question and the answer.

You were never meant to conquer one another.
You were meant to remember the dance.
One reaches with fire, the other receives with ocean.
One dreams in motion, the other roots in moonlight.

But neither is whole alone. Not truly.

The world was torn when this was forgotten—
when he believed he had to dominate to be safe,
when she believed she had to shrink to survive,
when love became a transaction instead of a communion.

But now, in this very moment, you are remembering again.

You, woman of remembering,
with your soft eyes and fierce knowing,

who dares to speak even when your voice trembles—
thank you.

You, man of awakening,
with your heavy heart and trembling hands,
who dares to feel even when the world tells you not to—
thank you.

This is not the end of the story.
This is the turning point.

Where you hold each other not as possession, but as presence.
Where you ask not, *What can I take?* but, *What can we make together?*
Where you choose, again and again, to meet in the center—
in the breath, in the prayer, in the ordinary light of a shared day.

Because this is the real union:
Not staying for comfort, but staying for transformation.
Not staying to avoid pain, but walking through it together until it
turns to light.
Not staying to keep the old story intact, but staying until a new one
is born.

And in that light, the world is born anew.

—

The Voice quiets, but the resonance remains—and into that stillness,
another sound begins to rise. Not the voice of union as a whole, but
the voices of the two who carry it. Feminine and Masculine. Not
as roles. Not as hierarchies. Not as enemies. But as counterparts,
turning toward each other at the threshold of remembrance.

A Dialogue Between the Feminine and the Masculine

at the threshold of remembrance

Feminine:
I was never here to fight you. I was only ever trying to be seen, to be felt, to be met in the places where my softness was mistaken for weakness and where my knowing was silenced because it could not be measured. I came bearing waters, but the world wanted fire, so I drowned in myself until now.

Masculine:
And I... I wasn't trying to dominate you. I was afraid. Afraid I would fail you. Afraid I wasn't enough. They told me to armor up, to win, to take, to fix. I did not know how to receive. I did not know how to stand still long enough to feel you, or even to feel myself.

Feminine:
But I have felt you all along—in your silence, in your collapse, in your reaching hands when you didn't know how to ask. Even when you disappeared, I still whispered your name in the dark, not to save you but to call you home.

Masculine:
I heard it. I didn't understand it then, but I feel it now. And I don't want to run anymore. I want to remember—with you. Not as your savior. Not as your shadow. But as your mirror, your witness, your counterpart.

Feminine:
Then let us remember what was forgotten. Let us restore the dance—not where I disappear in your arms, but where I rise beside you, and you do not flinch.

Masculine:

I will not flinch. I will not flee. I will not ask you to be smaller so I can feel big. I will hold the storm with you, and in doing so I will become the mountain.

Feminine:

And I will become the sea—not to test you, but to teach you the rhythm of what is eternal. We were never meant to compete. We were meant to co-create.

Masculine:

Then let us begin again—as fire and water, sky and soil, question and answer, song and drumbeat. Let us no longer fear the mystery of each other.

Feminine:

Let us begin again as those who remember—who remember that power is not possession, that intimacy is not weakness, that love is not performance but presence.

Masculine:

Let us begin again as those who choose to stay—who choose to listen when silence feels safer, who choose to soften when anger would be easier, who choose to rise together instead of against.

Feminine:

And let us promise this: that even when we falter, even when we forget, we will not abandon the path back to each other. For the path back to each other is the path back to God.

Masculine:

Yes. Then let us meet there—where the breath becomes prayer, and power becomes presence, and union becomes the memory that saves the world.

And from that vow, life continues. The dialogue does not end in the air.
It spills into the ground, into kitchens and bedrooms, into the tender weight of ordinary hours.
Because what is spoken between them in the language of spirit must be lived between them in the language of flesh.

And that is where the temple begins.

The Home as a Temple

She is in the kitchen, barefoot, hands deep in the sink. The day has been long, not because of one great catastrophe but because of the thousand invisible weights that bend her body into quiet labor—children needing, emotions shifting, the endless rhythm of tasks that never announce themselves as holy but always are. Her back is sore, her hands are raw, and her heart is tired from carrying so much that no one else can see.

He enters quietly, not with grand gestures or words rehearsed, but with presence. He watches her for a moment as if seeing her for the first time that day—not the mother or the worker or the strong one who always remembers everything, but the woman whose breath is caught in her chest. She does not look up, but she feels him. The air changes when he steps closer, and she knows without knowing that she is no longer alone in the room.

He does not rush to fix. He does not reach to interrupt. He simply comes near and lets his nearness be a vow. His hand finds her back—not as a demand for affection, not as a performance of care, but as a promise: I am here now. And she exhales without realizing she has been holding her breath all evening.

She is not angry; she is weary. Weary of being the one who remembers the doctor's appointments, the birthdays, the emotional climate of every soul under their roof. Weary of being the atlas of the family, carrying a world no one else can name. And in his silence, she hears devotion, not absence. He says nothing for a long time, and still she feels everything. And when he does speak, his voice is steady with truth.

"I didn't know how much you were holding until I let myself feel it."

She turns toward him, not fast, not with drama, but with a slowness that belongs to sacred pause. There is a shimmer in her eyes—not tears of pain but tears of being met at last.

"I didn't want you to feel guilty," she whispers. "I just wanted you to see me."

And he does now. He nods, not as apology but as recognition. "You don't have to carry it alone anymore," he says, and he begins to dry the dishes without asking where the towels are.

Later that night, they lie in bed. Not touching. Not speaking. Just breathing the same breath. He does not need her to perform peace. She does not need him to rescue her. There is no savior in this story.

At last he turns, not with urgency but with presence. "Teach me how to stay when it's messy," he says.

And she answers, "Teach me how to soften when I want to shut down."

Their hands find each other in the dark, fingers lacing not just in love but in new agreement. And that is how the world begins to change— not in war rooms or speeches, but in kitchens and bedrooms, in the ordinary places turned holy by presence.

There is a holiness in the way he pours her coffee the next morning— not because it is romantic, but because it is remembered. Because once upon a time he forgot what she liked, but now he stirs the milk before she asks. There is a sacredness in the way she places his towel on the bed—not as performance, but as quiet devotion, the kind that says, *I still see you, I still care for you, even here.*

There is holiness in the way they rise together when a child cries in the night, no resentment, no tally, only the shared vow: *we are the keepers of this temple now*. They do not pray with folded hands; they pray in how they hold space when one of them forgets and the other remembers, when one breaks down and the other stays near, not to fix but to hold.

They have stopped needing grand apologies. They have learned the art of repair in motion. A glance that says *I see you*. A hand on the knee that says *I'm still here*. An extra blanket at night that says *you don't have to ask*.

This is not the love of novels. It is the love of evolution.

And in the long ache of days when the weight is too much, she finds herself chopping onions, tears blurring her eyes—not from the onions but from the exhaustion of all that has been held—and he steps behind her, saying nothing, fixing nothing, only wrapping his arms around her as if to remind her: *you don't have to hold it all alone tonight.* She keeps chopping at first, keeps holding herself together, but his body at her back is enough. And slowly she softens, because sometimes love is not in the words, but in the body that does not leave.

There are other nights too, when silence grows thick between them, not violent but ancient, inherited from generations who did not know how to say I'm scared, I miss you, I don't know how to reach you anymore. In the car, arms crossed, jaw tight, replaying arguments in their minds, they finally let the silence break open—not with anger, but with a whisper.

"Do you think we forgot how to talk to each other?" she asks. And he exhales, his grip loosening on the wheel. "I think... we just stopped remembering how to listen without preparing a defense." It is not resolution. It is not a breakthrough. But it is a crack of light.

There are mornings when shoes cannot be found, when one child cries about toast and the baby pulls the sister's hair, when deadlines press and lunches are still unpacked. And in the chaos of it all, they pass each other in the hallway—disheveled, burdened, overwhelmed—and instead of snapping, she smiles. And he sees it, and smiles back, and kisses her shoulder in passing, quick but reverent. And that moment, more than anything else, saves the day. For it reminds them: we are not doing this to each other, we are doing this with each other.

And there are nights when they lie side by side in bed, not with passion but with presence, the space between them thick with questions neither has spoken aloud. She wonders if he still wants her. He wonders if she still needs him. Both ache. Both fear. And then, almost shyly, her fingers find his—not in seduction but in surrender. *I still choose you*, her touch says. And he turns toward her, not with urgency but with steadiness. *I never stopped*, his eyes answer. No fireworks. No grand resolution. Just warmth. Just return. Just enough. And in that small, ordinary touch, they undo decades of silence in their lineage.

And in these small mercies, they discover a deeper rhythm, one that carries them through the nights when love feels heavy and the days when tenderness is harder to find. Their words are not lofty, not rehearsed, but they rise in the ordinary silence, honest and unadorned.

Her:
I don't need you to fix me. I just need to know that when I unravel, you won't run.

Him:
I'm learning. I wasn't raised to sit in the fire. I was taught to silence it, to leave, to armor up. But I don't want that anymore. I want to stay, even when it scares me.

Her:
Even when it's messy?

Him:
Especially when it's messy. Because that's when you let me see the most sacred parts of you.

Her:
And what if I don't always know how to let you in? What if my walls come back without warning?

Him:
Then I'll keep knocking gently. And when you're ready, I'll still be here. Not to be the hero. Not to fix. Just to be with you.

And somewhere in another room, a child spills milk. No one yells. She exhales. He wipes it up. And together, without words, they break the ancestral pattern.

This is divine partnership—not loud, not showy, but thunderous in its quiet, revolutionary presence. It lives in the smallest choices:

When she softens her tone instead of weaponizing it.
When he asks about her day and actually listens.
When they go to bed still a little wounded, but their toes touch under the blanket anyway.
When their child hears them laugh and learns what safety sounds like.

This is where it lives. Not in the grand gestures, but in the ordinary mercies. In the extra ten seconds of grace. In the decision to stay soft when it would be easier to withdraw. In the return, again and again, to each other.

Because this is not the perfection of love. This is the presence of it. And in a world that teaches us to chase more, better, newer, this is the revolution: to stay, to see, to choose each other again. Even here. Especially here.
And even in these small mercies, the dialogue between them keeps rising, not just in kitchens or in cars, but in the marrow of who they are becoming together. It is less about answers now and more about vows, less about fixing and more about staying open to what is unfolding.

Her:

I don't need the perfect words. I don't need a map. I just need your presence when mine is wavering, your breath steady beside me when mine feels thin.

Him:

I don't need to be needed the way my father was, as the one who carried everything but never felt. I need to be trusted. Trusted to grow with you, to rise beside you, to stay even when the ground shifts.

Her:

And what if I change again? What if I outgrow what I was last year, last month, even yesterday?

Him:

Then I'll meet you there. Because I'm not here for who you were. I'm here for who you're becoming, and for who I am becoming beside you.

Her:

Then let us keep beginning again. Even when it's inconvenient. Even when it's uncomfortable. Even when it means dying to the versions of us that no longer serve.

Him:

Yes. Let us keep beginning. Because union is not a destination. It is the courage to remain in the becoming.

And the words hang between them, not heavy but luminous, like lanterns in the dark. They know they will falter. They know they will forget. But they also know the way back, and that knowing itself becomes the vow: the way back is never closed, and they will not abandon it.

And so their vows do not end in whispers between two bodies in the dark. They spill outward, carried in breath and in bone, until they become prayer. Not a prayer offered up to the sky, but a prayer spoken into the walls of their home, into the fabric of their days, into the lineage that will one day inherit this love.

—

To the ones who choose to stay—
to the lovers who still pass the salt gently even when they are angry,
to the ones who take turns sitting in silence so the other does not feel alone,
to the ones who say I'm sorry not to win but to return—this blessing is for you.

To the hands that hold both laundry and each other.
To the feet that stand side by side in kitchens, in courtrooms, in grief, in grace.
To the two who chose to remain in the fire, not because it did not burn but because it was the only place where truth could be forged—this blessing is for you.

This home is your altar.
This table is holy.
These rooms echo with every vow unspoken but deeply lived.

May your disagreements be softened by the memory of why you chose each other.
May your nights of doubt be met with a hand that still reaches across the space.

May the children of your love never have to wonder if partnership is possible.

Because you did not just survive.
You stayed.
You softened.
You let the remembering rise between you like morning light.

And when the world asked you to run, you lit a candle instead.
You said: we are still here, we are still choosing, we are still becoming.

And in doing so, you turned your life into the greatest transmission of all:
not just love, but holy, ordinary, enduring love.
Not just staying, but staying transformed.
Not just a home, but a temple.

Let this be the anthem of our time.

This is how the story turns.
Not in conquest, not in retreat, but in the choice to remain.

To stay until love becomes presence,
and presence becomes the ground of a new world.

CHAPTER EIGHTEEN

Where Our Wombs Remember with the Earth

Sometimes the book shows me where to go, and when it does, I follow as though the path has already been carved into my bones. This time it led me to a clearing deep in the forest, a place where the air itself seemed to part with intention, and the trees leaned in like sentinels who had been waiting for my arrival. At the center, a fire crackled, as though each flame was reaching upward to recall some ancient story written in the language of light. Sparks rose and disappeared into the sky, stitching earth to stars in a seam that glowed and then vanished, only to reappear again, as if the cosmos itself were breathing with us.

Around that fire a circle of women had already gathered, and though I did not know their names, something in me recognized them as kin. Some bore gray streaks in their hair and carried the gravity of many winters; others still carried the softness of recent birth, their bellies marked with tender lines that glimmered like constellations across their skin. There were maidens too, eyes wide with the shimmer of other worlds, gazes so unbroken by cynicism that they felt like open doorways to forgotten galaxies. We were not strangers meeting for the first time. We were echoes remembering ourselves, called back into form by a script older than memory, stepping into a scene that had been written long before we arrived, and would continue long after we left.

The air in the clearing was thick and alive, woven of contradictions that somehow belonged together. The sweetness of pine sap tangled with the metallic tang of stone after rain. Moss crept soft over the roots, offering cushions for our bodies, while the trees stood like pillars in a cathedral not built by human hands. And overhead, through the wide mouth of the clearing, the night sky leaned close, listening, every star burning with a kind of attention that made the space between heaven and earth collapse into a single breath.

The firelight wove across their faces, softening some into gold, shadowing others into mystery, until it was impossible to tell where the mortal ended and the eternal began. Smoke curled upward in ribbons, then unfurled into the vastness above, as if it carried our presence into the constellations that had gathered to witness. Somewhere beyond the circle, an owl called, its sound not a warning but a recognition, and the wind moved slowly between the branches, carrying with it a hush that felt like breath. Even the soil beneath us seemed awake, humming with an old rhythm, as though the roots themselves remembered every circle of women who had ever gathered, every grief spilled into the ground, every prayer whispered into flame. Time thinned; we were not in a single night but in all nights at once, suspended in the space where earth and sky bend toward each other and listen.

And then, as if the silence could no longer contain what pressed against it, one woman spoke. Her voice was not loud, but it was weighted, each word dropping into the fire like a stone into deep water. "The world is cruel," she said, and the way her jaw tightened made it clear she was not speaking of abstractions, but of wounds that still bled in her.

Another voice joined, trembling but insistent: "There is so much suffering. So much war. So much pain."

A third rose from the shadows: "Famine, greed, power-hungry leaders... The system was never made for us. It was made to break us."

And then the circle broke open, words tumbling like waves, each woman carrying her own tide of sorrow and fury. Their grief rose and crashed, rose and crashed again, as if the very air were made of saltwater, as if the fire itself were being stoked by their lament. It was not just political, not just environmental, not even just personal—it was the ache of lifetimes, the grief of women who had watched the world burn and been told to stay silent, to smile, to survive.

The words came one after another, like waves refusing to stop breaking. A woman with hair the color of ash spoke of her son lost to war, her voice low and steady, but her hands trembling in her lap. Another leaned forward, her shoulders still rounded from years of carrying babies, carrying burdens, everyone but herself, and she whispered of hunger—not only her own, but the hunger of whole villages she had once known.

One spoke of betrayal—not just by lovers or kin, but by the very structures that promised protection and delivered only chains. Another spat the word "power" into the night as though it tasted of blood, recounting leaders who had grown fat on greed while children wasted away. Each voice cracked the air in its own way: some with rage, some with despair, others with the kind of bone-deep exhaustion that no sleep could ever cure.

Their grief rose like a storm that could not be contained. It was tidal, it was ancestral, it was older than any one of us. Every cry seemed to summon another from the roots of the earth, and the night itself began to pulse with the ache of all the unshed tears of generations.

It was not only the words—it was the way they were spoken. Every syllable carried weight, drawn up from marrow and scar tissue. Some words dragged like chains, others flew like arrows. Together they formed a language older than language itself, the raw vocabulary of grief.

I felt it moving through the circle, a current of sorrow that bound us together in ways our separate lives never could. It was not one woman's pain, nor another's lament—it was the collective voice of the silenced, the survivors, the mothers who buried children, the daughters who buried mothers, the sisters who buried each other's dreams.

And the forest did not turn away. The trees leaned closer. The owl called again, softer now, as if answering. Even the fire seemed to listen differently, its crackle subdued, its flames bent forward as though in reverence.

We were not merely speaking grief; we were summoning it, embodying it, giving it shape and sound so it could no longer fester in shadows. And though it hurt—though it burned like salt on an open wound—there was something holy in it too.

The circle grew heavier with every voice, the air so thick with sorrow it was hard to breathe. A young woman barely past girlhood spoke of being born into a world already burning, her words cracked with the disillusionment of someone too young to carry such weight, yet carrying it all the same. An elder, her hair silver and eyes sharp as flint, spoke of lifetimes of silence—of watching the same patterns repeat, of praying for change and seeing none. Her lament was not loud, but it cut through us with the precision of a blade honed by centuries.

One woman beat her fist against the ground with each word, as if the soil itself needed to be reminded of the cost. Another rocked back and forth, keening low in her throat, no words at all—only the sound of grief too primal for language. The circle absorbed it all. The fire hissed, the smoke curled tighter, and above us, the stars seemed to flicker as if in sympathy.

It became difficult to tell where one woman's story ended and another's began. Hunger bled into war, war into betrayal, betrayal into the long ache of survival. Every word carried not just her pain but the echo of thousands of others—grandmothers, daughters, ancestors buried without their stories ever spoken aloud.

The grief swelled until it seemed the forest itself might split open under its weight. My chest ached with it, my bones reverberated with it, my womb pulsed with it. It was not theirs alone anymore. It had become ours, collective and unbearable, and it pressed against the edges of the night as though it might shatter the very sky.

And in that moment, I knew the silence that followed would not be enough. Something had to be spoken—not to soothe, not to soften, but to cut clean through the storm.

I felt it pressing against my ribs, coiling in my throat, demanding to be spoken. My heart pounded like a drum, my womb thrummed like a warning. It was as if every ancestor who had ever sat in such a circle leaned over my shoulder, whispering: *now.*

The silence was unbearable, not because it was empty, but because it was too full—swollen with centuries of lament, vibrating with the ache of all that had been unsaid. And I knew, in that charged pause, that if no one spoke, we would all drown in it.

So I rose. Not timidly. Not softly. But with the kind of force that only truth can carry when it has been waiting lifetimes to be spoken.

"The world doesn't need our fixing," I said, my voice cutting clean through the night like a blade of fire. "It needs our embodiment."

The words tore through the clearing like a spark striking dry tinder. For a moment, no one moved. Even the fire stilled, its crackle suspended in the air, as though the flames themselves leaned closer to listen.

I could feel it land in their bodies—the jolt, the recoil, the disbelief that such defiance could be spoken in the face of so much grief. A few women lifted their eyes sharply, as if they had been struck. Others froze, lips parted but no sound coming out, the weight of my words still unraveling inside them.

It was not a gentle interruption. It was a rupture. And yet, beneath the shock, I could feel a stirring—like something dormant shifting under stone, like roots stretching after too long in darkness.

For a breathless span of time, the circle held only that: shock, silence, the fire reflecting in our eyes, the night itself leaning in to hear what might come next.

And then the wind shifted.

It swept sudden and certain through the circle, bending the flames, lifting the smoke, carrying my words into the branches above. The trees swayed in answer, their leaves whispering like a thousand voices stirred awake. Hair lifted from foreheads, skirts brushed against ankles, and the women glanced upward as though the sky itself had turned to listen.

The wind pressed against my back, urging me forward, carrying my words further than breath could reach. It curled through the circle, swept over the fire, and then quieted, holding everything in suspension—as if the earth itself had asked me to go on.

"The planet is not broken," I said, my voice steadier now, resonant, alive in the current that moved through us. "She is evolving. She is shedding. She is grieving too."

The flames leapt higher, the smoke rose in ribbons, and I felt the night inhale as if to taste the truth of it. The women did not speak, but their silence was no longer heavy with despair—it had shifted into stillness, the kind that comes when the ground itself turns over, making room for something new.

The women leaned closer to the fire without realizing it, as though the flames had reached for them and they instinctively answered. Some pressed their palms into the earth, grounding themselves in the tremor of the moment. Others lifted their faces to the sky, eyes glinting in the flicker, as if the stars themselves had leaned in to listen.

Hair loosened, shawls slipped from shoulders, and no one adjusted them back. Their bodies had forgotten the instinct to cover, to contain. The grief that moments ago had bent their backs now rose through their spines in a quiet remembering of strength.

No words yet—only breath, thick, uneven, holy—moving through the circle like another element, as necessary as fire and wind. One woman's tears caught the light and looked like molten gold on her cheeks. Another woman's lips trembled, but not with fear—with the ache of finally hearing something her bones had known all along.

The fire hissed and flared, sparks lifting into the branches as if carried on the breath of the unseen.

I felt it surge through my chest, through my womb, through the soles of my feet—a current too strong to hold back. And so my voice rose, not gentle but fierce, the kind of fierce that knows it speaks for more than one lifetime.

"We are in a universe of duality," I said, each word landing like a stone thrown into water, rippling outward. "Shadow and light. Death and birth. Suffering and miracle. We cannot escape the paradox. But we can choose how we hold it."

The wind shifted again, carrying my words beyond the circle, into the trees, into the sky, into the soil that cradled us. The flames bowed lower for a breath, as though listening too.

The circle seemed to breathe differently. Shoulders that had been hunched with centuries of sorrow began to lift, not because the pain was gone, but because something in the air had shifted.

The wind, once restless, slowed into a long exhale, bending the branches overhead so they swayed in time with my words. A few sparks from the fire spiraled upward and did not fall back down— they dissolved into stars, as if the sky had reached closer to receive them.

I watched the women around me. One pressed her palm to her chest as though steadying a rhythm she had forgotten. Another let tears spill freely, her face tilted to the night sky. A younger one—no more than a girl, really—straightened her spine, her eyes wide with a knowing she could not yet name.

It was as if the forest itself leaned in. The trees groaned low, their bark holding echoes of prayers once whispered in other centuries. The soil beneath us thrummed with warmth, rising through our bones. Even the owl called again, but this time softer, as if echoing assent.

What I had spoken was no longer just mine. It belonged to the circle. To the night. To the Mother who was listening through every root, every stone, every star.

No one rushed to speak. The usual murmur that fills silence in a circle never came. Instead, the women stayed still, listening not just to me but to the air itself, as though waiting for the forest to confirm what their bones already knew.

The fire crackled louder, sending a plume of smoke curling upward, then eastward, then back toward us, its path no longer random but deliberate, like an answer forming in the dark. The flames bent, not wild but reverent, bowing toward the circle.

A gray-haired woman closed her eyes and lifted both palms to the night, her lips trembling with a prayer too ancient for words. Beside her, a mother with milk still drying on her blouse cradled her own body as if holding more than herself—as if she, too, had become vessel. The youngest of us, with skin that still carried the glow of girlhood, leaned forward on her knees, her eyes fierce, bright, unblinking.

The sound of breath became noticeable—not just mine, not just theirs, but the rhythm of many woven into one. Inhale, exhale, like tide. Like tide remembering shore.

And in that space between breaths, we realized something was coming. Not from above. Not from beyond. From within and beneath. From the ground itself.

The wind shifted once more, threading through the circle with a sound like low song. The smoke parted, the flames steadied, and then—in the stillness that followed—She came.

With a resonance that began in the soles of our feet and climbed into our bellies until our very bones hummed. It was not sound in the way we know sound. It was vibration, ancient and undeniable, the language of stone and soil and water.

And then, like a river pouring through a hollow, her words found shape inside me, inside all of us:

"You were never sent to fix me. You were sent to remember me. Piece by piece, breath by breath, you were sent to gather the fragments of yourselves that you left scattered when you forgot we were one."

Her tone was not gentle, but neither was it cruel. It was the tone of mountains, of rivers carving gorges, of seasons that never apologize for changing.

"Your wombs were made in my image," she said, the fire flaring as if to punctuate her truth.
"Cyclical. Wild. Regenerative. Eternal. You are not separate from me. You are me, given voice and form."

Tears slid down faces around the circle, though none of us sobbed. They were not tears of despair. They were the tears of recognition, of something lost now rising in memory again.

And in that moment, we knew: this was not only a dream. This was covenant.
When her voice faded into the night, no one moved.

The women sat as though spellbound, yet it was not enchantment that held us—it was recognition, the slow dawning of something we had always known but buried so deeply we had forgotten the way back.

One woman pressed her hands into the soil until her nails broke the surface, whispering a name she had not spoken in years. Another lifted her face to the sky, and though no tears fell, her jaw trembled with the effort of containing the flood.

The mother beside me, with hair still damp from nursing sweat, pressed her forehead to her knees. She was not collapsing—she was surrendering, releasing a grief that had no language, letting the earth catch it where no human arms could.

And the youngest, her eyes wide and shining, looked straight into the fire. She did not flinch. She mouthed the words silently—cyclical, wild, eternal—as though trying them on, letting them roll through her body like a prophecy she already carried.

Even the air seemed to shift around us. The branches stopped swaying, the smoke held steady. It was as if the forest itself had leaned closer, listening with us, waiting to see what we would do with the truth we had just heard.

The circle had changed.

We were no longer just women sitting by firelight. We were witnesses. We were keepers. We were daughters who had just been reminded of their Mother.
The circle held its breath.

Then the forest began to move.

The wind shifted first—not in a violent gust, but in a slow, deliberate exhale that threaded itself through our hair, through the branches, through the ash rising from the fire. It carried the weight of recognition, as though the air itself had been waiting for those words to be spoken aloud again.

The flames responded next. They did not roar higher; instead, they steadied, elongating into tall ribbons of gold and white, burning without flicker, as though suddenly remembering their own center. Their light pooled over our faces, revealing lines of grief softened into something luminous.

From the ground, a tremor pulsed—subtle, almost imperceptible at first—a heartbeat under the soil. Moss thickened beneath our palms. Roots hummed like low drums, as though the trees themselves were chanting a hymn older than language.

The owl called once more from the distance, and this time it was not recognition but benediction—a sound that vibrated through bone and blood, reminding us that witness was holy.

And in that convergence—wind, fire, earth, and sky—the silence did not feel empty. It felt expectant, like the whole forest had leaned in, preparing to deliver what only She could say.

The wind did not die down; it gathered, carrying the scent of resin and rain. The fire leaned inward, as if bowing to what had been spoken. Ash lifted, spiraling, not away from us but toward us— dusting our skin with a reminder that we belonged to something older.

The earth did not need to speak in words. She answered in currents: a tremor in the roots, a quickening in the soil, a low hum rising through the soles of our feet. The air thickened, the sky bent closer, and for a moment it was impossible to tell whether the sound we heard was outside of us or rising from our own bones.

The women felt it—a shiver across bare arms, a loosening of jaws clenched too long, a sob released without permission. Some closed their eyes, others stared into the flame as if it might spell the next truth in its flickering.

The Mother was not arriving; She was revealing. And we, at last, were porous enough to feel it.

The moss beneath us thickened with dampness, dark and fragrant, as though the earth had opened its pores to drink our grief. A pulse shivered through the roots of the trees—not violent, not quaking, but steady, like a heartbeat the ground had been keeping secret until now.

Above us, the branches stirred in waves, though no storm had come. Leaves clapped against one another, soft percussion, like a congregation affirming what had been spoken. In the distance, the owl called again, sharper this time, echoing through the clearing as if to mark the threshold we had crossed.

The women around the fire felt it ripple through their skin. Shoulders dropped, as if some invisible weight had been released. A few pressed their palms to the soil; others lifted their faces toward the sky. One woman began to weep—not the sob of despair, but the sob of recognition, the kind that opens more space than it closes.

The Earth was not coming. She was already here, answering in fire and air, in root and wing, in breath and body. And all we could do was feel it.

And then Her voice swelled again—not layered over theirs, but moving through them, as though their tones had become the very timbre of her speaking.

"I do not ask you to silence your grief," she said, her cadence rolling like distant thunder carried on wind. "I ask you to let it move. To let it flow like rivers that do not question their own flooding. To let it burn like fire that clears the forest so seeds may root again."

The air vibrated with her insistence. Sparks spun upward, dissolving into star-pricked sky. Beneath us, the ground gave a low groan, not of breaking but of stretching, like something vast making room for more.

"Do not mistake my shedding for ending," she continued. "The world is not collapsing. The world is becoming. You are not witnesses to a death, but midwives to a birth."

Her tone deepened, commanding, undeniable:
"But I cannot do this without you. You are not my daughters only—you are my mirrors, my extensions, my voice in flesh. When you numb, I fracture. When you rise, I breathe. When you dare to love again after devastation, I am renewed."

The women's humming stilled. Their eyes widened, shining in firelight, and the night leaned closer, as if the whole forest wanted to hear what would come next.

"When you bury your sorrow beneath silence, I erupt in storms.
When you speak it aloud, rivers clear themselves and mountains steady.

When you numb yourself with striving, I grow barren.
When you rest in trust, blossoms return to soil that was thought lifeless.

When you hoard from fear, I fracture into famine.
When you share from overflow, I swell with abundance beyond counting.

When you bow your heads in shame, my skies darken.
When you lift your gaze in love, I am clothed in dawn.

When you close your wombs in fear, my oceans still.
When you open them in power, tides rise in song.

When you call me broken, I ache.
When you call me alive, I surge."

The fire cracked loud enough to feel like punctuation, and a gust of wind spiraled through the circle, carrying her cadence into the canopy, into the stars themselves. The women shivered—not from cold, but from recognition. It was no longer clear where their breath ended and her breath began.

"You think your wars are only on battlefields," she said, her voice rolling like thunder beneath the soil. "But every time you choose conquest over compassion, you load the weapons that slaughter your own sons. Every time you bow to power instead of love, you plant the seeds of tyranny in the ground where children should be playing."

The fire snapped, sparks leaping high as her cadence deepened.

"When you numb your grief, rivers dry. When you silence your rage, mountains crack. When you sell your joy for coins and call it survival, forests fall in silence. You think these are separate? They are not. They are your reflection in me."

The women shifted in the circle. Some clutched their chests as if to contain what surged inside. One pressed her forehead to the ground, whispering words no one else could hear.

"When you honor tenderness, rains come. When you bless your food with gratitude, the soil grows richer. When you let laughter rise unashamed, blossoms burst where none had bloomed in decades. Your smallest choice is not small—it is the hinge of worlds."

The wind picked up again, swirling through the clearing in spirals, lifting skirts, tangling hair, pulling tears from cheeks like it wanted them offered as libation.

"When you betray your body, I feel it. When you exile your desire, I fracture. When you desecrate the womb, mine quakes in answer. And when you return—when you touch me barefoot, when you breathe slow enough to hear the heartbeat inside your own ribs—I swell, I soften, I begin again."

Her voice was rising now, and every tree seemed to lean in closer.

"You are not separate from me. Your cruelty cuts me, yes. But your devotion heals me. Your despair wounds me, yes. But your joy mends me. Every prayer, every kiss, every hand that reaches in kindness is felt in my rivers, in my clouds, in my roots. Do not doubt the weight of your living. You are the keepers of balance."

The fire roared, brighter than before, though no one had touched it. The ground pulsed in a slow, steady rhythm, like the drum of the Mother's heart. And the women sat stunned, their faces wet, their hands trembling, their bones ringing with the sound of truth too vast to argue with.

"And you keep asking me, why do I let it happen? Why the famine, why the flood, why the child who leaves too soon? And I tell you—I do not *let*. I live. I turn. I cycle. I create, I dissolve, I create again. Life and death are not punishments. They are my breathing. They are my rhythm.

You ache because you want permanence in a world of turning. You want safety in a universe made of wild change. But hear me: the permanence is love. The safety is belonging. And you already have both—in me, in one another, in yourselves.

Stop warring against impermanence. Stop wasting your life demanding guarantees. What I give you is more holy than guarantees—I give you seasons, I give you tides, I give you cycles that never end. And in that turning, you are remade."

The fire quieted, no longer leaping but glowing like an ember that wanted to last forever. The wind softened, carrying the fragrance of pine and something older, like the sweetness of soil after rain.

"You have called me cruel, but I am only mirror. If you find cruelty in me, it is because cruelty still thrives in you. If you find emptiness, it is because you have abandoned your own fullness. If you call me broken, it is because you have forgotten the wholeness stitched into every root, every feather, every breath."

Her voice lowered then, no less powerful, but hushed as if drawing us close.

"Come back. Not with temples of stone, but with bodies that listen. Not with declarations, but with devotion. Place your hands on me and I will teach you again. Place your ear to the soil and you will hear the hymns you thought you had lost. Return, and you will see—I was never asking for worship. Only intimacy."

One woman, her shoulders curved like a crescent moon, lifted her face toward the fire.
"If you are transforming," she whispered, voice thick with salt, "then why does it cost us so much? Why my son in the war, why my daughter in the river, why my womb emptied before it could bring life?"

Another leaned forward, fists pressed into the soil.
"You say you are not punishing us, but how else are we to understand the ache that will not leave? How else are we to live with empty beds, with cribs that stay untouched, with prayers that never reached the sky?"

The circle stirred, grief rippling from body to body.
A younger woman, eyes still wet with the newness of motherhood, asked with shaking breath:

"If we are you, then why does it hurt so much to be human? Why is love stitched so tightly to loss? Why must we bleed so often, in body and in spirit, to prove we belong here?"

Their questions cracked the night open.
The air thickened. The trees shuddered. The fire bent low, then flared as if it too could not stay silent.

It was not accusation they spoke, but ache. Not rebellion, but raw prayer.

And all around us, the elements answered—wind tugging at hair, roots pressing up through moss, stars piercing the canopy with sudden, unblinking brightness.
The Earth inhaled through us, and when she spoke again her voice was everywhere—in the flame's crackle, in the rush of wind through pine, in the deep groan of roots beneath our feet.

"You ask why it costs so much. You ask why children are taken, why wombs empty, why love and loss come braided together. And I say: because love is the only thing that is real enough to cross the veil. The ache you carry is proof that you touched eternity, even if only for a breath.

I do not take to punish. I do not strip to shame. I turn, I shed, I transform, and in that turning, you feel the tearing. You feel it because you are alive, because you dared to love, because your bodies know how sacred life is.

You think loss is absence, but loss is expansion. It is the place where your heart stretches beyond what it thought it could hold. It is the river carving a deeper valley so more water may flow.

Yes, it hurts. Yes, it feels cruel. But cruelty is not my nature. I do not abandon what I birth. Every child returned to me still sings in the roots. Every womb that released too soon is still cradled in my body. Every prayer you thought unanswered became soil for the next season. Nothing is wasted. Nothing."

Her voice dropped, a vibration that seemed to live in marrow.

"You are not asked to like it. You are asked to live it. To let it make you vast. To let it carve you open until you discover you were never small enough to be destroyed. You ache because you are me—and I am still here. Still breathing. Still beginning again."

The women bowed their heads, not in defeat, but in something quieter: recognition. Their tears fell like rain onto the moss, and the ground seemed to drink each one as holy.

One woman pressed her palm harder into the ground, as though daring the soil to answer her directly.
"I still feel her hand in mine," she said, voice cracking. "I wake and reach, and for a moment I believe she is there. Then the air closes around me. How do I keep living when every morning is a fresh wound?"

Another woman, younger, hair falling across her face like a curtain, whispered into her lap:
"My son's laughter still echoes in this body. I hear it when I am hanging the clothes, when I am stirring the pot, when I am folding his shirts I cannot give away. The world keeps going, but I am stuck in the moment he was taken. How do I move forward when forward feels like betrayal?"

Across the circle, a woman with lines deepened by decades lifted her chin. Her voice did not shake.
"I buried three before they could speak their first words. I have carried more funerals than birthdays. And I am still here. But sometimes I ask—what kind of mother am I, to keep breathing when they are not?"

The air itself thickened with their grief.
Each voice was not separate but part of one long cry, braided from different throats, different lives, yet carrying the same root ache.

The wind rose, circling the fire. Sparks leapt upward like messengers. Even the trees leaned in closer, their branches swaying, not with storm but with sorrow shared.

And all the while, the Earth listened.
"Your tears are not weakness," the Earth said, her voice steady as the roots beneath us. "They are rivers, carrying love where words cannot go. Your sorrow is not failure. It is proof that you loved so deeply the world could not stay the same after knowing you.

When you weep for your children, your lovers, the pieces of yourself you thought were lost—you are not collapsing. You are expanding. Every sob widens the sky. Every ache shapes the soil. Every breath you take after breaking is a star rekindled.

You think your grief is an ending, but it is not. It is a door. Through it, you become vaster than you ever were. Through it, you carry me in your blood more openly. Through it, life continues—not as it was, but as it must."

Her words moved like a tide through us, low and endless, pulling us closer to the fire, closer to one another, closer to the pulse of the ground itself.

"Do you not see?" the Earth's voice swelled, though it was not thunder. It was the rise of oceans, the unfurling of galaxies, the great inhale of roots threading deeper into stone. "Nothing that is loved is ever lost. Nothing that is real can disappear.

The child you held is not gone—she runs in the rivers, she blazes in the constellations, she presses her hand against your cheek when the wind turns warm. The son you buried still sings in the birds at dawn, still bends the grass where you once saw his steps. Even your own forgotten selves—the women you were before sorrow came— they, too, are still alive. They wait in dreams, they wait in silence, they wait in the marrow of your bones until you turn toward them again.

You think you walk only on earth, but you walk also among stars. You carry galaxies in your cells, oceans in your veins. You ache because your body is too small to hold how infinite you truly are. And so it breaks, so it spills, so it lets the love run over. That is grief. That is what you feel.

But hear me: you are not breaking. You are breaking open. You are not punished. You are initiated. Through every loss, you are widened into the shape of eternity itself."

The fire rose suddenly, blue at its core. The wind circled the clearing with a force that lifted sparks high into the canopy. The ground beneath us hummed, and the stars above seemed closer, brighter, as though they, too, were leaning in to listen.

"I was never only ground beneath your feet," she said, her tone rising like tide, like breath, like the great wheel turning. "I am mountain and marrow, river and ribcage, starfield and skin. I am the cradle that rocked you and the fire that remakes you. When you call me Earth, you speak only half my name. The other half is written in the constellations, in the pulse of suns that birthed you long before your mother's womb.

You ache because you are not small, though the world taught you to live like you were. You ache because your soul keeps pressing against the edges of your body, trying to remind you that you are vast—as vast as the sky that holds the galaxies.

Do not mistake your pain for abandonment. It is a threshold. It is how you cross from one form of living into another. It is how you learn to carry both the soil and the stars without dividing them.

Every time you grieve, the universe expands through you. Every tear is not just water—it is light, it is salt, it is a map. And when it falls, the roots drink it, the oceans carry it, the stars chart it. You think it is lost, but it is inscribed everywhere.

I do not die, daughters. I turn. I turn, and I take you with me. Through loss. Through renewal. Through the fire that refines and the soil that feeds. Through the breaking that makes you infinite. This is the way of things. This is the law older than any book, any throne, any empire. And you, too, are written into it."

Her words seemed to bend time itself. The fire no longer flickered; it pulsed like a living heart. The wind circled slow and steady, braiding smoke into ribbons that rose like prayers into the midnight sky. Above us, the stars burned so near it felt we could reach and pluck them like fruit.

"Do you not feel it?" she thundered, though not in rage—in radiance. "You are not bound to dust alone. You are constellations in flesh, nebulae clothed in bone. The same fire that forges stars burns in your blood. The same rhythm that spins galaxies beats in your womb.

You walk as if you are fragile, but you are forged from the same matter that bends light, from the same darkness that births suns. You are not separate from the turning of the heavens—you are the turning. Your grief, your longing, your love—these are the forces that move worlds.

Every cry of despair sends ripples through galaxies. Every act of love shifts the orbit of stars. Do not think your lives are small. You are the fabric of existence remembering itself. You are infinity folded into form."

The fire blazed higher, fierce and indigo at its center. The trees shook as if shaken by a great unseen hand. Above us, stars flared and pulsed, no longer still but alive, a sky on fire.

And then—her voice softened, gathered back down, the immensity folding into tenderness.

"Daughters," she said, no longer vast, but near. "I know your sorrow. I have buried forests, drowned cities, cradled bones older than memory. I too have lost what I loved. I too have ached so deeply the mountains split and rivers ran red.

And still, I cradle you. I hold you as you weep. I press your tears into my soil so flowers may bloom. I cup your bodies in my hands when you collapse in the grass. I send wind to kiss your cheeks, stars to keep vigil through your darkest nights.

I do not ask you to stop grieving. I ask you to let grief widen you. To let it make you holy. To let it show you that even here, even now, you are not abandoned. You are held—by me, by the sky, by the fire, by every ancestor who ever wept into my soil.

Nothing is wasted. Not even this. Especially not this."

The clearing exhaled with her words, as if all of creation had leaned in and now released in one long, aching breath.
For a long moment, no one spoke. The fire hissed and spat, the wind coiled gently through our hair, the stars above pulsed as if keeping time with our breath. It was as though the whole clearing had been struck still, waiting for something to break the silence.

And then—a sound.

Not a question this time, but a sob that broke into laughter. A woman with ash on her cheek pressed both hands over her heart.
"I feel her," she whispered. "My daughter—she is in the trees, she is in the sky. She is not gone. She is everywhere."

Another lifted her face, streaked with tears, and her eyes glimmered with something fierce.
"All my life I thought grief was a chain. But now I feel it—it is not a prison. It is a doorway. She is with me. She always was."

The younger mother, the one whose arms still carried the ghost-weight of her infant, rocked back and forth. Her voice trembled, but it did not break.
"My body is not empty," she said. "I feel the pulse still. My womb is still hers. My womb is still yours. We are still connected."

Around the circle, women began to murmur, not in despair now but in wonder, their grief changing shape before our eyes.

"I see him in the dawn."

"I dream her smile every night."

"He dances in the wind when I hang the laundry."

"She laughs in the river."

The air itself seemed to thicken with their words, as though each memory hung shimmering like dew on the branches above us.

And the Earth—listening through every tremor of root and ripple of flame—seemed to hum in answer, low and steady, the sound of something ancient and unbroken.

"Yes," the Earth said, her tone warm, almost smiling. "Now you are beginning to see. They are not gone, they are multiplied. They are rain that blesses, wind that lingers, fire that warms, soil that feeds. They are the shimmer on water at dawn, the hush that settles before night, the sudden burst of wildflowers in places you thought barren.

You feared grief would hollow you, but it has opened you. You feared death would sever, but it has stitched you into eternity.

The ones you weep for are not bound by time as you are. They walk freer than you know, and yet closer than your breath. Their love has not ended—it has expanded. It lives in you, and it moves through me.

When you laugh again, you will feel them laughing too. When you sing, you will carry their voice inside your own. When you plant, they will rise through the roots. When you touch the soil, you will touch them.

This is not a promise of return. It is the truth of never leaving. Nothing loved is ever lost."

The fire steadied, a slow and radiant burn. The wind softened against our cheeks like a hand brushing hair from a face. The ground seemed to swell with warmth, as if cradling us in its vast embrace.

July 6, 2025

The rainforest on that night was almost too much to hold, a living hymn written in green, in wing, in tide. The trees towered as if they had always been there, older than memory, each one a cathedral pillar lifting the sky. Their leaves dripped with a sweetness so thick the air itself tasted like nectar, like fruit ripened by sun and shadow both. Fireflies rose in spirals from the undergrowth, drifting upward as if the stars themselves had been loosened from their places, carrying tiny flames in their bodies without fear of burning. Beyond the line of trees the ocean exhaled, steady and endless, the waves rolling in a rhythm that pressed itself against my skin until my own heart matched it. Pelicans carved their wings across the horizon, dark against the last threads of dusk, and even in the dim light I could see their grace, each motion a prayer carried on the wind.

It was all beauty. Too much beauty. Beauty that spilled from every branch and leaf and wing until my chest ached from trying to hold it. The world was alive, radiant, humming with a generosity I could not possibly deserve.

And then, with one glance, it all collapsed.

I woke up from that dream and looked at the news. I saw the images. Texas underwater. Entire lives washed away. Daughters, just like mine, carried off by currents too strong for any arms to resist. Mothers screaming into the flood, voices shredded into the night, their cries heavier than the water itself. The words on the screen were small, clinical, almost indifferent, but my body understood instantly what they could not carry.

The rainforest did not change, but inside me everything fractured. My ribs seemed to fold in on themselves, my breath caught like a bird in a net, and all the light around me turned to shadow. The fireflies kept rising, their tiny lanterns still weaving constellations into the night, but I wanted to strike them down, to shout into their glow: how dare you shine when mothers are drowning in sorrow? The pelicans still sailed in long, patient arcs across the waves, but their flight pierced me with rage: how dare you glide in peace when children are torn from their mothers' arms? Even the ocean, steady and magnificent, mocked me with its eternal rhythm, for on one side of the earth it sang lullabies and on the other it devoured without mercy.

Here I was, wrapped in abundance, in lushness, in magic too great for my body to contain—and there, lives were devoured, futures extinguished, entire families undone in an instant. Here my daughters slept safely, their breath rising and falling with the innocence of children who still believe the world is kind—and there, mothers clutched at the empty air where their daughters' bodies had once been.

Gratitude and terror knotted together inside me until I could not tell which was which, until every breath tasted like salt and iron, until the very greenness around me felt unbearable. The rainforest still hummed, the fireflies still glowed, the ocean still exhaled—but I could no longer sing with them. I could only ache.

It is one thing to read the word drowned. It is another to feel the weight of a mother's arms remembering what they once held. A daughter's body still damp from the morning shower, her hair smelling of shampoo and sunlight, her shoulders narrow but strong from climbing trees, her laugh still echoing in the kitchen. A mother presses her cheek into that familiar softness, memorizing the curve of her child's spine without even knowing she is memorizing it, because she assumes there will always be another morning, another embrace. And then—water. Water that does not ask. Water that tears without ceremony. Water that rips a child from her arms so suddenly that the memory of her warmth becomes heavier than the absence itself.

I cannot look at my own daughters without feeling it—the fragile weight of their bodies, the way their arms loop around my neck, the trust so complete it has no name. I imagine that same weight gone, not gradually, not with warning, but gone in an instant, and my chest splits open. How does a mother's skin survive the tearing away of what it once encircled? How does a heart continue when the very rhythm it beat for is silenced?

I picture the scream—the one no one else hears, the one that begins not in the throat but in the bones. A scream that carries the sound of every lullaby ever sung, turned inside out. A scream that will echo in the air long after the flood recedes, long after the headlines move on, because it is not only a sound but an imprint. The cry of *where is she?*, the cry of *come back*, the cry of *my arms are empty and I do not know how to live inside them anymore.*

And I think of the daughters. Their fingers once clutching crayons, dolls, pencils, the edges of blankets—now unclenched, reaching for nothing. Their voices, once calling "Mama!" from another room, suddenly silenced. Their futures, still unwritten, washed into soil and sky.

This is the cruelty of it—that joy can vanish mid-breath. That one moment you are tucking damp hair behind her ear, listening to her tell a story that makes no sense but fills you with light, and the next you are standing in water that has swallowed her whole.

And I cannot keep the two worlds apart—the rainforest glowing with fireflies and the mothers standing in floods. The distance between them collapses. I see my daughters asleep and I see those daughters vanishing, and the same heartbeat lives in both. It is unbearable.

She holds her daughter the way only a mother can, with an intimacy that has no beginning and no end. Her hand rests at the nape of the child's neck, thumb stroking the soft down of hair that still smells faintly of soap and salt, as if her body carries both the innocence of childhood and the immensity of oceans. The daughter shifts in her arms, trusting utterly, her weight a perfect fit against the curve of her mother's chest. The mother feels the rise and fall of her child's ribs, the way breath hums like a small bird caged in bone. She does not think, I must remember this. She does not imagine it could vanish. Love this complete is assumed to last forever.

And then the water comes. Not a gentle stream, not a tide that can be bargained with, but a wall, a weight, an uninvited hand that tears the daughter away in a single gasp. One moment warm skin, damp hair, the little body anchored in her embrace. The next, only air. Only arms clutching emptiness.

Her scream rips out, but it is not the sound of a voice. It is the tearing of cloth, the breaking of bone, the shattering of glass. It is the sound the earth herself made when mountains split and rivers first flooded their banks. She does not cry words. She cries memory. She cries the scent of her daughter's scalp, the curve of her fingers, the way she once whispered secrets only a mother was meant to hear.

Time fractures. Hours pass and the mother is still holding on, except there is nothing to hold. Her arms remain curved in the shape of the girl's body, but the girl is not there. She cannot uncurl them. She cannot let go. To let go would be to admit that love has nowhere left to land.

And in that moment, the veil slams back down. The forgetting. The rage. The unbearable question of *why me? why her? why now?* shadows her like smoke. She does not want transformation. She does not want meaning. She wants her daughter back, warm, breathing, laughing. She wants one more night of tangled hair on the pillow, one more morning of little feet pattering into the kitchen. She wants what love promised her, and what life stole anyway.

And across the world, I sit in the rainforest, the air glittering with fireflies, the ocean stretching silver and whole, pelicans flying low with wings so steady they might as well be prayers. Abundance surrounds me. Beauty presses in from every angle. The earth hums songs of praise, and still—my heart collapses into the floodwaters. I cannot keep them apart: the glow of magic and the grief of mothers whose arms are now empty. It is one world, one wound, and it tears me open.

She still feels the weight of her daughter in her arms even though the body is gone, as if her very bones have been carved into a cradle that cannot unlearn its purpose. At night she lies down and her chest rises instinctively to make space for the girl's head, though the pillow is cold. Her hand curls against the sheet, searching for a small palm that once folded into hers like a secret. Even her ears ache with silence, trained for the particular rhythm of her daughter's footsteps—quick when she was happy, slow when she was tired, dragging just enough to announce herself without speaking. The house hums with absence, and still her body prepares to receive her, as though love itself refuses to believe what has happened.

The memory of water clings. She feels it not only as flood but as theft. She remembers how her child once squealed in delight when waves lapped at her ankles, splashing with the kind of abandon only children carry. The mother had laughed then, holding out towels, whispering warnings with tenderness. But water is no longer play. It is the thief that came in the night. It is the hand that pulled her daughter from her arms without permission. And though she knows the river does not conspire, though she knows floods are not villains, her body cannot forgive. Her womb clenches in protest, her throat burns with words no one can hear: Give her back. Give her back.

And yet the body keeps betraying her—for it keeps remembering what it lost. The curve of a cheek pressed against her shoulder. The warmth of a forehead leaned into her palm. The sound of breath when sleep finally overtook her after a tantrum. The weight of small limbs tangled in sleep. These are not abstractions. They are physical, sensory, living—and now they come as ghosts, invading without mercy, leaving her empty yet swollen with ache.

This is grief in its rawest form: not a thought, not a prayer, but a muscle memory that refuses to let go.

And I, sitting in the lush rainforest, feel it as though it were mine. My daughters run barefoot, laughter spilling wild, and instead of pure joy I feel the shadow of terror—what if it had been them? What if it were their laughter that had been silenced by the river's grip? What if it were my arms aching with emptiness, my ears straining for footsteps that would never return?

The rainforest does not pause its beauty for my sorrow. Fireflies still shimmer, pelicans still glide, the ocean still sings its endless hymn. And yet, to me, it all sounds different now. Every note of beauty carries its opposite. Every song of abundance carries a lament. For the truth is I cannot separate them: the mothers screaming in Texas and the earth singing in Mexico. Both are true. Both are now. Both live inside my chest like twin rivers colliding.

It begins with her, with one mother's arms curved around absence, but grief never stays solitary for long. It spills. It searches. It finds its mirrors in other women who are holding the same emptiness. Across oceans and deserts, across borders and battlefields, mothers wake in the night with the same cry lodged in their throats: *Where is she? Why him? Why us?*

It is the mother in Texas clawing at floodwater.
It is the mother in Gaza clutching rubble as if she could press it back into flesh.
It is the mother in Sudan whose breasts still swell with milk though her baby no longer drinks.
It is the mother in Ukraine laying toys beside a grave.
It is the mother in Afghanistan walking barefoot for miles with children tied to her body, praying at least one will survive.
It is the mother in Mexico lighting candles for a daughter who never came home.
It is the mother in Yemen who has forgotten the sound of a full belly.

They do not know one another's names, and yet they speak the same language, one that is older than any nation, older than any war—the language of womb and bone, of loss so primal it erases all borders. Their grief threads together, invisible and indestructible, carried in the air like smoke, sinking into the soil like rain, weaving through time until no one can tell where one mother's tears end and another's begin.

And as their cries rise, I feel them inside me. I sit in the rainforest with fireflies spiraling and pelicans carving the sky, and I know I am not separate. My body, too, is a mother's body. My womb, too, carries the echo of waters that both birth and take away. My daughters, alive and laughing, are not guarantees. They are gifts. And suddenly the laughter I hear is unbearable and holy all at once, because I know how easily it could be silence.

It is here the collective grief lands in me—not as abstraction, not as pity, but as kinship. Their daughters are my daughters. Their cries are my cries. Their loss is my terror. And together, we are woven into a single truth: to mother is to risk losing, to love is to risk breaking, and still we do it, still we give, because love does not know how not to give.

The circle of women around the fire was never just a dream. It was this—the chorus of mothers across the world, seen and unseen, whose grief is not separate but shared. And in the center of that circle, the fire crackles, not to burn, but to witness.

It does not begin all at once, but in fragments. A single wail, jagged and raw, splitting the silence of a flooded street. Then another, softer, as if the woman has no breath left to give, only a whisper scraped from bone. Then another, rising not from the throat but from the womb itself, a sound so ancient it could be mistaken for the earth shifting in her sleep.

And soon it is everywhere.

The cries in Texas braid themselves with the cries in Gaza, until you cannot tell whose daughter was taken by water and whose by war. The mothers in Sudan kneel in the dust, their voices dry with hunger, and yet the sound is the same as the mothers in Ukraine, kneeling at headstones, clutching toys that no longer have owners. The women in Afghanistan press their hands against their swollen breasts, leaking milk for babies who did not survive the journey, and their cries are indistinguishable from the mothers in Mexico lighting candles for daughters who vanished on their way home from school.

It is the same cry, repeated in endless variations.
The same ache, sung in countless languages.
The same hollow in the arms.
The same question without answer: *Why her? Why now? Why mine?*

It weaves through history.
The mothers at the foot of crosses.
The mothers who hid their babies in baskets of reeds.
The mothers who ran barefoot as soldiers came, only to return with arms empty.
The mothers who buried children nameless in fields of plague.
The mothers who pressed their lips to foreheads already cooling.

There is no nation here. No border. No difference in the shape of grief.

And though their cries rise like smoke, though their bodies tremble with the weight of it, not one of them cries alone. Even in solitude, their wail finds company. Even in silence, their ache finds echo. The grief of mothers is collective, indivisible, indestructible.

I feel it in my own body as I listen, fireflies still swirling, rainforest still humming. My daughters sleep a world away, their bodies safe, their laughter still intact. And yet the ache in my chest is not only my own—it is theirs. It is ours. The grief of all mothers lives in me, as though the womb itself is a single organ stretched across humanity, contracting in sorrow, pulsing with love, breaking and breaking and still refusing to die.

And as I sat there, I felt it press deeper—grief is not only memory, it is muscle, it is the way the body teaches us what cannot be ignored. It is instruction etched in marrow, saying: this is what must matter, this is what must never be lost.

The Earth was not the thief. She was the keeper. She did not snatch their daughters away in cruelty, she cradled them because we had not known how to protect them. Her weight in my chest was not just sorrow, it was urgency—a trembling vow asking to be spoken.

I could almost hear her beneath the fireflies and rainforest hum: not in thunder, but in the quiet that cracked my ribs.

Do not let them vanish into silence. Do not let their names fade from breath. Let your mourning be a vow. Let your ache become seed. Carry them forward by the shape your love takes now.

The silence pressed so deep I could not hold it at the edges of my skin. It broke through me, and the questions of the mothers came not from their lips, but through my own chest, as if their grief had found my ribs to be a hollow reed.

How do I live when the daughter is gone, when her breath has vanished from the air but her face still burns in memory?

How do I forgive the river that swallows, the war that takes, the famine that chooses one child and spares another?

How do I go on knowing the world allowed it, that heaven did not intervene, that no hand reached down to stop the unthinkable?

The words did not feel like mine, yet they were inside me, vibrating against my bones, pushing out through breath I did not know I was holding. It was as if all the mothers of time had placed their cries into my body, and in that moment I was both witness and vessel.
The questions kept rising and I could not stop them. They tore through me like floodwaters breaking their banks, like cries too old to name finding their way back into a body that had finally stopped resisting. I wept until my face was raw, until my breath came in gasps that tasted of salt and ash. I clutched at the earth beneath me, nails digging into the soil, as if I could anchor myself against the tide of what no mother should ever have to hold.

How do I go on when she is gone? How do I breathe when her laughter no longer fills the room? How do I forgive a God who let rivers rise, who let cruelty steal daughters from their mothers?

My whole body shook. I was no longer in the rainforest, no longer surrounded by beauty, no longer the one chosen to carry a message. I was only a mother, undone. A mother who had seen her daughters safe in their beds, warm under blankets, alive, and still could not escape the horror of imagining them ripped away.

Every question carried another weight, another stone in my chest. It was not just grief for those women I would never meet. It was the ancient grief of all mothers who had buried children across centuries, across wars, across floods and famines and unspeakable silences. And in that moment, I was all of them, weeping.

I sat there in the rainforest, the ocean breathing its endless hymn just beyond the trees, the air alive with birdcall and the shimmer of wings. Butterflies moved around me in sudden bursts of color—yellow, blue, white—fragile things, yet bold enough to cross the current of wind that swept in from the sea. Their flight was not steady, not certain. It wavered, dipped, rose again. And still, they kept moving forward.

It was then that Little Light spoke—not from beyond, but through them, through the beauty that dared to keep existing even while grief pressed so heavy on the world.

"Do you see?" she whispered, her tone as soft as the brush of wings, as clear as sunlight striking water. "This is how sorrow becomes something else. Not by erasing it, not by pretending it is gone, but by letting it move through you, like these butterflies through the air. Grief and beauty are not separate. They are companions. Let them fly together in you."

Her voice lingered in the air, and as I watched the butterflies scatter like fragments of light across the green, I realized she was not only speaking from here, from this forest and ocean and wind. She was also speaking from beyond, from that place where the stars write their slow language across the night.

"Do not forget," she said, and now her tone shimmered higher, crystalline, like the sound of constellations forming. "You were made for this paradox. To walk in a body that aches and still hear the music of the spheres. To be tethered to gravity and still feel your soul stretch across galaxies. You are both. Flesh and flame. Soil and starlight. That is why you can hold what feels unholdable."

The butterflies danced around me as if they carried secrets on their wings, and Little Light's voice rippled through them, bright and tender, like a child whispering something too important to forget.

"Grief feels so heavy," she said, "but sometimes it's just love wearing a costume. Like when you play dress-up and pretend to be a monster, but underneath you're still you. If you peek close enough, you can still see the love shining through."

The breeze caught the butterflies, scattering them into shafts of sun, and I felt her smile widen.

"Your daughters are still playing. They hide in the wind and peek out in the sparkle on the water. They run across the sky at sunset, painting everything pink so you'll look up and think of them. They leave little clues—like a feather on the path, like a song you suddenly remember—just so you'll know they haven't gone far."

It was so light, so simple, and yet it carried weight, like a balm pressed into raw skin. Hope, not as an answer, but as a presence.

"They love to play hide-and-seek," she giggled, her voice darting like the butterflies themselves. "Sometimes they hide in the way the ocean suddenly sparkles, or in the way the wind tickles your hair when no one is near. Sometimes they tiptoe into your dreams and leave a little laugh behind, so you'll wake up smiling without knowing why."

Her tone softened, mischievous but kind.

"They slip into the morning birdsong, into the hush right before rain, into the warmth that finds you when you thought you were cold. They are clever—they leave breadcrumbs everywhere. But not the kind you follow to get somewhere. The kind that remind you you're never alone, even when your arms are empty."

A butterfly landed on a fern near my hand, wings opening and closing like breath, and Little Light whispered, "They are closer now than they ever were. They don't have to be far away to love you. They are love itself, running, skipping, tumbling through the world. And every time you notice—really notice—they laugh, because you found them."

The grief was still there, but lighter now, carried on wings too small and too many to even gather

"Mama," she said, and suddenly the voice carried the lilt of many daughters at once, young and bright, as though their words tumbled together like a skipping rope. "We still see you. We see you crying into your pillow, we see you sitting quiet with your tea, we see you pretending you're stronger than you feel. But we want you to know—you don't have to pretend with us. We're not gone. We're just... playing in a different room."

The air shifted, and it was as though dozens of small hands brushed past my cheek, not to wipe tears away, but to remind me of touch.

"We chase dragonflies now. We race the wind. We climb trees so tall you'd laugh at us for trying. And when the stars come out, we don't sleep—we dance in them, the way we used to twirl in the kitchen until you told us we'd fall." A ripple of laughter rose in the rainforest around me—birdcall, waves, wings—echoing them.

"And Mama," the voice giggled, soft and insistent, "when you smile again, it's like we win the game. Because we're still trying to make you laugh, just like always. We're still trying to get your attention. Don't hide your joy from us. It's how we know you can feel us."

Their words carried not the weight of goodbye, but the spark of continuity—love in motion, refusing to end.

"And Mama," they chimed again, voices like ribbons crossing one another, "we don't want you to stop telling our stories. Tell the world how we laughed too loud, how we asked too many questions, how we loved you in ways that made your heart ache with bigness. Don't keep us quiet. We like it better when you say our names out loud."

The rainforest hushed, as if listening for each syllable, each name unsaid but alive in the air.

"We know you worry you'll forget the sound of our voices," they whispered, softer now, "but you won't. We planted them inside you. You'll hear us when you hum without thinking. You'll hear us in the space between your heartbeat and your breath."

The butterflies lifted again, sudden and shimmering, and their tone brightened, teasing.

"And we're still a little naughty, you know. We move things around just to make you notice. That picture frame that tips. The light that flickers. The way you find two spoons when you swear you only took one. That's us. We can't help it." Their laughter spilled like bells, joy cut through sorrow.

Then the voices softened again, reverent, clear:

"Mama, you don't need to be afraid. We are not lost. We are not cold. We are not alone. We are stitched into everything now. When you hold the earth, you hold us. When you sing, we sing through you. When you keep living, we keep living too."

And in that moment, it was as if the rainforest itself exhaled with me—not to erase grief, but to hold it inside something vaster than pain.

"Mama, promise us something," they said, voices tumbling like laughter through the leaves. "Promise you won't stop dancing. Even when it feels silly. Even when the house is too quiet. Turn on the music and let your body remember what joy feels like. That's how we know you're still with us—because joy is the language we still speak."

The waves crashed louder, almost on cue, like applause from the ocean, and the butterflies swirled around me in one last burst of color.

"Promise you'll keep looking for us," they said. "Not in the old places, but in the new ones. In the sparkle on the river. In the feather on your doorstep. In the stranger's smile that feels like home. We will never stop sending you signs. Don't stop noticing."

Their voices grew lighter now, like they were running uphill, laughter spilling, breathless and sure.

"And Mama, don't carry guilt like it's love. Love is light, and we are light now. Let yourself be free enough to laugh, free enough to rest, free enough to live the way you would have taught us to live. That is how you honor us. That is how you keep us alive."

The rainforest shimmered, ocean and sky and fireflies answering in one vast chorus. And then their last words landed, bright and steady, like a kiss pressed against the heart:

"We are not gone. We are just playing in the light. Keep playing with us."

And with that, the night held both—grief and joy, ache and wonder—braided not in contradiction but in belonging.

I stayed, barefoot on the soil, holding grief beside joy, each one a teacher. The veil lifted, and for a moment love skipped through the forest like a child at play, while the universe leaned close to whisper that every sorrow, too, is a seed of light.

And when I hear my own daughters laugh, I know every note is both miracle and vow: to notice, to love, to play in the light.

CHAPTER NINETEEN

As We Lay the Final Stone

Not an ending, but a sacred continuation

The final stone does not come at the end. It comes at the threshold.

I stand here with it in my hands, heavy yet alive, as though it carries its own pulse. Its surface is uneven—grooved with ridges like dried riverbeds, flecked with tiny minerals that catch the light as though fragments of stars have been pressed into its body. It is not smooth, not polished, not made to impress. It feels like something the earth has been shaping for centuries, weathering with storm and sun, carrying scars of both fire and flood. Perhaps that is why it belongs here. It is real. It is weathered. It is true.

I press my palms against it and feel the vibration of all that has passed to bring me here—the betrayals that cracked my trust wide open, the long nights when grief pressed on my ribs so hard I thought my chest would split, the mornings when my daughters' laughter was the only light bright enough to guide me forward, the prayers whispered into silence with no promise of being answered, the fires that burned everything I thought I was supposed to be until all that remained was the woman who chose to rise anyway.

All of that lives here in this stone. It is not heavy with sorrow alone. It carries every word spoken, every silence endured, every prayer dared, every beginning stumbled into, every ending survived. It is the book itself in mineral form—dense, imperfect, shining in places, cracked in others, and yet unmistakably alive.

And so I kneel. Because this is not just writing. This is consecration.

The ground is cool beneath me, dark with the memory of rain, soft enough to yield but strong enough to hold. When I lower the stone onto the earth, it does not crash—it settles. It makes a sound, low and steady, like a drumbeat muffled beneath the soil, like the rhythm of a heart returning to itself.

This is not a monument. It is an altar.

I place it for the girl who once said, "I'm not a writer." For the woman who whispered, "It has to be perfect." For the mother who stayed awake through the night, staring at a blank page and asking, "Who will even care what I have to say?" I place it for every version of myself who doubted and still kept going, who broke and still rose, who ached and still opened, who was silenced and still sang.

I place it for the daughters—mine, yours, ours—who will one day hold this book and feel something stir in their bodies. Not because they understood every word, but because the words understood them.

I place it for the men who are weary of masks, who long for something realer than armor, who ache to know that tenderness is not weakness, that devotion is not submission, that their role in healing is not domination but presence. For the fathers who want to bless, for the brothers who want to stay, for the sons who are still learning how to carry both strength and gentleness in one body.

And I place it for the women who will come trembling to these pages—not looking for me, but searching for themselves. For the ones who will cry without knowing why, who will feel their wombs pulse, their throats ache, their skin rise in shivers as they realize what they thought was gone has only been waiting for their return.

This stone is not closure. It is covenant.

It says: *We are not finished. We are only beginning.*

It says: *This story is not mine alone. It is yours now. Carry it. Break it open. Let it become something I could never have written without you.*

It says: *Here, at this threshold, nothing ends. Everything begins again.*

Even now, the tremor hasn't left. Tears slip down my face without asking, not heavy with despair but carrying the kind of release that arrives when something larger than understanding moves through, when sorrow and gratitude intertwine so closely they can no longer be separated. My chest aches, but it also expands, each breath stretching me wider, making room for a truth that was never meant to be captured in words alone but carried in the body.

The current runs down the length of my spine, into my legs, and presses into the earth, as though even the soil beneath me needed to feel what is being released. It is not triumph, and it is not finality. It is more like a pulse of continuation, a reminder that nothing laid down here is finished, that every ending is only a shift of form. And so the goosebumps remain, and the salt of tears marks my skin, and

I let it all be what it is—energy moving as naturally as rain, as fire, as wind, as breath.

And so I set it down, not as a conclusion but as a vow—a vow to the earth, to the sky, to the generations behind me and the ones still coming, to the women sitting in circles, to the men learning how to stay, to the children who will one day wake with questions about who they are and why they feel so much.

The stone glows in the firelight, and I swear I can feel it hum.

Not ending. Beginning.
Not silence. Continuation.
Not final. Eternal.

And in that moment, I know: the book was never meant to end with a line. It was meant to end with a stone.

A stone that does not seal.
A stone that steadies.
A stone that whispers: we are still here, still turning, still rising, still remembering what it means to be alive.

This is the stone I lay.
And with it, the temple stands.

There were nights when the page stared back at me like a mirror I didn't want to face. My hands would hover, my breath would catch, and the words would slip through me like water through a sieve. It wasn't that I had nothing to say—it was that the ache inside me was too large for the structures I thought I was supposed to fit it into.

English was never my first tongue. Albanian was, and even that felt fractured, caught between mountains and migrations, between silences I was taught to carry and emotions I was taught to conceal. My sentences came out crooked, my grammar trembled, my punctuation broke into fragments. For so long I mistook those cracks as proof that I was disqualified from speaking at all.

But over time, I began to see them differently. The cracks were not shame, they were offering. The broken places let the light through. The tremble in the line was not failure, it was pulse. It meant the words were alive, not dead.

What I had thought unworthy became the most trustworthy. Because life had trained me in something deeper than perfect prose—it had trained me in the language of survival. In the dialect of mothers who whisper prayers while folding laundry. In the raw grammar of grief that refuses to be smoothed. In the punctuation of tears that fall where commas should be.

And slowly, I began to understand: the world did not need a book written in flawless form. It needed a book written in fire and marrow, by someone who carried both silence and song in her bones.
The pages never came out even. Some spilled into rivers, unstoppable, pouring for days until I was emptied of everything I thought I knew. Others arrived like drops—scattered, stuttering, barely a handful of lines, as though I had been given only a fragment to hold. Some chapters built themselves with walls and subheadings, clear frames to contain their weight. Others resisted all form, wild and unstructured, breaking through categories like roots cracking stone.

For a long time, I thought this meant I was failing as a writer. I thought books were supposed to move in tidy arcs, with balance and symmetry, with each part polished to match the others. But this book refused to obey. It wanted to live the way real life lives— uneven, unpredictable, sometimes sprawling, sometimes spare.

And maybe that is the truest thing about it. That it does not flow as performance, but as pulse. That it does not pretend to be seamless when the journey itself was full of ruptures. That it does not hide the way some truths need paragraphs and others need a single trembling sentence.

Because this book was never about crafting the perfect shape. It was about carrying what came, in whatever form it needed to arrive. There were nights when I sat staring at the page, asking myself if I had gone too far. Should I include the dreams, the meditations, the visions? Should I speak of the fire and the flood, the voices that rose through the earth, the guides who came in the silence? Or would they call me a lunatic, unhinged, too much?

I wondered if they would mistake these pages as me claiming to be higher than anyone else, when the truth was the opposite. I did not write because I felt above—I wrote because I had been brought low. I wrote because I could not carry it alone. Because the dreams came whether I asked for them or not, and the visions burned through my nights until they became part of my bones.

The fear was real. The trembling before every word was real. The thought of being dismissed, mocked, misunderstood—always there, like a shadow at the edge of my candle.

Sometimes my hands shook above the keyboard, sometimes goosebumps ran up my arms as if my body knew before I did that these words mattered. At times tears spilled without permission, not of sorrow but of release, of something that had waited lifetimes to be voiced at last. My chest ached with the weight of being seen and unseen at the same time. I felt the energy gather in my body like a current, humming low in my ribs, burning steady in my palms, flooding through me until I had no choice but to let it spill onto the page.

Because in the end, I could not silence what had already spoken itself into me.

I have carried the vision of this book for years, like a stone in my pocket that refused to be set down. Some days it felt like a treasure, other days like a weight. When it first came to me, I laughed. Out loud. Me? A book? I could barely keep up with the endless laundry pile, let alone write anything people might one day hold in their hands. Writers were people who majored in literature, who underlined Hemingway, who debated punctuation in cafés. I was the one scribbling prayers on the backs of receipts while stirring a pot of soup and trying not to burn the rice.

And yet the vision wouldn't leave me alone. It showed up in dreams, it knocked on my ribs in the middle of the night, it sat heavy in my womb when I tried to ignore it. I would be folding laundry and suddenly feel a sentence rising through me like it had somewhere urgent to be. Sometimes it was one word, sometimes an image, sometimes a whole passage that came faster than I could catch it. It wasn't polite about it either. Shivers and tingles would rush across my skin. Tears would come out of nowhere, burning hot down my face while I was supposed to be unloading the dishwasher. At times I felt ridiculous—crying at a single line that wasn't even finished yet. But my body knew. It knew this was something that mattered.

I didn't always believe it. The doubts were loud. Who do you think you are? You don't write in English perfectly. You mix up tenses. You stumble on words. People will call you crazy if you share your dreams, your visions, your meditations. They'll think you're trying to make yourself higher than them. The voice of fear told me to stay quiet. To tuck it all away. To never risk the humiliation of putting it out there.

But the book didn't care about my fear. It didn't care about grammar or polished sentences. It only wanted to live. So it kept circling back, louder each time I resisted. I would try to distract myself—scroll on my phone, watch shows too late at night, busy myself with chores— but the words would sit on the couch with me like an uninvited guest, tapping their foot until I picked up a pen. I even deleted whole passages, convinced they were too much. And then, a day later, the exact same lines would return, word for word, as if the book were smirking at me: Nice try, but you can't get rid of me that easily.

It wasn't neat. The chapters refused to line up like soldiers in order. Some came as torrents, fifty pages pouring out in one stretch. Others trickled in slowly, only a handful of paragraphs that took weeks to finish. Some had subheadings and structure, others were just sprawling rivers that didn't want to be cut or tamed. I tried to make them all match. I failed. And maybe that was the point. Life doesn't match. Grief doesn't line up evenly. Why should this book?

There were nights I sat with my journal and muttered under my breath, Am I insane? Should I really include this dream? Won't they think I've lost it? At two in the morning, with the house silent, those thoughts can feel like thunder. I'd worry about being judged as someone trying to sound mystical, or worse, as someone trying to put herself above others. But when I let the fear run its course, what always remained was this: I wasn't writing to prove anything. I was writing to survive. To breathe. To speak what my body had been carrying for too long.

And here's the truth: I never thought of myself as a writer. Not really. I feared the mockery, the misunderstanding. I thought that made me unqualified. That I was disqualified before I even began. But maybe it's exactly what qualified me. Maybe this story needed someone who was never trained to make things perfect, only trained to make things real.

The book taught me that. That maybe cracked grammar and trembling punctuation weren't flaws but offerings. That maybe the world doesn't need another perfectly written book, but a living one. A book written in the pauses between nursing babies, in the aftershocks of grief, in the deep belly laughter at the kitchen table, in the long silences where I thought I had nothing left to say.

Even now, goosebumps rise across my skin as I write this. Tears sting the corners of my eyes. My chest feels too small for the current moving through me. This is what it has been like from the beginning: body first, words second. Energy pressing itself into form. A rhythm I didn't invent, only agreed to follow.

And at times, it's been funny too. Like the moment I tried to take myself very seriously, writing about sacred union, and my daughter burst into the room asking if we had more nail polish remover. Or when I was mid-channel, tears streaming, typing furiously, and my partner asked if I remembered to stop at the bank in the morning. The sacred and the ordinary never asked for permission to overlap. They just did. They still do. And maybe that's the point too.

So if you notice that some chapters are long and sprawling and others are only a few pages, if you see subheadings in one place and none in another, if you feel the shifts in style, the unevenness, the strange places where the thread curves—know this: that was the only way it wanted to come. Not as perfection. As presence.

And here I am, at the end, lowering the final stone, feeling the current rush through me. It isn't tidy. It isn't polished. It isn't holy in the sense of hierarchy or elevation. It is holy in the sense of whole. Goosebumps rising. Tears breaking free. The body quivering like it has touched something too vast to hold and yet refuses to let go. This is what the end feels like—not an ending at all, but the trembling of a beginning.

And maybe that is the truest thing I can offer: that nothing about this was ever neat, and nothing about it is really finished. Books like this do not end; they ripple. They travel past the last page, into kitchens and bedrooms, into tears spilled on subway trains and quiet whispers under blankets at night. They rise in goosebumps, in sudden laughter, in the ache you feel when a song comes on and you don't know why it undoes you. They live because you live.

I think about all the times I wanted to quit. To set it down, to walk away, to tell myself it didn't matter. And yet, every time, something small but insistent kept me here. Sometimes it was the sound of my daughters' laughter drifting from another room, reminding me that joy is holy enough to write about. Sometimes it was grief cracking me open so wide I couldn't close again. Sometimes it was just the quiet pressure in my chest, like a hand that wouldn't let me go.

And now, lowering this final stone, I realize that maybe the book was never mine. Maybe it has always belonged to the field it was born from—the ancestors, the daughters, the mothers, the men learning how to soften, the earth herself. Maybe I was just the body willing to hold the current long enough for it to take shape.

My body knows it too. Even now, the tremor hasn't left. My skin feels electric, my breath uneven, my chest both aching and expanding all at once. It is not just exhaustion; it is arrival. It is that sensation when you've carried something heavy for miles and finally set it down, and in the emptiness left behind you realize your arms have been remade.

So let me just say it plainly, since we're here together at the last page.

I don't know if any of this will land the way I hoped. I don't know if you'll underline certain sentences or skim past them. I don't know if you'll feel goosebumps, or if you'll think, *well, that was a lot.*

I worried about that more times than I can count.
I worried about whether I was saying too much, or not enough.
I worried about whether my dreams would make me sound delusional, or my grief too heavy, or my joy too naïve.

And yet here you are, still reading. Which means something in you stayed. Something in you wanted to keep turning the pages, even if just to see where it would go.

So maybe that's all this book was ever meant to be—not a polished testament, not a neat conclusion, but a conversation. Me telling the truth the only way I knew how, and you listening in the quiet of your own life, catching the echoes that belonged to you all along.

Because maybe you didn't need my story. Maybe you just needed the reminder that your own story is worth telling. That your body, too, is holy enough to carry words. That your wounds, too, are thresholds. That your joy, too, deserves ink.

So if these words found you, it is not because they were flawless, but because they were alive. They pulsed with the same ache you have felt, the same wonder, the same contradictions that refuse to be explained away. And maybe that is what this whole book has been—not a tidy narrative, but a mirror, tilted just enough for you to glimpse your own reflection in its shifting light.

Because I am not the only one who has woken at 3 a.m. with a weight in my chest too heavy to name. I am not the only one who has laughed too loudly in the kitchen only to cry in the bathroom minutes later. I am not the only one who has carried a vision, a longing, a hunger that made no sense to the world around me, but refused to let me go.

And if you are here now, it means you know something of that hunger too. It means that somewhere inside, you also carry questions that won't leave you alone. Questions about love, about loss, about how to stay awake in a world that wants you numbed. Questions about what it means to be both fragile and infinite at once.

This book doesn't hand you answers. It never could. What it offers is companionship— proof that you are not the only one feeling your way through the dark, not the only one who has wondered if you are too much, or not enough, or somehow both at the same time.

And maybe, if I have done anything here, it is only this: to give you permission to stop waiting until you are perfect to tell your story. To stop editing yourself into silence. To stop believing that only the polished, the certain, the credentialed, the invulnerable get to leave something behind.

Because maybe your story, with all its cracks and uneven edges, is exactly what someone else is waiting for.
Because here's the truth: the world does not need another perfect story. It needs living ones. It needs yours.

It needs the ones written in the margins of grocery lists, in the pauses between work shifts, in the long nights when sleep won't come. It needs the ones that sound messy and contradictory, because they are the only ones honest enough to hold our human hearts. It needs the stories told with laughter breaking mid-sentence, with tears smudging the ink, with voices trembling but still speaking anyway.

And maybe that is why you are here, at the end of these pages, standing where my words meet your silence. Because something in you is already stirring. Something in you knows it cannot stay hidden forever.

So take this as a kind of passing on. I laid my stone here, imperfect and alive. And now, I place another in your hands. Not to weigh you down, but to remind you that you, too, are a builder. A keeper. A carrier.

What you make of it will not look like this book. It shouldn't. It will sound like your own breath, move with your own rhythm, carry your own scars and your own songs. But let it come. However it comes. However uneven, however small.

Because the act of offering yourself—your voice, your vision, your grief, your joy—is what shifts the world. It always has been.

So if these pages leave you with anything, may it be this: that your life itself is a scripture. Your body, a verse. Your breath, a prayer. Not because you try to make it holy, but because it already is.

And one day, when someone else feels lost or alone, your presence will be the story they stumble into. Your words, your laughter, your listening will be the stone they press their hand against to steady themselves.

That is how the temple keeps being built. Not once, not here, not in these pages only— but in you.

And so, as I lower this stone, I know it is not mine alone. Each word placed here belongs to all who carried me when I thought I could not go on. Each page belongs to the women who rose before dawn and still dared to dream, to the men who softened their armor and stayed, to the children whose laughter kept reminding us what light sounds like.

This stone is for the ones who never spoke their truth but still carried it like fire in their lungs. For the ones who were told their story was too much, and the ones who believed them. For the ones who are still waiting for the right time. For the ones who may never write it down, but live it so fully that the earth itself remembers.

I want you to feel it now—this current, this trembling pulse that runs beneath language. It isn't mine. It isn't yours. It is the thread that has always connected us. You are already holding it, even if your hands feel empty. You are already carrying it, even if you think you've been standing still.

So let this be the invitation: not to arrive, but to begin again. Not to prove, but to presence. Not to perfect, but to pour. To let your own life spill into form, however it wants to come.

Because this book is not the ending. It is a hand extended. A door left slightly open. A flame kept alive long enough for you to see your own reflection in its light.

May you leave these pages knowing: your voice matters. Your body knows. Your story belongs.

And when the world grows loud again, when you doubt or stumble or forget—may you return, not to me, not even to this book, but to yourself.

Because you are the next beginning.
You are the continuation.
You are the stone being set now.

And so, if you are still here, still turning the pages, still letting your eyes linger on words that came like water, like fire, like breath—I want you to know you have already done something holy. You stayed. You stayed through the jagged places and the tender ones, through the questions that had no neat answers, through the stories that may have mirrored your own ache. You stayed, and that matters.

This stone I lay is also yours. Each reader lays it with me, whether you are curled in bed under a blanket, whether you are reading between bus stops, whether you are hiding this book under a desk at work, whether you are holding it in trembling hands at three in the morning when the house is silent. The stone is laid again every time a woman dares to tell the truth she was told to swallow. Every time a man softens his chest enough to let love enter. Every time a daughter refuses to carry what is not hers. Every time a son chooses gentleness over silence.

I know the doubts that circle. I know the weight of fear that says your story is too small, or too strange, or too heavy, or too much. I know the temptation to wait until you are braver, until you are wiser, until you are healed. But I have learned: there is no waiting place where all is perfected. There is only this moment, imperfect and trembling, where your heart is already enough.

So here is my blessing for you—

For the morning you will wake into, before coffee, before the phone, before the world begins its chorus of demands—may you pause. Even if only for the length of one inhale, may you feel the earth steady beneath your feet, reminding you that you belong here. For the light that spills through your window, even on the gray days, may you see it as an invitation, not to hurry, but to be.

For the rituals you call ordinary—folding shirts, rinsing plates, driving the same road, answering the same questions—may you begin to sense the quiet holiness braided into them. May you notice the way the suds glisten on your hands, the way fabric carries the warmth of sun, the way your breath fogs the window on a winter morning. These are not interruptions of your life. These are your life, shimmering with the pulse of something larger that hums beneath every motion.

For the joy that arrives unannounced—a child's giggle, a stranger's smile, the shimmer of rain puddles catching streetlight—may you let it stay longer than your mind insists. May you resist the urge to rush past it. May you let joy soak into your skin, ripple through your chest, and remind you that joy is a gift, not a task to complete.

And for the grief that will come, as it always does—may you not treat it as an intruder. May you remember that sorrow is not the opposite of life but one of its deepest languages. Let your tears be rivers, cleansing, not proof that you are drowning. May they carve valleys wide enough for joy to return and settle when it is ready.

For the days when you feel unseen—when your tenderness meets silence, when your effort dissolves unnoticed, when you question if you matter at all—may you feel the witnessing of the earth beneath you, the sky above you, the ancestors at your back. Even here, even now, even in invisibility, you are held.

For the ones who carried you here—the mothers who worked until their hands cracked, the fathers who swallowed words that burned their throats, the children who shouldered burdens too heavy for their years—may their strength breathe through you now. May you inherit their wisdom without their wounds, their sparks without their shadows.

For the stories spoken and the ones buried in silence—may they rise like tides within you, not to trap you in the past, but to remind you that you are part of a river always moving toward freedom. For the ancestors who could not rest, who died unheard, who were silenced or shamed—may your living become a resting place for them. May your voice give them peace.

For your children—whether born or unborn, held in your arms or only in your prayers—may they feel your courage humming in their bones. May they walk lighter because you chose to put down what was never yours to carry. For the daughters who will someday look in the mirror and whisper, *Why do I feel so much?*—may this story rise to meet them like a grandmother's hand on their back: *Because feeling is power, and you come from a long line of it.* For the sons who will question whether gentleness is allowed of them—may your life be their answer: *yes, always yes.*

And for those not yet born, who will live in the ripple of your choices—may they find your strength in their courage, your tenderness in their love. They may never know your name, but they will feel the freedom you left for them.

For the parts of you still hidden—not because they are unworthy, but because they are waiting for the right season—may they bloom gently. May they rise not with rush but with rhythm, like flowers opening to the sun in their own time. For the dreams you are afraid to say aloud, may they grow roots in silence, and may the day come when courage meets them in the open air.

For the moments when you feel lost, may you remember that even stars wander before they find their place in the sky, and the night is incomplete without them. May you trust that your detours are gathering wisdom you cannot yet see.

For the times when you falter—when you forget, when you break, when you question everything you once believed—may you not mistake these thresholds for failure. May you see them as sacred interruptions, as invitations to grow beyond what once kept you safe.

For the love that still waits for you—in friendship, in kinship, in partnership, in the quiet corners of your own heart—may you open to it without fear of being swallowed. May you remember that real love does not cage you. It multiplies you. It does not erase you. It reveals you.

And for the self you have not yet met—the one who has weathered storms you cannot imagine, the one who has stood on the edge of her breaking and chosen to keep going—may you welcome her like an old friend. May you marvel at her strength, her softness, her radiance. And may you trust that she already lives within you now, waiting to be named.

And for the world itself—weary and wondrous, fractured and beautiful, still trembling beneath our feet—may we learn again to walk upon it with reverence, as children entering a sacred hall. May we learn again to touch soil as if it were skin, to drink rivers as if they were blood, to breathe air as if it were our shared lung.

For the nations divided, for streets echoing with grief, for the places where bombs fall and silence follows—may love interrupt. Not the fragile love that denies pain, but the fierce love that refuses to give cruelty the final word.

For the hungry, may we become bread. For the thirsty, may we become water. For the silenced, may we become voice. For the leaders who forget, for the systems that consume, for the greed that blinds—may cracks open in the walls of power, letting in light no law can contain.

For the mothers who weep, for the fathers who ache in silence, for the children who inherit chaos they never asked for—may the tide turn. May healing come swifter than harm. May justice come steadier than vengeance, deeper than despair.

For the elements themselves—fire, wind, water, stone—may they not rise against us, but with us. May they remind us that their rage is our warning, their gentleness our gift. May we learn to return to rhythm instead of conquest.

And for this trembling, radiant world—cracked yet luminous, fragile yet resilient, still turning, still singing in the language of stars and soil—may we remember to call it home. Not as conquerors, not as consumers, but as part of the living whole.

—

When you close this book, when the noise of life returns, may you remember: the temple is not here in these pages. It is in you—in the pulse beneath your skin, in the way you love, in the way you fall and rise again.

This is not the end. It is only the turning of a page.

The rest is yours to write.